P9-DOF-192

ON MENCKEN

Essays by

William Manchester

Huntington Cairns

Alistair Cooke

Charles A. Fecher

Malcolm Moos

William H. Nolte

Carl Bode

Alfred A. Knopf

On MENCKEN

Edited by JOHN DORSEY

ALFRED A. KNOPF
NEW YORK 1980

THIS IS A BORZOI BOOK
PUBLISHED BY ALFRED A. KNOPF, INC.

 Published in the United States by Alfred A. Knopf, Inc., New York, and simultaneously in Canada by Random House of Canada Limited, Toronto. Distributed by Random House, Inc., New York

Library of Congress Cataloging in Publication Data
Main entry under title:
On Mencken.
Includes various pieces by H. L. Mencken.
1. Mencken, Henry Louis, 1880–1956—Addresses, essays, lectures. 2. Authors, American—20th century—Biography—Addresses, essays, lectures. I. Manchester, William Raymond. II. Dorsey, John R. III. Mencken, Henry Louis, 1880–1956.
PS3525.E43Z76 1980 818'.5209 [B] 80-7639
ISBN 0-394-51253-7

Manufactured in the United States of America
Published September 12, 1980
Second Printing, October 1980

CONTENTS

INTRODUCTION

Henry Louis Mencken was born in Baltimore on September 12, 1880, the first of four children of August and Anna Mencken. His father and his uncle Henry, after whom he was named, ran a cigar factory in West Baltimore.

When he was three, Mencken's family moved from the Lexington Street house in which he was born to 1524 Hollins Street, a comfortable red brick rowhouse similar to thousands of others in Baltimore, then and now. It faced Union Square, one of several block-square areas reserved as modest urban parks in the western part of the city. Much has changed in Baltimore since then, but the house is still there, and so is Union Square. With the exception of the five years of his marriage, this was to be Mencken's home for the rest of his life. The childhood that he spent in that proper middle-class neighborhood and wrote so lovingly about later engendered in him, as Huntington Cairns describes in "Mencken of Baltimore," a devotion to the city and its slow, comfortable, Southern ways.

The family was of German extraction, and in those days the city had a large German community. The first school that Mencken attended, many of the shops his parents patronized, the music he was brought up on were German, and so he quite naturally grew to feel an identification with the country and people of his origins.

When he wasn't roaming the nearby alleys and vacant lots with his brother Charles, he spent most of his time reading. At the age of eight he discovered *Huckleberry Finn* and thus began his lifelong love affair with the works of Mark Twain, whose humor and distinctively American way of writing were to be major influences on Mencken's literary opinions and on his writing style. About the same time, his father bought him for Christmas a small printing press, which he later cited as the genesis of his desire to be a newspaperman. It is probably safe to say that no one ever wanted to be a newspaperman more than Henry Mencken did.

At sixteen he graduated with high honors from the Baltimore Polytechnic Institute, one of the city's leading public high schools, and reluctantly went to work in his father's factory. After the elder Mencken's death in 1899, he began to haunt the city room of the Baltimore *Morning Herald* and persisted until Max Ways, the paper's city editor, gave him a job. He immediately showed his talents for the work, and advanced from Southern Police District reporter to City Hall reporter to city editor of the paper in about three years. When the Baltimore fire of 1904 consumed the *Herald* building along with much of the city's center, Mencken put out the paper from three different places during the next week and contributed to what has been called the best contemporary account of the fire. His memory of that experience later became the chapter "Fire Alarm" in *Newspaper Days;* in the present volume, it accompanies William Manchester's essay, "Mencken in Person."

In 1906 the *Herald* failed, and Mencken joined the Baltimore *Sun* as its Sunday editor, contributing a column on the theater as well. In 1910, when the *Evening Sun* was launched, he went to work for its editorial page and soon began writing a daily column, "The Free Lance." The highly controversial column, primarily concerned with local issues, continued until 1917, when Mencken's pro-German sympathies—he had gone to Germany as a war correspondent and had advocated American entry on the German side—made it advisable for him to leave the paper temporarily. In 1920 he returned, and began a series of Monday editorial page articles which continued until 1938 and which dealt with every topic from national politics to local streetcars. He also continued to cover such major stories as the national political conventions and the Scopes trial in Tennessee in 1925. But it should not be thought that Mencken's "coverage" of such events was, or was meant to be, straight reporting. Like his columns, his dispatches, even when they appeared on page one, were clearly pieces of opinion, written by Mencken in his role as critic of the American scene.

His vivid accounts of the Scopes trial, and his ridicule of the performance of the aging, half-mad William Jennings Bryan as champion of the law against teaching evolution in the schools, only enhanced the national reputation Mencken had already achieved. He was by then, Alistair Cooke has said, as famous in America as Bernard Shaw was in England. From the beginning, without any slacking of attention to his newspaper work, he had sought a larger stage than the Baltimore press could provide. As early as the first decade of the century, he was publishing fiction and verse. The first of his 30-odd books was a collection of poems called *Ventures into Verse*, and he even wrote a one-act play. But he was essentially a critic—of politics, literature, society, and, as he said, of "ideas."

In 1905 he wrote a book on Shaw's plays, and three years later one on Nietzsche's philosophy. Both brought their respective subjects to the attention of the American public for the first time. Shortly thereafter he became a contributor to the *Smart Set*, a popular and sophisticated New York magazine, and in 1914 was made co-editor with his friend, the drama critic George Jean Nathan. Ten years later the two launched the *American Mercury*, with Alfred A. Knopf as publisher. (Mr. Knopf's essay includes an account of the birth of the magazine and of the subsequent quarrel between Mencken and Nathan.) The *Mercury* became the bible of college students and the American literary set of the 1920s.

In the *Smart Set*, Mencken established his prominence as a critic by challenging what was known as the Genteel Tradition in American letters, as represented by those writers who aped the styles and social attitudes of British Victorian authors, and those critics who applauded such work. As William Nolte describes, Mencken supported instead a new generation of American writers whose works more realistically reflected American life.

Even the status of national celebrity could not lure Mencken away from his beloved Baltimore. He customarily spent two or three days at his New York office, then returned to Hollins Street to pursue the orderly, quiet pattern of his life. One person, however, upset the pattern.

In 1930, to almost everyone's surprise, he gave up bachelorhood to marry Sara Powell Haardt, Goucher College graduate and Southern writer. They moved into an apartment at 704 Cathedral Street, just off the once-elegant but then declining Mount Vernon Place. When the fragile Sara died five years later, Mencken moved back to Hollins Street for good.

During the Depression, Mencken fell out of fashion. One reason may have been the often bellicose style of his criticism, more suited to the iconoclastic 1920s than to the idealistic

1930s. But, as Malcolm Moos notes, a principal contributing factor was the consistency of his thought, which many took for the opposite. A self-styled libertarian, he found himself on the side of the liberals with regard to the social issues of the 1920s, but allied with the conservatives in his opposition to the New Deal. Both positions sprang from his dislike of government interference in the life of the citizen. He was, for example, against both Prohibition and the attempt to eradicate prostitution, on the grounds that human nature cannot be altered by government fiat and therefore all such crusades are bound to fail.

Mencken had a contempt for democracy, because he thought it tended to promote mediocrity. But his contempt was an amused one most of the time; nor did he have much love for other forms of government. He championed individual liberty through the conviction that if men were left to sink or swim for themselves the best would rise to the top and produce an intellectual aristocracy equipped to lead the social order. Governments tended, he thought, to get in the way of that process, and the bigger the government the more it got in the way.

During the 1930s he worked on revisions and supplements to his monumental treatise *The American Language*, which had made him the foremost authority on the subject. He also contributed to *The Sunpapers of Baltimore*, published on the occasion of the *Sun*'s centennial in 1937. In the early 1940s he produced three volumes of reminiscences, which Mencken lovers call "the *Days* books." In *Happy Days, Newspaper Days,* and *Heathen Days,* he eschewed political and social comment almost entirely and produced a superb if unconventional autobiographical work. It is neither complete nor, as William Manchester points out, completely factual; but it is Mencken to the life.

Always a lover of political conventions, Mencken covered

three of them in 1948, including that of the Progressive Party, at which Henry Wallace was nominated for the presidency. In the fall of that year, Mencken suffered a severe stroke, from which he appeared to recover physically; but he was left with an inability to read, write, or remember proper names. For such a writer, this was hell on earth. He wanted "out," but it took more than seven years. He died in his bed at Hollins Street on the night of January 26, 1956.

When a famous artist dies, his reputation—and his prices—do not immediately go up. Rather, as has been said, there is a pause while a necessary adjustment is made, for people must have time to stop thinking of the artist as an active participant on the contemporary scene and begin to consider his place in the history of art. It is somewhat the same with Mencken. Although he has scarcely been forgotten in the quarter-century since his death, it seems likely that more years will pass before we know the final verdict on his place in American letters.

Recently there has been a feeling in certain circles that he is due for a renaissance. Some critics have pointed out that we are undergoing a conservative resurgence in our political thought, and that Mencken's ideas, which were considered out of date for half a century, are once again gaining popularity. Such may be the case, but it seems to me both an oversimplification and an injustice to Mencken to call him a conservative and leave it at that. It has been noted that the rigid consistency with which he applied his ideas as one set of issues gave way to another altered his political bedfellows. It should be remembered that he was thought a liberal in the conservative 1920s and a conservative in the liberal 1930s. If the nation's center of gravity is indeed shifting to the right, Mencken the immovable object may appear to be farther to the left the farther right we go. To cite but one modern example, Mencken's hatred of change would undoubtedly put him on the side of the preservationists, who are, by and large, liberals.

What may be happening, if a renewal of interest in Mencken is in fact taking place, is simply that enough time has passed to begin to change the focus of our interest in his writings, and that as a result he is no longer passé. I doubt if the reader of Mencken today either approaches him to find out what he had to say about Roosevelt or Dreiser or, conversely, puts him aside because the particular battles that he fought are old hat. The present-day reader's interest tends to lie in one or both of two more general areas: to discover the point of view from which Mencken's opinions sprang (which is why we are witnessing the appearance of such books as Charles A. Fecher's *Mencken: A Study of His Thought*); or to read him for the sheer joy of it.

That joy, in my opinion, is the chief reason Mencken will continue to be read, and if so then his principal claim to immortality rests upon his style. As William Nolte points out, critics who last beyond their own time do so because of the way they write, and not because of their opinions. For his writing style, Mencken was indebted, as Alistair Cooke shows, to Thomas Henry Huxley as well as to Mark Twain, and undoubtedly he learned from others in some degree. But the distillation was his own; its liveliness, its humor, its clarity, the marvelous cadences which demand to be read aloud, the sheer rolling beauty of the writing may well earn Mencken a place in American literary history as one of our best prose stylists. Whether Joseph Wood Krutch (as quoted by William Nolte) was right in believing that "it will be generally recognized . . . that Mencken's was the best prose written in America during the Twentieth Century," surely it is more encouraging to think that his reputation will rest upon the strength of his writing than that it will be dependent upon such extraneous factors as the political climate.

But there is another facet to the joy mentioned above, one that has as much to do with Mencken's style as the strictly literary values of his writing. It is the style of the man himself. To read Mencken at his best, whether it is the *Days* books or old newspaper columns or anything else, is to encounter not just Mencken the mind but Mencken the man: to feel oneself—almost physically—in the presence of this enormous and engaging personality. It is not only understandable but appropriate that several of the contributors to this volume, although their task was to address themselves to various aspects of Mencken's writing, felt impelled to include an anecdote or two about the Mencken they remembered; for, to a degree that may be unparalleled among critics, the man and his writing are one. And the fact that Mencken the man is compellingly alive in his writings adds a level of enjoyment to reading him that one does not have with most critics. On the page, Mencken's personality and writing skill combine to produce a *style* as fascinating as it is—his would-be followers have found—inimitable.

But whatever the judgment of history on Mencken as a critic, on one point at least there can be no doubt. H. L. Mencken was one of the best journalists this country has produced. The opinion is given without reference to his ideas; it has to do with the qualities he brought to the profession of journalism. It is hard to imagine another person so single-mindedly determined to pursue a particular career and so ideally qualified for it.

He had everything: He had a fine mind. He loved his work. He had curiosity, combined with industry. He wanted to go where the story was and follow it to the end, no matter what the hours or personal inconvenience involved. No man without those qualities could have loved national political conventions, one of the most taxing of all newspaper assignments. He had that skepticism of men and their motives so necessary to this profession; and, as has often been said, he not only despised pretense, hypocrisy, and sham but was totally incapable of them himself. He was an omnivorous reader, and whether reading or writing he had an astonishing breadth of interest. He had speed, a quality essential to a newspaperman. Mencken claimed that in his early years he often wrote 5,000 words a day, and anyone familiar with the size of his total output must realize how extraordinarily high the volume remained. Carl Bode cites August Mencken's estimate that in addition to everything else his brother wrote 100,000 letters.

Some journalists are good writers and some are good reporters, but it is hard to find both qualities combined in one person. Mencken claimed that he wasn't a good reporter. It's true that he wasn't "objective," but that only means he wasn't hypocritical enough to pretend to be. It's true that often his conclusions and prognostications were notably wide of the mark, as Malcolm Moos amply demonstrates. But was there ever anyone more supremely capable of communicating the essence, the *flavor*, of what he witnessed? Reading someone else's account of this or that, one who was there might well say, "Yes, that's what happened." Reading Mencken's, one would be more likely to say, "Yes, that's the way it was."

Alistair Cooke shows that as a writer Mencken had an uncommon virtue: He kept getting better. He never ceased to work on his style, gradually ridding it of some of its early complexities and redundancies, making it ever more direct and cleaner. From early to late, however, his meaning, as he correctly boasted, was always clear—once you knew the meanings of all the words he used.

Above all, he possessed in concert two qualities which together formed the keystone of his greatness: honesty, and what another of the country's leading journalists, Gerald W.

Johnson, called "his unfreezing courage." The first of these qualities has often been remarked upon by those who knew Mencken. If the second has been cited less often, that may be because Mencken seemed so utterly fearless, and it is part of our popular psychology to associate courage with overcoming fear.

Only robots and madmen are without fear, but, as Carl Bode points out, Mencken rarely betrayed any deep emotion even in his letters. And William Manchester states that when Mencken was low he went away by himself and didn't rejoin the world until he was on top of things again. Taken together, the two observations are revealing. Despite his love of company, Mencken was a private person, and to a remarkable degree self-sufficient. He could deal with fears and anxieties alone, without demanding sympathy or understanding. His courage, I think, was a product of that self-sufficiency, in that he was free from the need to be sustained by the approbation of others. He never had to hesitate in apprehension over how his opinions might be received in this quarter or that. Consequently, he was free to say exactly what he thought, boldly and fully. That he did, and for that he will be remembered.

To be a Baltimorean, or a newspaperman, is to live to some degree in the shadow of Mencken. When one is both, the shadow is larger and deeper. But curiously—or perhaps understandably—I scarcely felt this immense presence until I was well into my own newspaper career, long after the years when I was born and grew up in Baltimore, and long after my double connection with the most famous Baltimorean of the twentieth century might have been expected to produce a lively and serious interest in him. I think this was probably due to what might be called the Local Monument Phenomenon, which keeps New Yorkers from taking in the Statue of

Liberty until a visiting cousin from out of town demands to see it, and which assures that dear, absent-minded old Arthur will still be dear, absent-minded old Arthur to his family even after he has won the Nobel Prize. The fact is that, except among those who might be said to be to some extent his devotees, Mencken isn't noticed much in Baltimore, or even on the *Sunpapers*. His room in the Enoch Pratt Free Library is open to the public on the occasion of his birthday each September, when there is also a Mencken lecture; the day draws a few hundred people to the Pratt, many of whom come regularly almost every year. One sees perhaps half-a-dozen people from the *Sun* at the lecture, rarely more.

In the lobby of the *Sun* building there is a small plaque in Mencken's memory, but so far as I know, no one points it out to the new employee; and I daresay no one points it out to the busloads of school children who are trooped through the building on most weekdays. That is as it should be, no doubt, for Mencken scorned the idea of any sort of memorial to him; it is merely put forward in weak defense of the fact that I grew up in a newspaper (indeed, a *Sunpaper*) family in the city of Baltimore and attained my majority in almost total ignorance of Mencken as anything more than a name. My father, who worked at the paper for more than 35 years, 15 of them while Mencken was still active there, rarely mentioned him at home. When I joined the *Sunday Sun* in 1962, just six years after Mencken's death, there was less talk about him than there is today, and that isn't much.

It was not until sometime in the mid-1960s, when I discovered (I forget how) the *Days* books, that I got hooked on Mencken; and it was not until 1975, when I was given the assignment to draw up a small booklet of selections from Mencken's writings on the subject of Baltimore, published by the paper that fall, that I did any work on him at all. But I was by that time—and remain—a captive, and so was delighted when Richard H. Hart, former head of the humanities department at the Pratt and as such keeper of the Mencken Room there, asked me to join the committee being formed to plan the celebration of the Mencken centennial.

Out of that invitation grew this book. Thinking about what such a celebration might include, it occurred to me that it would not be inappropriate to have a book of some sort, which could be available at the time of the ceremonies and which might remain as one of the more or less permanent products of the centennial.

Two things were obvious from the start: Since the book, because of its timing, ought to be in the nature of a celebration, it seemed best to look for a number of contributors already known for their Mencken connections. And it would hardly do to have a Mencken book without any Mencken in it. From these ground rules evolved a book of selections and essays, divided into chapters. Each chapter, with one exception, consists of an essay dealing with some aspect of Mencken's work,* accompanied by selections from Mencken's writings in that area, chosen in each case by the author of the essay.

Now it goes without saying that there have been numerous books of selections from Mencken's writings before this, including ones by most of the contributors to the present volume. But none has been done in quite this way before. It was thought that such a book could serve two purposes: It could bring together in one place essays by people who have been known for their interest in Mencken, but whose contributions have until now been available only in many different books; and it could serve as a lively introduction to Mencken for those who want to read a bit of him and a bit about him at the same time.

* The exception is the chapter contributed by Alfred A. Knopf, which contains his account, much of it published here for the first time, of his longtime professional relationship and friendship with Mencken.

The success of such a venture depends, of course, on its contributors. Of the eight in this volume, each is known for his association in one way or another with Mencken's work; each is distinguished in his own field; and five knew Mencken personally.* Their essays speak for themselves, and need no comment here; but I do want to express my gratitude to them all for having given so much time and effort to the project. Most of them told me it was a labor of love, but it was a labor nevertheless.

Among those to whom I am most indebted are Harold A. Williams, editor of the *Sunday Sun,* who got me started on Mencken in the first place, and who gave his permission for my participation in the work of the centennial committee; Neil Jordahl, current head of the Pratt Library's Humanities Department, who answered every call for assistance promptly and helpfully; the other members of the Mencken Centennial Committee, who gave their enthusiastic approval to the project; Robert W. Armacost, who never failed to shout encouragement whenever it seemed for one reason or another that the whole thing was about to fall apart; and Alice Phillips, who did much of the final typing of the manuscript, and who worked not just efficiently but thoughtfully as well.

Finally, it is my pleasure to acknowledge my deep debt to Richard Hart. It is impossible to do justice to the magnitude of his contribution, from the time some three years ago when I first asked him what he thought of the idea and he encouraged me to go ahead. Since then he has been an invaluable resource through every step of the process, giving me free use of his time, his knowledge of the work of all the contributors, his familiarity with Mencken's work, his excellence as a critic. To cite but two examples of the aid he has so liberally given, it was he who suggested to me the names of

* Mr. Knopf, Mr. Cairns, Mr. Cooke, Dr. Moos and Mr. Manchester.

several of the contributors, and as the essays came in he read each one and gave me his unfailingly incisive comments upon it. But, practical matters aside, I am above all grateful for the opportunity I have had to observe, to learn from, and to become more closely acquainted with a man of such erudition and wisdom, whose speech is as elegant as his mind.

JOHN DORSEY

Baltimore
October, 1979

John Dorsey is a native of Baltimore and a reporter for the Baltimore *Sun*.

ON MENCKEN

Mencken *in* PERSON

William Manchester

Scott Fitzgerald once observed that a writer's childhood is his capital. Certainly that was true of Mencken; he accumulated an immense principal in his youth and drew handsome dividends to the end. One reason for his solvency was that he rarely wandered far from the bank. In the last year of his life he and I sat each morning in the backyard of his home at 1524 Hollins Street, surrounded by memorabilia of his earliest years. On rainy days we moved into his old green-and-white pony shed, and wintry evenings were spent by the sitting-room fireside while flickering shadows played charmingly on the dark rosewood of the old-fashioned secretary where, seventy years earlier, he had, in his words, entered "thc larval stage of a bookworm." Now and then he would glance thoughtfully up at the shelves, protecting, so to speak, his investment.

From whom, or what? It seems inconceivable that he, of all

William Manchester, a former foreign correspondent for the Baltimore *Sun*, is adjunct professor of history at Wesleyan University. He wrote the first biography of Mencken, *Disturber of the Peace*.

men, might have felt threatened. Yet he did. He feared change and battled it to the end. No doubt the spring of his life was less serene than he would have had us believe. His father didn't want him to become a newspaperman, and it cannot be said that the old man's death left the boy grief-stricken; the day after the funeral he applied for a job on the Baltimore *Morning Herald*. But most strong men go through king-of-the-mountain struggles with their fathers. The fact remains that the young Mencken, growing up in the 1880s and 1890s, had fallen in love with the world around him—his house, his neighborhood, his city, and most of the city's inhabitants. Anachronistically, we may say that he enjoyed their life-style. He rejected his paterfamilias' hope that he would become a cigar-maker, but he approved of the product; I can still smell those ghastly Uncle Willies he kept thrusting at me.

Enemies of change are conservatives, and although he championed new writers and attacked the establishmentarians of his time, he remained a Bourbon in private life. Just as he preferred the Old Testament to the New, so he believed that life was more pleasant in the nineteenth century than in the twentieth. That wasn't true for ordinary men, but it was valid for extraordinary men like him. Possessing, in his words, "a kind of caginess that has dissuaded me, at all stages in my life, from attempting enterprises clearly beyond my power," he fought his battles on his own soil, surrounded by friends and allies. He thus followed the oldest of Teutonic martial principles. The first *Feldmarschallen* stood on little hummocks of earth rather like pitcher's mounds, and directed their troops from there, safe from ambushes or flanking movements. If you must fight, that's the way to do it.

Mencken had to fight. Aggression came as naturally to him as self-pity to Richard Nixon. But since his social instincts were gentlemanly, and since he liked most men anyhow, he jousted on the battlefield of ideas. No warrior ever displayed less malice. He rejoiced in combat for its own sake, and he seldom lost, because his weapon, an unsurpassed mastery of the language, never failed him. He knew precisely how to pirouette on a semicolon, when to lunge with a metaphor, where to swat a non sequitur. And once these had decided the issue, he would rout the foe with battalions of derision. When time has enshrouded the rest of his work, his comic genius will still leer across the ages, brightening dark moments with flashes of Menckenian mirth.

Here, however, a caveat is in order. Many who knew him, even many who saw him almost daily, recall his exuberance and believe his spirits were always high. That is precisely what he wanted them to think. He was a proud man. But in a naked moment he wrote: "like any other author I have suffered from recurrent depressions." That is an aspect of writing which writers would rather not explore. Theirs is, quite simply, a desperate business. Mencken was cheerier than most in the trade; nevertheless, I have seen him so despondent that he could scarcely speak, when his eyes were moist with unspeakable sorrow. When the shadow was upon him, he would hoist his drawbridge and struggle back to sanity in his home. Only the innocent—and they are lucky—will consider this a weakness. In fact, such spells afflict the mightiest of men. Lincoln had them; so did Bismarck; so did Churchill, who called them "Black Dog." At such times many men turn to drink, which explains why so many Nobel laureates are alcoholics. Mencken found solace in illusions, and it is this jollity which illumines the pages of the *Days* books.

One morning he and I were awaiting an elevator when Frank Kent strode up brandishing a copy of *Newspaper Days*. "Harry, this isn't true," he cried, riffling the pages with his thumb. "You *know* it isn't!" "No," Mencken hoarsed, beaming benevolently, "but it makes a good story, doesn't it?" In the prefaces to his *Days* books he more or less concedes that he is serving up apocrypha here and there. First he writes that his memory is "more or less accurate," then acknowledges that it is "not always photographically precise," then that "no one is more aware than I am of the fallibility of human recollection," and finally that his autobiography "is not sober history but yarning, and is devoid of any purpose save to entertain."

Elsewhere he calls himself "a poor reporter." The literal-minded agree. What other conclusion can be drawn, they argue, about a correspondent who wrote from Philadelphia in 1948 of "the traditional weather of a national convention . . . a rising temperature, very high humidity, and lazy puffs of gummy wind from the mangrove swamps surrounding the city"? Philadelphia, they solemnly observe, hasn't a single mangrove. They are the sort that protests Renoir as unrepresentational and T. S. Eliot because he doesn't scan; they are color-blind to pyrotechnics and tone-deaf to symphonies. In fact the mangrove passage is vintage Mencken: pure fiction and pure delight. Of course, he got away with it because he was who he was. I doubt that he would even have made the *Sun* payroll in my day. For one thing he had, by the late 1940s, come to admire the Newspaper Guild and recommend that I join it, asking only that I keep his endorsement to myself rather than offend his old friends in the paper's front office. For another thing, he had no patience with stylebook pedantry. In *Newspaper Days* he proudly sets down the eight-column ribbon he wrote on his most exciting day as a city editor:

HEART OF BALTIMORE WRECKED BY
GREATEST FIRE IN CITY'S HISTORY

That would have been rejected by the copy desk I knew because the first line ends in a preposition.

William H. Nolte writes in *The American Spectator* of the folly of "trying to discover whether Mencken's ideas were true or not." He continues: "One may as well try to discover 'truth' in vital force, or a storm that blows down houses on the seashore, or in a bell that wakes us in the morning. [He was] a profound artist in the way that Swift and Voltaire and Mark Twain were profound. . . . He made us see and feel and know things that we had not seen, felt, or known before he came along. In all his work . . . there is instruction for the sober researcher and entertainment for the heavy laden."

Especially there is the entertainment. We may say of the *Days* books, as Huck Finn said of *Tom Sawyer*, that the author "told the truth mainly," that there were "some stretchers," but "I never seen anybody but lied, one time or another." And why not? Frank Kent got his facts straight and yet, by his selective use of them, he systematically distorted the news from Washington for half a century. Mencken manipulated facts in a different spirit and achieved greater goals. At the heart of his work there was an irresistible, primitive drive older than Gutenberg, older even than the written word. Like the Teutonic story-tellers who spun their fantastic tales as fellow tribesmen sat entranced round fires deep in the Hercynian forest, he held his audience spellbound by sorcery which touched chords far deeper than such chronicles as, say, the Domesday Book. If you want to know the names, addresses, and lodge affiliations of forgotten politicians, read Kent. But if you hunger for the feel, the smell, the taste, and the sheer vitality of life, told by a genius whose vowels soar, whose consonants crash, and whose matchless skill holds you transfixed until the last breath, reach for Mencken and you will find that you haven't exceeded your grasp.

. . .

I first met him in the spring of 1947, in the Maryland Club. ("The cooks here do a swell job with soft-shell crabs," he rasped, peering at me over his spectacles. "They fry them in the altogether; then they add a small jockstrap of bacon.") I had written my dissertation on his literary criticism; he liked it, and when I suggested that I write his biography, he agreed and persuaded the *Sunpapers* to hire me while I worked on the book. Of his own days on the defunct *Herald* he had written: "A newspaper reporter, in those remote days, had a grand and gaudy time of it, and no call to envy any man." Now he told me: "You'll love it, but be sure you get out before you're thirty-five." That was one of two incomparable pieces of practical advice he gave me. The other was: "Never regard royalty checks as income. Fitzgerald did, and it led to his ruin. Royalties are equity; just spend the interest." I did, with the result that by the time I was forty I was financially independent and could write exactly as I pleased.

In that last year before his stroke the old man was still robust, alert, and quick; his lexical machete continued to be long and sharp and heavy, and he had never swung it with greater gusto. He was a marvel to watch. Once he remarked that there would be no point in erecting a statue of him, because it would just look like a monument to a defeated alderman, but actually he was a man of great physical presence. To be sure, his torso was ovoid, his ruddy face homely, and his stubby legs thin and bowed. Nevertheless, there was a sense of dignity and purpose about all his movements, and when you were with him it was impossible to forget that you were in the company of a great original, a writer *sui generis*. Nobody else could stuff stogies into a seersucker jacket with the flourish of a Mencken, or wipe a blue bandanna across his brow so dramatically. His friends treasured everything about him, because the whole of the man was manifest in each of his aspects—the tilt of his head, his close-fitting clothes, his high-crowned felt hat creased in the distinctive fashion of the 1920s, his strutting walk, his abrupt gestures, his habit of holding a cigar between his thumb and forefinger like a baton, the roupy inflection of his voice, and, most of all, those extraordinary eyes, so large, and intense, and merry.

We talked in the club, his home, the Pratt Library, Miller Brothers' restaurant, and on long walks through downtown Baltimore. There was, of course, no pretense to conversation between equals; like Winston Churchill during my latter days as a foreign correspondent, he addressed me as though I were a one-man House of Commons. I treasured these hikes and also his letters to me, which were even more frequent than our talks, for he loved correspondence, always preferring the written word to the telephone. And I kept elaborate notes on all our contacts, which, he being Mencken, really were notable.

One warm day when I was covering a fire in his neighborhood he appeared friskily, carrying a pencil and perspiring happily. "I'm like the hippopotamus," he said in greeting, "an essentially tropical animal." Like the hippo, he was also a creature of exaggeration. He never asked me to join him for a beer; I was invited to "hoist a schooner of malt." He couldn't order sweetbreads at Millers' without explaining that they were taken from "the pancreases of horned cattle, the smaller intestines of swine, and the vermiform appendix of the cow"—thereby causing me to choose something else on the menu. Anthony Comstock hadn't merely been a censor; he had been "a great smeller." Mencken was forever stuffing letters to me with advertisements for chemical water closets, quack-remedy broadsides, and religious pamphlets. He found the comic lining in every somber cloud. One afternoon on Charles Street we encountered two sedate women from the *Sun*'s library coming the other way, and he cried out heartily, "Hello, girls! How's the profession?" (Later one of them said to me, "Of course, he didn't mean it the way it sounded." I knew that was exactly how he had meant it.) In the library itself he advised a man updating the Mencken obituary to, "Leave it as it is. Just add one line: 'As he grew older, he grew worse.' " Once, while showing me the collection of his papers in the Pratt Library, he said he was worried about its security; the stack containing it was locked, but he wanted a sign, too. "Saying 'KEEP OUT'?" I asked. "No," he said, "Saying: 'WARNING: TAMPERING WITH THIS GATE WILL RELEASE CHLORINE GAS UNDER 250 POUNDS PRESSURE.' "

Mencken was fascinated by the frailties of the human body, his own and everybody else's. He was constantly studying medical journals, reading up on diseases of the bronchial tubes, gall bladder, etc., and he was the most considerate visitor of the sick I have ever known. Acquaintances who, in health, would not see him for weeks, found him at their hospital doors each evening, as long as they remained bedridden, fascinated by their progress, or, even more, by their lack of it. His letters to me and others reflected his preoccupation with illness and anatomy. "Imagine," he wrote typically, "hanging the stones of a man *outside*, where they are forever getting themselves knocked, pinched, and bruised. Any decent mechanic would have put them in the exact center of the body, protected by an envelope twice as thick as even a Presbyterian's skull. Moreover, consider certain parts of the female—always too large or too small. The elemental notion of standardization seems to have never presented itself to the celestial Edison."

On Wednesday, November 24, 1948, a reserved table in the Maryland Club awaited four parties: Mencken, Evelyn

Waugh, a Jesuit priest, and me. Waugh and Mencken had never met; the priest and I had arranged everything, like seconds before a duel. The encounter never took place, however, because disaster had struck the old man the evening before. He was having a cocktail with Rosalind Lohrfinck, his secretary, when, in the middle of a lucid sentence, he began to babble incoherently. Alarmed, she called his physician, Ben Baker. At Johns Hopkins Hospital, Ben found that his "star patient," as he always called HLM, had been stricken by a cerebral thrombosis affecting his speech center and paralyzing his entire right side. Paul Patterson, the *Sunpapers'* publisher, somehow regarded this as a horrid secret. He wouldn't allow a word of it in his papers. Equally remarkable, he persuaded the AP to observe this blackout. I wasn't even allowed to explain what had happened to Waugh and the priest, with the result that Waugh left Baltimore believing that Mencken had insulted him.

The burden of caring for the invalid—and it was to be a heavy one—fell on Mencken's unmarried younger brother, August, with whom he shared the Hollins Street house. Later I took a leave of absence from the *Sun* to read to the old man. One day the *Sun* carried a story about a husband who had killed his wife, her lover, and himself. "You know," Mencken reflected—there were days when he could speak haltingly, and this was one of them—"it's probably the only decent thing he did in his life." Another high point was Dr. Samuel Shepard's trial for the murder of his wife. For Mencken it had everything: high theater, the physician who wasn't really a physician, the pillar of the community exposed as a hypocrite. Of Mrs. Shepard, Mencken said with a deep sigh, "Well, she's a goner now. She's up there with the angels." We sat for a moment in contemplation of the sublime. Then Mencken gestured at the paper. "Come on," he said impatiently, "how the hell did he do it?"

Shortly before his death I said my last good-bye at Hollins Street; I was leaving Baltimore for my native New England. We both knew that we would never meet again, despite all our talk of reunions. He was failing rapidly now. Yet he rallied gallantly that afternoon, and as I turned to leave through the vestibule he struck a pose, one foot in front of the other, one hand on the banister and the other, fisted, on his hip. "You know, I had a superb time while it lasted," he said in that inimitable voice. "Very soon it will stop, and I will go straight to heaven. Won't that be exquisite? It will be very high-toned."

We shook hands; he trudged up the stairs into shadow, and I departed carrying two farewell gifts, an Uncle Willie (which I have never smoked), and a log from his hoard of chemically treated firewood which, when ignited, displayed the colors of the rainbow. Several months later an AP reporter called me in Connecticut to tell me that the old man had died in his sleep. His ashes were deposited in Baltimore's Loudon Park Cemetery. Afterward I read of August's death, and then word reached me that the Hollins Street house—"as much a part of me as my two hands," Mencken had once said of it—was temporarily occupied by the University of Maryland's School of Social Work. That evening I laid the piece of treated firewood in my fireplace. I didn't expect much; after all that time, I thought, the chemicals would have lost their potency. But I was wrong. Instantly a bright blue flame sprang up. Blue changed to crimson, and after a few minutes there was another change; it was eerie: from end to end the wood blazed up in a vivid green which would have been familiar to anyone who had ever held a copy of the *American Mercury*.

Fleetingly I thought: *If only the* Mercury *were still being published!* And: *If only he were still alive!* I remembered him lamenting the fact that there was no decent memorial service for nonbelievers. This little fire, I realized, was the closest I would ever come to one for him. Now his home had become a headquarters for a profession he had ridiculed. Miller Bros.' eating house, where we had drained steins of pilsener, was being torn down; the name of the restaurant lived on ignominiously in a sterile new Hilton Hotel. The Baltimore which had delighted Mencken as a young reporter, when, he wrote, "the days chased one another like kittens chasing their tails," was swiftly vanishing; soon the Baltimore I had known would disappear, too. For a moment I was near tears. And then I checked myself. I realized what Mencken's reaction to my maudlin fireside scene would have been. He would have split it into sentimental flinders with one vast gravelly chuckle.

◇◇◇

IN THE FOOTSTEPS OF GUTENBERG

On November 26, 1887, my father sent his bookkeeper, Mr. Maass, to the establishment of J. F. W. Dorman, at 217 East German Street, Baltimore, and there and then, by the said Maass's authorized agency, took title to a Baltimore No. 10 Self-Inker Printing Press and a font of No. 214 type. The press cost $7.50 and the font of type $1.10. These details, which I recover from the receipted bill in my father's file, are of no conceivable interest to anyone else on earth, but to me they are of a degree of concern bordering upon the super-colossal, for that press determined the whole course of my future life. If it had been a stethoscope or a copy of Dr. Ayers' Almanac I might have gone in for medicine; if it had been a Greek New Testament or a set of baptismal grappling-irons I might have pursued divinity. As it was, I got the smell of printer's ink up my nose at the tender age of seven, and it has been swirling through my sinuses ever since.

The press and type, of course, were laid in by my father against Christmas, and were concealed for the nonce in a cupboard at home, but my brother Charlie and I had a good look at them before early candlelight of November 27. We decided that they were pretty nifty, or, as the word was then, nobby. If Charlie, comparing them to the velocipede that lay in wait for him, was bemused by envy, he had only himself to blame, for he had delayed his coming into the world for twenty months after my own arrival, and was still virtually illiterate. It was barely three months, in fact, since he had begun to attend the sessions of F. Knapp's Institute, and he yet had some difficulty in distinguishing, without illustrative wood-cuts, between the words *cat* and *rat*. Compared to him, I was so far advanced in *literae humaniores* as to be almost a savant. During the previous Summer I had tackled and got down my first book, and was even then engaged in exploring the house library for another. No doubt this new and fevered interest in beautiful letters was marked in the household, and set afloat the notion that a printing press would be to my taste. Indeed, I probably hinted as much myself.

If my mother approved, which she undoubtedly did, she must have developed a certain regret on Christmas Day, for my father undertook to show me how to work the press, and inasmuch as he knew no more about printing than Aristotle and had so little manual dexterity that he could not even lace a shoe, he made a ghastly mess of it. Before he gave it up as a bad job all the ink that came with the outfit had been smeared and slathered away, and at least half the type had been plugged with it or broken. I recall clearly that we ran out of white cards before noon, and had to resort to the backs of his business cards. By that time all the brass gauge-pins had been crushed, one of the steel guides that held cards against the platen was bent, and the mechanism operating the ink-roller was out of order. It was a sad caricature of a printing press that went to the cellar at midday, when my mother ordered a halt and a clean-up.

Next morning, after my father shoved off for his office, I unearthed it and set to work to scrub the ink off it and make it go. Unfortunately, I had almost as little skill with my hands as my father, so it must have been New Year's Day, at the earliest, before I succeeded. My cash takings, that Christmas, had been excellent; in fact, I had amassed something on the order of $2. With this money I went down to Dorman's, bought a new can of ink and a large bottle of benzine, and also laid in a new font of type. With the press there had come a font of Black Letter and to it, apparently on the advice of Mr. Maass, who was an aesthete, my father had added one of Script. My own addition was a prosaic font of Roman, with caps only. I now had enough faces to begin printing on a commercial scale, and early in 1888 I was ready with the following announcement:

H. L. Mencken

Card Printer

1524 HOLLINS ST.
BALTIMORE, MD.

Up to this time I had always written my name Henry L., or Harry, which last, as I have noted, has been my stable-name all my life. My change to H. L. was not due to any feeling that the form better became the dignity of a business man, but simply to the fact that my father, in the course of his Christmas morning gaucheries, had smashed all my Black Letter lower-case *r*'s, and I had to cut my coat to fit my cloth. During the ensuing months I had some accidents of my own, and by the time I began to print billheads I had wrecked the penultimate cap *M* in my Roman font, and was forced to abbreviate Baltimore to Balto. But I still had an undamaged & in Black Letter and also a serviceable though somewhat mangey cap C, so I added "& Co" to the style and designation of my house.

So far as I can remember, my father was my only customer. His taste in typography, as in the other arts, was very far from finicky, and his pride in the fact that I could print at all sufficed to throttle such feeble qualms as he may have had. In February, 1888, he set off to one of the annual deliriums of the Knights Templar, and I applied for, and got, the contract for printing his fraternal *cartes de visite*. These cards were exchanged by brethren from North, East, South and West whenever two or more of them happened to be thrown together in the saloons of the convention town. They followed a rigid model. Each showed the name and home-town of the bearer, and a series of colored symbols representing his Masonic dignities.

The symbols were naturally lacking in my composing-room, and I had no idea where they were to be obtained. Moreover, my Baltimore No. 10 Self-Inker was hardly fitted for work in six or eight colors. But such impediments could not stump a really up-and-coming business man. I simply put in the symbols by hand, and colored them with the water-colors that had also been among my Christmas presents. My father professed to be delighted with the cards, and on his return from the convention told me that he had presented specimens of them to Freemasons from points as far distant as Key West, Fla., Duluth, Minn., and Ogden, Utah, and that among the recipients were some of the most puissant and austere dignitaries of the order, including two Governors and a dozen United States Senators. This was my first attempt upon a national audience. My bill for the job survives. It shows that I charged my father 8½ cents a dozen for the cards, including the hand-painting. Of the cards themselves, two or three also survive. They will go to the Bodleian after they have made the round of the American galleries.

In a little while I was branching out. On the one hand I issued a circular offering to print advertising at what, even in the primitive West Baltimore of that remote era, must have seemed to my competitors to be cut rates. And on the other hand, I launched into the publication of a newspaper in rivalry to the celebrated Baltimore *Sunpaper*, the news Bible at 1524 Hollins Street as it has always been in every other respectable Baltimore household, then, now and forever. My circular offered to produce advertisements 2 by 2 inches in area, in any quantity below the astronomical, at the uniform rate of 4 cents a hundred. For an additional 2 cents a hundred I offered to blow them up to the magnitude of 3 inches by 3¼. This was as far as I could go, for it was the full size of the chase of my press. For business cards on plain white stock, "any size," I asked 5 cents a dozen, or 2 cents a quarter of a dozen. Why I assumed that anyone would want as few as a quarter of a dozen, or even a dozen, I don't recall: there must have been some reason, but it has slipped me. The "any size," of course, was only a euphemism: as I have said, my maximum size was 3 inches by 3¼. I never got any orders for these goods. I solicited my mother's trade, but she replied coldly that she was not in any commercial business, and had no use for cards or circulars. I also solicited my brother Charlie, but he was poor in those days, and believed that it was a kind of lunacy to lay out money on printed matter. He much preferred the black licorice nigger-babies sold by Old Man Kunker in Baltimore Street, and commonly went about with his face mired by their exudations.

The newspaper I set up against the *Sunpaper* also came to nothing. It was doomed from the start, for it was afflicted by every malady that a public journal can suffer from—insufficiency of capital, incomplete news service, an incompetent staff, no advertising, and a press that couldn't print it. No copy of it survives, but I remember that it consisted of four pages, and was printed on scraps of wrapping-paper filched from the hired girl's hoard in the kitchen. I had to print each page separately, and to distribute the type between pages, for I hadn't enough to set up all four at once. Having no news service whatever, and not knowing where any was to be had, I compromised by lifting all of my dispatches out of my rival. In those days the Associated Press foreign report consisted largely of a series of brief bulletins, and the *Sunpaper* printed them on its first page every morning under the standing head of "Latest Foreign News." I chose the shortest, and when there were none short enough, chopped down the longer. Thus the most important item I ever printed was this:

BERLIN, March 9—William I is dead aged 91.

This came out in my paper on March 15 or thereabout, a week after the *Sunpaper* had made it generally known in Baltimore, Washington, Virginia, West Virginia and the Carolinas. My domestic news came from the same source, and consisted wholly of telegraphed items, for they were usually short. I made no effort to cover local news, though there was then plenty of it in West Baltimore. Almost every day Murphy the cop made one of his hauls of ruffianly Aframericans in Vincent Alley, and I could sit at my third-story office-and-bedroom window and see him drag them through Union Square to the watch-house at Calhoun and Pratt streets. It was common, also, for car-horses to fall dead in their tracks, for children to get lost, and for great gang-wars among the neighborhood dogs to tear up the Union Square lawns. But I never attempted to report any of these things. I remain a bad reporter, in fact, to this day. During my term of servitude as city editor of a Baltimore daily, long after my own paper blew up, I blushed inwardly every time I had to excoriate a member of the staff for failing to get the age, weight, color and address of a lady jugged for murdering her husband, or the names of the brave cops who had tracked her down.

Rather curiously, I can't recall the name of my paper, if, in fact, it had one. The chances are at least even that it didn't, for I was chronically short of what printers call sorts, and never wasted a single piece of type if I could help it. A little while later, probably during the ensuing Autumn, I discovered a perfect mine of supplies in the hell-box that stood outside the printing plant of Isaac Friedenwald & Son, in Paca Street, across narrow Cider Alley from my father's factory. It was Mr. Maass who directed me to this Golconda, and I began to work it diligently. From it I recovered all sorts of mangey wood-cuts, many empty ink-cans with a little ink remaining in them, a great deal of scrap paper and cardboard, and an occasional piece of condemned type, always badly battered. Unfortunately, this type was of small use to my newspaper, for the Friedenwalds were printers to the Johns Hopkins University, and laid claim to having the largest stock of foreign type-faces in the Western World, so when my eye lighted upon what looked to be a likely *E* it sometimes turned out to be a Greek *sigma* or a Hebrew *lamedh*. I could make nothing of these strange characters; in fact, I didn't know that they were characters at all, but took them to be the devices of unfamiliar branches of the Freemasons.

The Friedenwalds did not stop with such relatively intelligible alphabets, but boasted that they could print any language ever heard of on earth, and often surprised and enchanted the Johns Hopkins professors by making good. They had fonts of Arabic, Sanskrit, Russian, Coptic, Armenian and Chinese, not to mention Old Norse runes and Egyptian hieroglyphs. The specimens of these types that I recovered were always cruelly damaged, but nevertheless some of them were still legible, and if I had given them due study I might have become a linguist. But I usually traded them for marbles, chewing-tobacco tags or cigarette pictures with a neighbor who made lead soldiers of them in a mold he had somehow acquired, so I made no appreciable progress in the tongues.

Despite all these griefs and burdens, I stuck to my printing press through 1888, and it remained my favorite possession for several years afterward. Why my father, seeing my interest in it, did not buy me a larger and better one I do not know; probably it was because I wasn't aware that a larger and better one existed, and hence did not ask for it. I have found out since that Dorman had them with chases up to 6 by 8 inches, and that his catalogue listed two or three dozen different fonts of type, some of them with highly ornate faces in the rococo taste of the time. But though my press was a poor thing and my type gradually wore out to the point where all the letters printed like squashed O's, my enthusiasm for printing did not die, and even when a rage for photography and then for chemistry began to challenge it, in my early teens, it managed to continue a sturdy undercover existence. When, on my father's death, as I was eighteen, I was free at last to choose my trade in the world, I chose newspaper work without any hesitation whatever, and, save when the scent of a passing garbage-cart has revived my chemical libido, I have never regretted my choice. More than once I have slipped out of daily journalism to dally in its meretricious suburbs, but I have always returned repentant and relieved, like a blackamoor coming back in Autumn to a warm and sociable jail.

Aside from the direct and all-powerful influence of that Baltimore No. 10 Self-Inker and the Friedenwald hell-box, I was probably edged toward newspapers and their glorious miseries by two circumstances, both of them trivial. The first was my discovery of a real newspaper office in the little town of Ellicott City, where we spent the Summers of 1889 and 1890. Ellicott City was then a very picturesque and charming place, and indeed still is, despite the fact that the heavy hand of progress is on it. It is built along the two steep banks of a ravine that runs down to the Patapsco, and many of the old stone houses, though four stories high in front, scarcely clear their backyards in the rear. It is the local legend that dogs, pigs, chickens and even children have been known to fall out of these backyards into and down the chimneys. The Baltimore & Ohio Railroad's old main line to the West runs beside the river on a viaduct spanning the main street, and from this viaduct, in 1889, a long balcony ran along the second story of a block of houses, with an entrance from the railway station's platform. I naturally explored it, and was presently rewarded by discovering the printing-office of the weekly Ellicott City *Times*.

The *Times*, even in those days, must have been an appreciably better paper than my own, but its superiority was certainly not excessive. The chief article of equipment in its gloomy second-story office was a Washington handpress that had probably been hauled in on mule-back in the twenties or thirties, when the town was still Ellicott's Mills, and a famous coaching-station on the road to the Ohio. I have seen many Washington handpresses since, but never a hoarier one. Its standards were oaken beams, and it looked to a marvelling boy to be as massive as a locomotive. It was operated by a young man and a boy, and I watched enchanted as the white paper was placed on the chase, the platen was brought down, and the printed sheets were lifted off. The circulation of the *Times* at that time was probably not more than 400, but it took the man and the boy all day to print an edition, for only one side could be printed at a time, and yanking the huge lever was a back-breaking job. I noted that the young man left most of the yanking to the boy, and encouraged him from time to time by loud incitements and expostulations. I found out that Thursday was press-day, and I managed to be on hand every time. If my mother had no commission for me in the village on a Thursday I always suggested one.

I was captivated not only by the miracle of printing, but also by the high might and consequence of the young man in charge of the press. He was genuinely Somebody in that remote and obscure village, and the fact radiated from him like heat from a stove. He never deigned to take any notice of me. He might give me a blank glance when he halted the press to take a chew of tobacco, but that was all. He became to me a living symbol of the power and dignity of the press—a walking proof of its romantic puissance. Years later I encountered him again, and got to know him very well, and to have a great affection for him. I was by then city editor of the Baltimore *Morning Herald,* now dead and forgotten, and he was the assistant foreman of its composing-room. No man in all my experience has ever met more perfectly the classical specifications for that office.

On a rush night he gave a performance that was magnificent. Arising in his pulpit, he would howl for missing takes in a voice of brass, always using the formula hallowed since Gutenberg's time: "What --- -- - ----- has got A 17?" His chief, Joe Bamberger, was also a foreman of notable talents, and knew how to holler in a way that made even the oldest printer gasp and blanch, but Josh Lynch—for such was his name—could out-holler Joe a hundred to one, on the flat or over the jumps. He was a grand fellow, and he taught me a lot about the newspaper business that was not on tap in the *Herald* editorial-rooms. Above all, he taught me that a newspaper man, in the hierarchy of earthly fauna, ranked only below the assistant foreman of a composing-room, and that neither had any reason or excuse in law or equity to take any lip from any ——— in the whole ——— world. He is dead now, but surely not forgotten. If I miss him in Hell it will be a disappointment.

The second experience that served to cake the ink upon me and doom me to journalism took the form of an overheard conversation. My father's Washington agent, Mr. Cross, paid a visit to us at Ellicott City one Sunday, and he and my father and my uncle Henry put in the afternoon drinking beer on the veranda of our house. They fell to talking of the illustrious personages they were constantly meeting in Washington—Senators who had not been sober for a generation, Congressmen who fought bartenders and kicked the windows out of night-hacks, Admirals in the Navy who were reputed to be four-, five- and even six-bottle men, Justices of the Supreme and other high courts who were said to live on whiskey and chewing tobacco alone. They naturally admired these prodigious men, and I crept up to hear them described and praised. But in the end Mr. Cross, who knew Washington far better than my father or my uncle, permitted himself a caveat of doubt. All such eminentissimos, he allowed, were mere passing shapes, as evanescent as the morning dew, here today and gone tomorrow. They had their effulgence, but then they perished, leaving no trace save a faint aroma, usually bad. The real princes of Washington, he said, were the newspaper correspondents. They outlasted Senators, Congressmen, judges and Presidents. In so far as the United States had any rational and permanent government, they were its liver and its lights. To this day, though reason may protest bitterly, I still revere the gentlemen of the Washington corps.

Other Christmas presents came and went, but there was never another that fetched and floored me like Dorman's Baltimore No. 10 Self-Inker Printing Press. The box of water-colors that set me to painting I have mentioned, and I have also alluded to the camera that aroused in me a passion for photography, and then, by way of developers and toning solutions, for chemistry. But my career as a water-colorist was brief and not glorious, and the camera came after the period covered by this history. I recall a year when some one gave me a microscope, but it, too, held me only transiently, for one of the first things I inspected through it was a drop of vinegar, and the revolting mass of worms that I saw kept me off vinegar for a year afterward, and cured me of microscopy. Another year I received an electric battery, and for a while I had a swell time with it, but I began to neglect it when I discovered that it could not work a small arc-light that I had made of two charred matches. Yet another year I was favored with a box of carpenter's tools, but they must have been poor ones, for the saw would not saw, the plane would not plane, the hammer mashed my thumb, and the chisel cut my hand.

Nor was I greatly interested in the steam-engine that appeared at Christmas 1889, or the steam railroad that followed the year after. The latter, indeed, was probably my brother Charlie's present, not mine, for he spent much more time playing with it than I did, and in later life he took to engineering, and laid many a mile of railroad line, and worked on many a bridge and tunnel.

It was the printing press that left its marks, not only upon my hands, face and clothing, but also on my psyche. They are still there, though more than fifty years have come and gone.

from Happy Days (*Alfred A. Knopf, 1940*).

◇◇◇

FIRE ALARM

At midnight or thereabout on Saturday, February 6, 1904, I did my share as city editor to put the *Sunday Herald* to bed, and then proceeded to Junker's saloon to join in the exercises of the Stevedores' Club. Its members, having already got down a good many schooners, were in a frolicsome mood, and I was so pleasantly edified that I stayed until 3:30. Then I caught a night-hawk trolley-car, and by four o'clock was snoring on my celibate couch in Hollins Street, with every hope and prospect of continuing there until noon of the next day. But at 11 a.m. there was a telephone call from the *Herald* office, saying that a big fire had broken out in Hopkins Place, the heart of downtown Baltimore, and fifteen minutes later a reporter dashed up to the house behind a sweating hack horse, and rushed in with the news that the fire looked to be a humdinger, and promised swell pickings for a dull Winter Sunday. So I hoisted my still malty bones from my couch and got into my clothes, and ten minutes later I was on my way to the office with the reporter. That was at about 11:30 a.m. of Sunday, February 7. It was not until 4 a.m. of Wednesday, February 10, that my pants and shoes, or even my collar, came off again. And it was not until 11:30 a.m. of Sunday, February 14—precisely a week to the hour since I set off—that I got home for a bath and a change of linen.

For what I had walked into was the great Baltimore fire of 1904, which burned a square mile out of the heart of the town and went howling and spluttering on for ten days. I give the exact schedule of my movements simply because it delights me, in my autumnal years, to dwell upon it, for it reminds me how full of steam and malicious animal magnetism I was when I was young. During the week following the outbreak of the fire the *Herald* was printed in three different cities, and I was present at all its accouchements, herding dispersed and bewildered reporters at long distance and cavorting gloriously in strange composing-rooms. My opening burst of work without a stop ran to sixty-four and a half hours, and then I got only six hours of nightmare sleep, and resumed on a working schedule of from twelve to fourteen hours a day, with no days off and no time for meals until work was over. It was brain-fagging and back-breaking, but it was grand beyond compare—an adventure of the first chop, a razzle-dazzle superb and elegant, a circus in forty rings. When I came out of it at last I was a settled and indeed almost a middle-aged man, spavined by responsibility and aching in every sinew, but I went into it a boy, and it was the hot gas of youth that kept me going. The uproar over, and the *Herald* on an even keel again, I picked up one day a volume of stories by a new writer named Joseph Conrad, and therein found a tale of a young sailor that struck home to me as the history of Judas must strike home to many a bloated bishop, though the sailor naturally made his odyssey in a ship, not on a newspaper, and its scene was not a provincial town in America, but the South Seas. Today, so long afterward, I too "remember my youth and the feeling that will never come back any more—the feeling that I could last forever, outlast the sea, the earth, and all men . . . Youth! All youth! The silly, charming, beautiful youth!"

Herald reporters, like all other reporters of the last generation, were usually late in coming to work on Sundays, but *that* Sunday they had begun to drift in even before I got to the office, and by one o'clock we were in full blast. The fire was then raging through a whole block, and from our fifth-floor city-room windows it made a gaudy show, full of catnip for a young city editor. But the Baltimore firemen had a hundred streams on it, and their chief, an old man named Horton, reported that they would knock it off presently. They might have done so, in fact, if the wind had not changed suddenly at three o'clock, and begun to roar from the West. In ten minutes the fire had routed Horton and his men and leaped to a second block, and in half an hour to a third and a fourth, and by dark the whole of downtown Baltimore was under a hail of sparks and flying brands, and a dozen outlying fires had started to eastward. We had a story, I am here to tell you! There have been bigger ones, of course, and plenty of them, but when and where, between the Chicago fire of 1871 and the San Francisco earthquake of 1906, was there ever one that was fatter, juicier, more exhilarating to the journalists on the actual ground? Every newspaper in Baltimore save one was burned out, and every considerable hotel save three, and every office building without exception. The fire raged for a full week, helped by that bitter Winter wind, and when it fizzled out at last the burned area looked like Pompeii, and up from its ashes rose the pathetic skeletons of no less than twenty overtaken and cremated fire-engines—some of them from Washington, Philadelphia, Pittsburgh and New York. Old Horton, the Baltimore fire chief, was in hospital, and so were several hundred of his men.

My labors as city editor during that electric week were onerous and various, but for once they did not include urging lethargic reporters to step into it. The whole staff went to work with the enthusiasm of crusaders shinning up the walls of Antioch, and all sorts of volunteers swarmed in, including three or four forgotten veterans who had been fired years before, and were thought to have long since reached the dissecting-room. Also, there were as many young aspirants from the waiting-list, each hoping for his chance at last, and one of these, John Lee Blecker by name, I remember brilliantly, for when I told him to his delight that he had a job and invited him to prove it he leaped out with exultant gloats—and did not show up again for five days. But getting lost in so vast a story did not wreck his career, for he lived to become, in fact, an excellent reporter, and not a few old-timers were lost, too. One of the best of them, sometime that afternoon, was caught in a blast when the firemen began dynamiting buildings, and got so coagulated that it was three days before he was fit for anything save writing editorials. The rest not only attacked the fire in a fine frenzy, but also returned promptly and safely, and by four o'clock thirty typewriters were going in the city-room, and my desk was beginning to pile high with red-hot copy.

Lynn Meekins, the managing editor, decided against wasting time and energy on extras: we got out one, but the story was too big for such banalities: it seemed like a toy balloon in a hurricane. "Let us close the first city edition," he said, "at nine o'clock. Make it as complete as you can. If you need twenty pages, take them. If you need fifty, take them." So we began heaving copy to the composing-room, and by seven o'clock there were columns and columns of type on the stones, and picture after picture was coming up from the engraving department. Alas, not much of that quivering stuff ever got into the *Herald*, for a little before nine o'clock, just as the front page was being made up, a couple of excited cops rushed in, howling that the buildings across the street were to be blown up in ten minutes, and ordering us to clear out at once. By this time there was a fire on the roof of the *Herald* Building itself, and another was starting in the pressroom, which had plate-glass windows reaching above the street level, all of them long ago smashed by flying brands. We tried to parley with the cops, but they were too eager to be on their way to listen to us, and when a terrific blast went off up the street Meekins ordered that the building be abandoned.

There was a hotel three or four blocks away, out of the apparent path of the fire, and there we went in a dismal procession—editors, reporters, printers and pressmen. Our lovely first edition was adjourned for the moment, but every man-jack in the outfit believed that we'd be back anon, once the proposed dynamiting had been done—every man-jack, that is, save two. One was Joe Bamberger, the foreman of the composing-room, and the other was Joe Callahan, my assistant as city editor. The first Joe was carrying page-proofs of all the pages already made up, and galley-proofs of all the remaining type-matter, and all the copy not yet set. In his left overcoat pocket was the front-page logo-type of the paper, and in his left pocket were ten or twelve halftones. The other Joe had on him what copy had remained in the city-room, a wad of Associated Press flimsy about the Russian-Japanese war, a copy-hook, a pot of paste, two boxes of copy-readers' pencils—and the assignment-book!

But Meekins and I refused to believe that we were shipwrecked, and in a little while he sent me back to the *Herald* Building to have a look, leaving Joe No. 2 to round up such reporters as were missing. I got there safely enough, but did not stay long. The proposed dynamiting, for some reason unknown, had apparently been abandoned, but the fire on our roof was blazing violently, and the press-room was vomiting smoke. As I stood gaping at this dispiriting spectacle a couple of large plate-glass windows cracked in the composing-room under the roof, and a flying brand—some of them seemed to be six feet long!—fetched a window on the editorial floor just below it. Nearly opposite, in Fayette Street, a sixteen-story office building had caught fire, and I paused a moment more to watch it. The flames leaped through it as if it had been made of matchwood and drenched with gasoline, and in half a minute they were roaring in the air at least 500 feet. It was, I suppose, the most melodramatic detail of the whole fire, but I was too busy to enjoy it, and as I made off hastily I fully expected the whole structure to come crashing down behind me. But when I returned a week later I found that the steel frame and brick skin had both held out, though all the interior was gone, and during the following Summer the burned parts were replaced, and the building remains in service to this day, as solid as the Himalayas.

At the hotel Meekins was trying to telephone to Washington, but long-distance calls still took time in 1904, and it was fifteen minutes before he raised Scott C. Bone, managing editor of the Washington *Post*. Bone was having a busy and crowded night himself, for the story was worth pages to the *Post*, but he promised to do what he could for us, and presently we were hoofing for Camden Station, a good mile away—Meekins and I, Joe Bamberger with his salvage, a copyreader with the salvage of the other Joe, half a dozen other desk men, fifteen or twenty printers, and small squads of pressmen and circulation men. We were off to Washington to print the paper there—that is, if the gods were kind. They frowned at the start, for the only Baltimore & Ohio train for an hour was an accommodation, but we poured into it, and by midnight we were in the *Post* office, and the hospitable Bone and his men were clearing a place for us in their frenzied composing-room, and ordering the press-room to be ready for us.[1]

Just how we managed to get out the *Herald* that night I can't tell you, for I remember only trifling details. One was that I was the principal financier of the expedition, for when we pooled our money at Camden Station it turned out that I had $40 in my pocket, whereas Meekins had only $5, and the rest of the editorial boys not more than $20 among them. Another is that the moon broke out of the Winter sky just as we reached the old B. & O. Station in Washington, and shined down sentimentally on the dome of the Capitol. The Capitol was nothing new to Baltimore journalists, but we had with us a new copy-reader who had lately come in from Pittsburgh, and as he saw the matronly dome for the first time, bathed in spooky moonlight, he was so overcome by patriotic and aesthetic sentiments that he took off his hat and exclaimed "My God, how beautiful!" And a third is that we all paused a second to look at the red glow over Baltimore, thirty-five miles away as the crow flies. The fire had really got going by now, and for four nights afterward the people of Washington could see its glare from their streets.

Bone was a highly competent managing editor, and contrived somehow to squeeze us into the tumultuous *Post* office. All of his linotypes were already working to capacity, so our operators were useless, but they lent a hand with the make-up,

[1] Bone was an Indianan, and had a long and honorable career in journalism, stretching from 1881 to 1918. In 1919 he became publicity chief of the Republican National Committee, and in 1921 he was appointed Governor of Alaska. He died in 1936.

and our pressmen went to the cellar to reinforce their *Post* colleagues. It was a sheer impossibility to set up all the copy we had with us, or even the half of it, or a third of it, but we nevertheless got eight or ten columns into type, and the *Post* lent us enough of its own matter to piece out a four-page paper. In return we lent the hospitable *Post* our halftones, and they adorned its first city edition next morning. Unhappily, the night was half gone before Bone could spare us any press time, but when we got it at last the presses did prodigies, and at precisely 6:30 the next morning we reached Camden Station, Baltimore, on a milk-train, with 30,000 four-page *Heralds* in the baggage-car. By eight o'clock they were all sold. Our circulation hustlers had no difficulty in getting rid of them. We had scarcely arrived before the news of our coming began to circulate around the periphery of the fire, and in a few minutes newsboys swarmed in, some of them regulars but the majority volunteers. Very few boys in Baltimore had been to bed that night: the show was altogether too gaudy. And now there was a chance to make some easy money out of it.

Some time ago I unearthed one of these orphan *Heralds* from the catacombs of the Pratt Library in Baltimore, and gave it a looking-over. It turned out to be far from bad, all things considered. The story of the fire was certainly not complete, but it was at least coherent, and three of our halftones adorned Page 1. The eight-column streamer-head that ran across its top was as follows:

HEART OF BALTIMORE WRECKED BY
GREATEST FIRE IN CITY'S HISTORY

Well, brethren, what was wrong about that? I submit that many worse heads have been written by pampered copyreaders sitting at luxurious desks, with vassals and serfs at their side. It was simple; it was direct; there was no fustian in it;

and yet it told the story perfectly. I wrote it on a make-up table in the *Post* composing-room, with Meekins standing beside me writing a box for the lower right-hand corner of the first page, thanking the *Post* for its "proverbial courtesy to its contemporaries" and promising formally that the *Herald* would be "published daily by the best means it can command under the circumstances."

Those means turned out, that next day, to be a great deal short of ideal. Leaving Joe Callahan, who had kept the staff going all night, to move to another and safer hotel, for the one where we had found refuge was now in the path of the fire, Meekins and I returned to Washington during the morning to make arrangements for bringing out a larger paper. We were not ashamed of our four pages, for even the *Sunpaper*, printed by the Washington *Evening Star*, had done no better, but what were four pages in the face of so vast a story? The boys had produced enough copy to fill at least ten on the first day of the fire, and today they might turn out enough to fill twenty. It would wring our gizzards intolerably to see so much good stuff going to waste. Moreover, there was art to consider, for our two photographers had piled up dozens of gorgeous pictures, and if there was no engraving plant left in Baltimore there were certainly plenty in Washington.

But Bone, when we routed him out, could not promise us any more accommodation than he had so kindly given us the first night. There was, it appeared, a long-standing agreement between the *Post* and the Baltimore *Evening News*, whereby each engaged to take care of the other in times of calamity, and the *News* staff was already in Washington cashing in on it, and would keep the *Post* equipment busy whenever it was not needed by the *Post* itself. Newspapers in those days had no such plants as they now boast: if I remember rightly, the *Post* had not more than a dozen linotypes, and none of them could chew up copy like the modern monsters. The prospect seemed depressing, indeed, but Bone himself gave us a shot of hope by mentioning casually that the Baltimore *World* appeared to have escaped the fire. The *World?* It was a small, ill-fed sheet of the kind then still flourishing in most big American cities, and its own daily editions seldom ran beyond four pages, but it was an *afternoon* paper, and we might hire its equipment for the night. What if it had only four linotypes? We might help them out with hand-set matter. And what if its Goss press could print but 5,000 six- or eight-page papers an hour? We might run it steadily from 6 p.m. to the middle of the next morning, bringing out edition after edition.

We got back to Baltimore as fast as the B. & O. could carry us, and found the *World* really unscathed, and, what is more, its management willing to help us, and as soon as its own last edition was off that afternoon Callahan and the gentlemen of the *Herald* staff came swarming down on its little office in Calvert Street. The ensuing night gave me the grand migraine of my life, with throbs like the blows of an ax and continuous pinwheels. Every conceivable accident rained down on us. One of the linotypes got out of order at once, and when, after maddening delays, Joe Bamberger rounded up a machinist, it took him two hours to repair it, and even then he refused to promise that it would work. Meekins thereupon turned to his desperate plan to go back to Gutenberg and set matter by hand—only to find that the *World* had insufficient type in its cases to fill more than a few columns. Worse, most of this type appeared to be in the wrong boxes, and such of it as was standing on the stones had been picked for sorts by careless printers, and was pretty well pied.[2]

[2] Perhaps I should explain some printers' terms here. The stones are flat tables (once of actual stone, but now usually of steel) on which printers do much of their work. Type is kept in wooden cases divided into boxes, one for

Meekins sent me out to find more, but all the larger printers of Baltimore had been burned out, and the only supply of any size that I could discover was in the office of the *Catholic Mirror*, a weekly. Arrangements with it were made quickly, and Joe Bamberger and his gallant lads of the union rushed the place and proceeded to do or die, but setting type by hand turned out to be a slow and vexatious business, especially to linotype operators who had almost forgotten the case. Nor did it soothe us to discover that the *Mirror's* stock of type (most of it old and worn) was in three or four different faces, with each face in two or three sizes, and that there was not enough of any given face and size to set more than a few columns. But it was now too late to balk, so Joe's goons went to work, and by dark we had ten or twelve columns of copy in type, some of it in eight-point, some in ten-point and some in twelve-point. That night I rode with Joe's chief of staff, Josh Lynch, on a commandeered express-wagon as these galleys of motley were hauled from the *Mirror* office to the *World* office. I recall of the journey only that it led down a steep hill, and that the hill was covered with ice. Josh howled whenever the horse slipped, but somehow or other we got all the galleys to the *World* office without disaster, and the next morning, after six or eight breakdowns in the press-room, we came out with a paper that at least had some news in it,

---

a character. As it is set up by the compositor it is placed in galleys, which are brass frames, and then the galleys are taken to the stone and there made up. Sometimes, after the printing has been done, the type is returned to a stone, and left there until a convenient time to return it to the cases. To "pick sorts" is to go to such standing type and pick out characters that are exhausted in the cases. Pied type is type in such confusion that it cannot be returned to the cases by the usual method of following the words, but must be identified letter by letter. To "forget the case," mentioned below, is to lose the art of picking up types from the boxes without looking at them. The boxes are not arranged alphabetically, and a printer learns the case as one learns the typewriter keyboard. A face of type is a series of sizes of one design.

though it looked as if it had been printed by country printers locked up in a distillery.

When the first copy came off the *World*'s rickety Goss press Meekins professed to be delighted with it. In the face of almost hopeless difficulties, he said, we had shown the resourcefulness of Robinson Crusoe, and for ages to come this piebald issue of the *Herald* would be preserved in museums under glass, and shown to young printers and reporters with appropriate remarks. The more, however, he looked at it the less his enthusiasm soared, and toward the middle of the morning he decided suddenly that another one like it would disgrace us forever, and announced at once that we'd return to Washington. But we knew before we started that the generous Bone could do no more for us than he had already done, and, with the *Star* monopolized by the Baltimore *Sun*, there was not much chance of finding other accommodation in Washington that would be better than the *World*'s in Baltimore. The pressure for space was now doubled, for not only was hot editorial copy piling up endlessly, but also advertising copy. Hundreds of Baltimore business firms were either burned out already or standing in the direct path of the fire, and all of them were opening temporary offices uptown, and trying to notify their customers where they could be found. Even in the ghastly parody printed in the *World* office we had made room for nearly three columns of such notices, and before ten o'clock Tuesday morning we had copy for ten more.

But where to turn? Wilmington in Delaware? It was nearly seventy miles away, and had only small papers. We wanted accommodation for printing ten, twelve, sixteen, twenty pages, for the *Herald* had suffered a crippling loss, and needed that volunteer advertising desperately. Philadelphia? It seemed fantastic, for Philadelphia was nearly a *hundred* miles away. To be sure, it had plenty of big newspaper plants, but could we bring our papers back to Baltimore in time to distribute them? The circulation men, consulted, were optimistic. "Give us 50,000 papers at 5 a.m.," they said, "and we'll sell them." So Meekins, at noon or thereabout, set off for Philadelphia, and before dark he was heard from. He had made an arrangement with Barclay H. Warburton, owner of the Philadelphia *Evening Telegraph*. The *Telegraph* plant would be ours from 6 p.m., beginning tomorrow, and it was big enough to print any conceivable paper. Meekins was asking the Associated Press to transfer our report from Baltimore to Philadelphia, and the International Typographical Union to let our printers work there. I was to get out one more edition in Washington, and then come to Philadelphia, leaving Callahan in charge of our temporary office in Baltimore. But first I was to see Oscar G. Murray, president of the B. & O. Railroad, and induce him to give us a special train from Philadelphia to Baltimore, to run every night until further notice.

The B. & O.'s headquarters building in Baltimore had been burned out like the *Herald* office, but I soon found Murray at Camden Station, functioning grandly at a table in a storage warehouse. A bachelor of luxurious and even levantine tastes, he was in those days one of the salient characters of Baltimore, and his lavender-and-white striped automobile was later to become a major sight of the town. When he gave a party for his lady friends at the Stafford Hotel, where he lived and had his being, it had to be covered as cautiously as the judicial orgies described in Chapter XII. He looked, that dreadful afternoon, as if he had just come from his barber, tailor and haberdasher. He was shaved so closely that his round face glowed like a rose, and an actual rose was in the buttonhole of his elegant but not too gaudy checked coat. In three minutes I had stated my problem and come to terms with him.

At two o'clock, precisely, every morning a train consisting of a locomotive, a baggage-car and a coach would be waiting at Chestnut Street Station in Philadelphia, with orders to shove off for Baltimore the instant our *Heralds* were loaded. It would come through to Camden Station, Baltimore, without stop, and we could have our circulation hustlers waiting for it there.

That was all. When I asked what this train would cost, the magnificent Murray waved me away. "Let us discuss that," he said, "when we are all back home." We did discuss it two months later—and the bill turned out to be nothing at all. "We had some fun together," Murray said, "and we don't want to spoil it now by talking about money." That fun consisted, at least in part, of some very exuberant railroading. If we happened to start from Philadelphia a bit late, which was not infrequent as we accumulated circulation, the special train made the trip to Baltimore at hair-raising speed, with the piles of *Heralds* in the baggage-car thrown helter-skelter on the curves, and the passengers in the coach scared half to death. All known records between Philadelphia and Baltimore were broken during the ensuing five weeks. Finally the racing went so far beyond the seemly that the proper authorities gave one of the engineers ten days lay-off without pay for wild and dangerous malpractice. He spent most of his vacation as the guest of our printers in Philadelphia, and they entertained him handsomely.

But there was still a paper to get out in Washington, and I went there late in the afternoon to tackle the dismal job. The best Bone could do for us, with the Baltimore *News* cluttering the *Post* office all day and the *Post* itself printing endless columns about the fire still raging, was four pages, and of their thirty-two columns nearly thirteen were occupied by the advertisements I have mentioned. I got the business over as soon as possible, and returned to Baltimore eager for a few winks of sleep, for I had not closed my eyes since Sunday morning, and it was now Wednesday. In the *Herald*'s temporary office I found Isidor Goodman, the night editor. He reported that every bed in downtown Baltimore was occupied two or three deep, and that if we sought to go home there were no trolley-cars or night-hacks to haul us. In the office itself there was a table used as a desk, but Joe Callahan was snoring on it. A dozen other men were on the floor.

Finally, Isidor allowed that he was acquainted with a lady who kept a surreptitious house of assignation in nearby Paca Street, and suggested that business was probably bad with her in view of the competing excitement of the fire, and that she might be able in consequence to give us a bed. But when we plodded to her establishment, which was in a very quiet neighborhood, Isidor, who was as nearly dead as I was, pulled the wrong door-bell, and a bass voice coming out of a nightshirt at a second-story window threatened us with the police if we didn't make off. We were too tired to resist this outrage, but shuffled down the street, silent and despairing. Presently we came to the Rennert Hotel, and went in hoping to find a couple of vacant spots, however hard, on a billiard-table, or the bar, or in chairs in the lobby. Inside, it seemed hopeless, for every chair in sight was occupied, and a dozen men were asleep on the floor. But there was a night-clerk on duty whom we knew, and after some mysterious hocus-pocus he whispered to us to follow him, and we trailed along up the stairs to the fourth floor. There he unlocked a door and pointed dramatically to a vacant bed, looking beautifully white, wide and deep. We did not wait to learn how it had come to be so miraculously vacant, but peeled off our coats and collars, kicked off our shoes, stepped out of our pants, and leaped in. Before the night-clerk left us we were as dead to this world and its sorrows as Gog and Magog. It was 4 a.m. and we slept until ten. When we got back to the *Herald*'s quarters we let it be known that we had passed the night in the house of Isidor's friend in Paca Street, along with two rich society women from Perth Amboy, N.J.

That night we got out our first paper in Philadelphia—a gorgeous thing of fourteen pages, with twenty columns of advertising. It would knock the eyes out of the *Sun* and *Evening News*, and we rejoiced and flapped our wings accordingly. In particular, we were delighted with the *Evening Telegraph*'s neat and graceful head-type, and when we got back to Baltimore we imitated it. Barclay Warburton, the owner of the *Telegraph*, came down to the office to see us through—elegantly invested in a tail coat and a white tie. Despite this unprofessional garb, he turned out to be a smart fellow in the press-room, and it was largely due to his aid that we made good time. I returned to Baltimore early in the morning on the first of Oscar Murray's special trains, and got a dreadful bumping on the curves and crossings. The circulation boys fell on our paper with exultant gurgles, and the next night we lifted the press-run by 10,000 copies.

We stayed in Philadelphia for five weeks, and gradually came to feel almost at home there—that is, if anybody not born in the town can ever feel at home in Philadelphia. The attitude of the local colleagues at first puzzled us, and then made us snicker in a superior way. Save for Warburton himself, not one of them ever offered us the slightest assistance, or, indeed, even spoke to us. We were printing a daily newspaper 100 miles from base—a feat that remains unparalleled in American journalism, so far as I know, to this day—and it seemed only natural that some of the Philadelphia brethren should drop in on us, if only out of curiosity. But the only one who ever appeared was the managing editor of one of the morning papers, and he came to propose graciously that we save him a few dollars by lending him our halftones of the fire.

Inasmuch as we were paying his paper a substantial sum every day for setting ads for us—the *Evening Telegraph* composing-room could not handle all that crowded in—we replied with a chilly nix, and he retired in a huff.

There was a press club in Philadelphia in those days, and its quarters downtown offered a convenient roosting-place for the hour or two after the night's work was done. In any other American city we'd have been offered cards on it instantly and automatically, but not in Philadelphia. At the end of a week a telegraph operator working for us got cards for us in some unknown manner, and a few of us began using the place. During the time we did so only one member ever so much as spoke to us, and he was a drunken Englishman whose conversation consisted entirely of encomiums of Barclay Warburton. Whenever he saw us he would approach amiably and begin chanting "Good ol' Bahclay! Good ol' Bahclay! Bahclay's a good *sawt,*" with *sawt* rhyming with *caught*, and apparently meaning *sort*. We agreed heartily, but suffered under the iteration, and presently we forsook the place for the saloon patronized by the *Herald* printers, where there was the refined entertainment described in Chapter XI.

Meekins's arrangements for getting out the *Herald* so far from home were made with skill and worked perfectly. Callahan remained in Baltimore in charge of our field quarters outside the burned area, and on every train bound for Philadelphia during the afternoon he had an office-boy with such copy as had accumulated. At six o'clock, when the *Evening Telegraph* men cleared out of their office, we opened a couple of private wires, and they kept us supplied with later matter. Even after the fire burned out at last Baltimore was in an appalling state, and there were plenty of old Baltimoreans who wagged their heads despairingly and predicted that it would never be rebuilt. One such pessimist was the Mayor of the town: a little while later, yielding to his vapors, he committed suicide. But there were optimists enough to offset these glooms, and before we left Philadelphia the debris was being cleared away, many ancient and narrow streets were being widened, and scores of new buildings were started. All these debates and doings made for juicy news, and the men of the local staff, ably bossed by Callahan, poured it out daily. Meekins would come to Philadelphia two or three times a week to look over his faculty in exile, and I would drop down to Baltimore about as often to aid and encourage Joe. We had our own printers in Philadelphia and our own pressmen. Our circulation department performed marvels, and the advertising department gobbled up all the advertising in sight, which, as I have said, was plenty. The *Herald* had been on short commons for some time before the fire, but during the two or three months afterward it rolled in money.

Once I had caught up on lost sleep I prepared to do a narrative of the fire as I had seen it, with whatever help I could get from the other *Herald* men, but the project got itself postponed so often that I finally abandoned it, and to this day no connected story has ever been printed. The truth is that, while I was soon getting sleep enough, at least for a youngster of twenty-four, I had been depleted by the first cruel week more than I thought, and it was months before I returned to anything properly describable as normalcy. So with the rest of the staff, young and old. Surveying them when the hubbub was over, I found confirmation for my distrust, mentioned in Chapter XI, of alcohol as a fuel for literary endeavor. They divided themselves sharply into three classes. Those who had kept off the stuff until work was done and it was time to relax—there were, of course, no all-out teetotalers in the outfit—needed only brief holidays to be substantially as good as new. Those who had drunk during working hours, though in moderation, showed a considerable fraying, and some of them had spells of sickness. Those who had boozed in the classical manner were useless before the end of the second week, and three of them were floored by serious illnesses, one of which ended, months later, in complete physical and mental collapse. I pass on this record for what it is worth.

from Newspaper Days (*Alfred A. Knopf, 1941*).

A DIP INTO STATECRAFT

[1912]

Some time ago, in writing a book for the edification of the young, I let fall the remark that, in the now forgotten year of 1912, I was a candidate for the Democratic nomination for Vice-President of the United States. It is almost incredible that an author of my experience should have made such a slip. I must have been very well aware, even in the cachexia of composition, that the only effect of my statement would be to provoke a storm of snorts, and get me classed among the damndest liars on earth. That, indeed, is exactly what happened, and during the month after the book came out (it had a very fair sale) I received 30,000 or 40,000 letters full of hoots and sneers. Nevertheless, my statement was true in the most precise and literal sense, and I hereby reiterate it with my hand upon the Holy Scriptures. I was actually a candidate as I said, but I should add at once, before historians begin to rush up with their proofs, that I did not get the nomination.

Perhaps the best way to tell the story, which is mercifully brief, will be to start out with a cast of characters. Here it is:

The Hon. J. Harry Preston, mayor of Baltimore, and a man of aggressive and relentless bellicosity.

Charles H. Grasty, editor of the Baltimore *Sunpapers*, an enemy to Preston, and a sly and contriving fellow.

H. L. Mencken, a young journalist in the employ of Grasty as columnist and trigger-man.

Scene: Baltimore.

Time: The weeks preceding the Democratic National Convention of 1912.

That was the year when the late Woodrow Wilson was nominated and so began his dizzy rise to immortality. Grasty was for him, but Preston was against him and in favor of Champ Clark of Missouri. This difference was only one of hundreds that lay between them. They quarreled all the time, and over any proposition that could be dissected into alternatives. If Preston, as mayor, proposed to enlarge the town dog-pound, Grasty denounced it in both morning and evening *Sunpapers* as an assault upon the solvency of Baltimore, the comity of nations, and the Ten Commandments, and if Grasty argued in the *Sunpapers* that the town alleys ought to be cleaned oftener Preston went about the ward clubs warning his heelers that the proposal was only the opening wedge for anarchy, atheism and cannibalism. It was impossible to unearth anything against Preston's private character, though every *Sun* reporter, under Grasty's urging, made desperate efforts to do so, for he was a respectable family man, a vestryman in an Episcopal church with a watchful rector, and a lawyer of high standing at the bar. But in his rôle of politician, of course, he was an easier target, and so his doings in the City Hall were gradually assimilated (at least in the *Sunpapers*) to those of Tweed in New York, the *ancien régime* in France, and the carpetbaggers in the South.

Grasty, on his side, was vulnerable in the reverse order. That is to say, he could not be accused of political corruption, for it was notorious that he had no political ambitions, but in his private life there was more encouraging material, for several times, in the past, he had forgotten himself. The dirt thus dredged up was gradually amalgamated into the master charge that he had been run out of Kansas City (where he formerly lived) for a series of adulteries of a grossly levantine and brutal nature. This charge Preston not only labored at great length in his harangues to the ward clubs; he also included it in his commencement addresses to the graduates of the Baltimore high-schools and his speeches of welcome to visiting Elks, Shriners, Christian Endeavorers and plumbers' supply dealers; moreover, he reduced it to writing, signed his name to it with a bold flourish, and printed it as paid advertising in the *Sunpapers* themselves.

The revenues from this advertising were gratefully received by Grasty, for the *Sunpapers*, in those days, were using up almost as much red ink in the business office as printer's ink in the press-room. But against that pleasant flow of the wages of sin there had to be set off the loss from the municipal advertising, which Preston, though a Democrat, diverted to a Republican paper. It took him a long while to clear it out of the *Sunpapers*, but clear it out he did at last. Any City Hall functionary who, by force of old habit, sent in an announcement of a tax sale or a notice of an application to open a hat-cleaning parlor was fired forthwith and to the tune of loud screams of indignation. To meet this devastating attack the whole staff of the two *Sunpapers* spent half its time in concocting reprisals. No story against Preston was too incredible to be printed, and no criticism too trivial or irresponsible. If the blackamoors in the death-house at the Baltimore City Jail had signed a round robin accusing him of sending them poison in cornpone or snuff, it would have gone into type at once.

My own share in this campaign of defamation was large and assiduous. In my daily column on the editorial page of the *Evening Sun* I accused Preston of each and every article in my private catalogue of infamies. Once I even alleged that he was a Sunday-school superintendent—and was amazed to discover that it was true. I had nothing against him personally; on the contrary, I was fond of him, thought he was doing well as mayor, and often met him amicably at beer-parties. But in his character of enemy of Grasty, and hence of the *Sunpapers*, I was bound by the journalistic code of the time to deal him a lick whenever I could, and this I did every day. On some days, in fact, my whole column was devoted to reviling him. Why he never hit back by accusing me of adultery, or, at all events, of fornication, I do not know, but no doubt it was because he was too busy amassing and embellishing his case against Grasty.

The plain people of Baltimore naturally took his side against the *Sunpapers*. They are always, in fact, against newspapers, and they are always in favor of what reformers call political corruption. They believe that it keeps money in circulation, and makes for a spacious and stimulating communal life. Thus they cheered Preston every time he appeared in public, and especially did they cheer him every time the *Sunpapers* published fresh allegations that he and his goons, having made off with everything movable in the City Hall, were beginning on the slate roof and the doorknobs. This popularity had a powerful effect on the man himself, for he was not without the vanity that afflicts the rest of us. He began to see himself as a great tribune of the people, ordained by God to rescue them from the entrapments of a dissolute journalism, by libel out of crim. con. More, he began to wonder if the job of mayor of Baltimore was really large enough for his talents. Wasn't there something grander and juicier ahead? Didn't the Bible itself guarantee that a good and faithful servant should have a reward? What if the people of Maryland should decide to draft the man who had saved the people of Baltimore, and make him their Governor and Captain-General? What if the people of the whole United—

But this last wayward thought had to wait until, early in 1912, the Democrats of the nation decided that Baltimore should be their convention city. Preston, as mayor, had a large hand in bringing the party national committee to that decision. He not only made eloquent representations about the traditional delights of the town, especially in the way of eating and drinking; he also agreed to raise a fund of $100,000 to pay the costs of the show, and made a big contribution to it himself, for he was a man of means. During the Spring the wild fancies and surmises that were devouring him began to emerge. One day the Republican paper getting the city advertising suggested that he would make a magnificent candidate for the Vice-Presidency, the next day he received hundreds of spontaneous letters and telephone calls from his jobholders, urging him to accept the plain call of his country, and the third day his campaign was in the open, and throwing out dense clouds of sparks and smoke. It soon appeared that he had an understanding with Champ Clark. Clark had already rounded up a majority of the delegates to the coming convention, but he needed more, for the two-thirds rule still prevailed. Why couldn't the Baltimore gallery, packed and fomented by Preston, panic enough waverers to give Clark the nomination? It seemed an enlightened trade, and it was made. If Preston delivered the goods and Clark became the standard-bearer, Preston would have second place.

It was at this point that Grasty conceived his hellish plot, and the rest of the story is soon told. Under the presidential primary law then on the books in Maryland every candidate for the Presidency who itched for the votes of the state's delegates had to file his name "before the first Monday in May" preceding the convention, and with it deposit $270 in cash money. Under the same law candidates for the Vice-Presidency lay under the same mulct. If no candidate submitted to it, the state convention was free to instruct the delegates to the national convention to vote for anyone it fancied, but if there were two who had paid up it had to make its choice between them, and if there was but one it had to instruct the delegates to vote for him. The agents of Wilson, Clark and all the other contenders for first place on the ticket had entered their appearances and paid their fees, but no candidate for the Vice-Presidency had been heard from. Preston, of course, knew the law, but he was a thrifty fellow and saw no reason why he should waste $270, for he figured with perfect plausibility that he would be the only aspirant for second place before the state convention.

Grasty's sinister mind grasped this point a day or two before I was sailing for Europe on a holiday. Summoned to his office, I sat enchanted while he unfolded his plan. It was to wait until the very last minute for filing names of Vice-Presidential candidates, and then rush an agent to Annapolis, properly equipped with $270 in cash, to file *mine*. "Go back to your office," he instructed me, "and write a letter of acceptance. Say in it that you are sacrificing yourself to save the country from the menace of Preston. Lay it on with a shovel, and take all the space you want. To be sure, you'll be in the middle of the Atlantic when the time comes, but I'll send you a wireless, so you'll know what to say when the New York *Herald* reporter meets you at Cherbourg. The joke will wreck Preston, and the shock may even kill him. If he actually shoots himself I'll tone down your statement a bit, but write it as if he were still alive and howling. Imagine the scene when the state convention is forced to instruct the delegates to the national convention to vote for you! Here is the law: read it and laugh. It is really too rich, especially this point: the delegates to the national convention will have to vote for you *as a unit* until 'in their conscientious judgment' you are out of the running. That may not come until days and even weeks after the convention starts. All the Wilson men will throw you votes to annoy Clark. Now get busy with your letter of acceptance before I laugh myself to death."

On the fatal evening I was aboard ship in lat. 50 N, long. 15 W, gulping down beer with my traveling companion, A. H. McDannald, another *Sunpaper* man, and keeping a sharp lookout for a page-boy with a radio envelope. McDannald was in on the plot, and helped me to itch and pant. We got through beer after beer—one, two, three, six, ten, *n*. We wolfed plate after plate of sandwiches. We returned to beer. We ordered more sandwiches. The hours moved on leaden feet; the minutes seemed to be gummy and half dead. Finally, we were the only passengers left in the smokeroom, and the bartender and waiters began to shuffle about pointedly and to douse the lights. Just as darkness closed in on us the page-boy came at last. He had two messages for McDannald and three for me. Both of McDannald's read "Sorry to have missed you; bon voyage," and so did two of mine. The third read: "Everything is off. Say nothing to anyone."

It was not until I got home, four weeks later, that I found out what had happened. Grasty, it appeared, had been so taken by the ingenuity and villainy of his scheme that when he went to the Maryland Club the next afternoon for his daily ration of Manhattan cocktails he couldn't resist revealing it—in strict confidence, of course—to one of the bibuli there assembled. I should say that the bibulus was normally a very reliable man, and carried in his breast a great many anecdotes of Grasty that Preston would have given gold and frankincense to hear, but this time he was so overcome by the gorgeousness of the secret that he took a drop too much, and so blabbed. This blabbing was done in the sanctity of the club, but Preston had his spies even there. Thus, when Grasty's agent appeared at the office of the Secretary of State at Annapolis, at the very last minute for filing names, with $270 in greenbacks held tightly in his fist, it was only to find that Preston's agent had got there two minutes before him, and was engaged with snickers and grimaces in counting out the same sum.

I thereby missed my purple moment, and maybe even immortality. Now that the facts are before a candid world, let the publicists of the *Nation*, the *New Masses* and the *New Republic* speculate upon the probable effects upon history—nay, upon the very security and salvation of humanity—if Grasty's scheme had worked. I offer them the job without prejudice, for no matter how powerfully their minds play upon it their verdict will be only moot. It was not until years later that I discovered that the Constitution of the United States, Article II, Section 1, provides that no person shall be eligible for the Presidency, and *pari passu* for the Vice-Presidency, "who shall not have attained to the age of thirty-five years." On that July day of 1912 when the Hon. Thomas R. Marshall of Indiana got my job I was precisely thirty-one years, ten months and twenty-three days old—and the Constitution was still in force.

from Heathen Days (*Alfred A. Knopf, 1943*).

Mencken *of* BALTIMORE

Huntington Cairns

Mencken's vigor is astonishing. It is like an electric current. In all he writes there is a crackle of blue sparks . . . that give you a sense of enormous hidden power.

JOSEPH CONRAD

When Henry L. Mencken was born in 1880 in Baltimore, the then fourth largest city in the United States was not noted for a literary tradition. It possessed a number of writers, but only one had achieved distinction. This exception was Edgar Allan Poe, who remains today the city's most famous writer, with an international reputation. Mencken is the first Baltimore writer since Poe who possessed the qualifications for a place on this roster.

Huntington Cairns was for many years secretary of the National Gallery of Art in Washington, D.C. He edited *H. L. Mencken: The American Scene.*

But Mencken's association with Baltimore is far more intimate than that of Poe, who lived at one time or another in several cities. Mencken would live in no other city than Baltimore. His phrase for the attraction of the town was that it had charm, and it was the right comment. The city cast a spell over those who knew its daily life, its cobblestones, its streets, alleys, horse-drawn cars, and other complements to the civilized living of Mencken's early days. During his lifetime many offers came to him as a newspaperman to establish a connection with some paper elsewhere, but he was never really tempted. He was deeply attached to his home, his parents and brothers and sister, and he saw Baltimore with the friends he made there as an extension of his home life. He observed in the Baltimore *Evening Sun* in 1931 that a Baltimorean was a special kind of person, he was not an average man. He was *of* Baltimore in the European fashion of the Middle Ages and the Renaissance, when the best men were marked by adding their geographical localities to their names.

Not even the attractions of Periclean Athens could have taken him away from his native city, and his undying love for it despite all the changes it underwent during his lifetime is but one example of his extraordinary consistency. The unity of his thought, his work, and his life was phenomenal. It extended from his basic ideas to his manner of living. Early on, he settled into a pattern of life which he was to follow the rest of his days. It was built on two rocks—coherent unity in every detail of his life, and arduous work.

Mencken's love for Baltimore was not only manifest, but manifold. Many times, in the *Sunpapers* and elsewhere, he wrote of his good fortune in having learned from its institutions, prospered from its food and drink, savored its atmosphere, suffered amiably its climate, enjoyed its people and the music he made with them and of them. The merest glimpse at a few aspects of his life reveals many of these tender relationships.

A BALTIMORE EDUCATION

A tireless reader from a very early age, Mencken learned far more from his own reading than from any schooling, though he appreciated both his schools and his teachers. So far as I can recall, he spoke disparagingly of only one, Richard Uhrbrock, who taught mathematics at the Polytechnic Institute, the Baltimore high school from which Mencken graduated at the age of sixteen. A generation later I was in Uhrbrock's class at the Baltimore City College and remonstrated mildly with Mencken that he may have underestimated Uhrbrock's ability. Mencken remained firm; perhaps Uhrbrock meanwhile had learned some mathematics.

When he was seventeen, Mencken enrolled in a correspondence course which purportedly taught aspirants how to become writers. For such enterprises, the instructors were reasonably competent, and Mencken always spoke well of them.

But it was what he got on his own that constituted the bulk of his education. In *Happy Days* he records that *Huckleberry Finn* was the great discovery of his early years, and it came from a shelf at home. It has often been noted how much influence Twain had on Mencken's development as an American humorist. One short passage from his memoirs of his West Baltimore childhood will serve to illustrate the point.

One day, he recorded, he was held up by two tough boys and relieved of his "all: five keys, a horse chestnut, the snapper of a buggy whip, a dried cockroach in a pill box, a small shell, six agate marbles, a top, and a handkerchief used mainly for dusting my shoes. I also had two cents, but the bandits, after a long debate, decided not to take them, it would be stealing."

Throughout his life Mencken, who never went to college, took advantage of two excellent libraries which served him well. The Enoch Pratt Free Library was a circulating library with an astonishing collection of scholarly books of a high order. In addition, it catered to the general public. The Peabody Library was also a scholarly library; its books did not circulate, but its patrons were assigned cubicles where they could work in privacy and quiet, and the books they were using could remain on their desks until they were no longer needed. The staffs of both libraries were friendly and efficient in their relations with the public.

The philosopher Alfred North Whitehead held that the educated man was the self-educated man, and Mencken was a prime example of that insight. It is rare for a student to fall into the hands of a stimulating teacher, and one of the important services a competent teacher can perform is to tell a student, "Don't read that book, read this one." Mencken had no one to tender him such advice. Long ago, Havelock Ellis in his study of British genius found that the sons of ministers constituted the largest class of such lucky persons, because their fathers usually had well-stocked libraries. Mencken had to separate the good books from the bad on his own, with the consequence that he read much popular trash, but one must admit that, Mencken being Mencken, he got reams of good copy from them.

He made no systematic study of prose, but he read widely among the standard English stylists, particularly the Augustans. He was not especially familiar with Shakespeare, but he thought Mistress Quickly's account of Falstaff's death one of the finest pieces of prose in the language, and that the opening of *Hamlet* would be difficult to better as a piece of stagecraft. I once tried to draw him out on the merits of *A Comedy of Errors*, but he injected into the conversation the name of Hazlitt, who did not regard the play with pleasure, and then discoursed on the dullness of articles which showed the influence of Hazlitt on Lamb and vice versa.

In the end, Mencken graduated *magna cum laude* from Baltimore's two great libraries.

NEWSPAPER DAYS

Mencken believed that the life of a young newspaper reporter in his day was the "maddest, gladdest, damndest existence ever enjoyed by mortal youth." He maintained that he had no more public spirit than a cat. In one sense the statement is true, in another false. He could no more have thought of a career devoted to improving the public good than he could have of becoming a Prohibitionist. Nevertheless, he wrote hundreds of thousands of words which advised and cajoled the Baltimore public into following courses which he thought beneficial to the public welfare. He spoke freely on the relative merits of political candidates, sewer plans, educational methods, executions, and all other business which interested the public, and some which did not. But he always put his views forward as an informed man giving freely of opinions, and with no impulse to improve mankind.

The ancient Athenians held that a citizen who did not give voice to his views on public matters belonged elsewhere. During World War I, there were patriotic efforts in Baltimore to cause Mencken to move elsewhere for *giving* his views —i.e., for expressing his German sympathies. Unpopular as they were, none could deny that he gave them the same forceful and fearless expression that he gave to all his opinions.

Rumors of Mencken's omniscience were widespread, and he did nothing to discourage them. Movie stars, hopeful writers, city planners, even a nearby mortician, sought his counsel. Some of his suggestions alarmed the sanest politicians. Governor Albert Ritchie, a literal-minded man, asked Mencken's advice on some issues in a coming campaign. Mencken arranged a meeting at his home on Hollins Street with two or three members of the *Sun* hierarchy present. As the discussion moved forward, the governor became more and more alarmed as he reflected upon the impact on the voters if some of the suggestions ever reached the public. Mencken's humor probably bubbled over with a remark which reminded the governor of his host's famous proposal that defeated candidates for the presidency should be promptly hanged on the ground that otherwise they would be infernal nuisances for the rest of their days. The governor resorted to a telephone and was overheard to demand that an assistant call back and inform him that the State House in Annapolis was on fire. Shortly thereafter the governor fled.

As a humorist of the first order, Mencken's contributions to the rich American tradition in that field were abundant. Goethe's remark that "men always show their character in nothing more clearly than by what they find laughable" is applicable to many first-rate writers, but to none more so than Mencken. He certainly added to the merriment of his city, in almost countless ways—including in the "letters to the editor."

On one occasion the publisher of a four-volume history of American literature withdrew a volume under pressure from the Christian Science church in order to revise a chapter on Mary Baker Eddy which the church found offensive. This action provoked a caustic article from Mencken denouncing the action and commenting on Mary Baker Eddy, whom he did not hold in esteem. The church answered at once through its committee on such matters, and complained that Mencken had offended the memory of an elderly New England lady who had benefited thousands. Mencken replied in the letters column that he did not know whether the committee was talking about Mary Baker Eddy or Lydia Pinkham. At once the committee asked for a meeting with Paul Patterson, the paper's publisher. Patterson and Mencken received the delegation, and Patterson inquired what they could do for them. The chairman of the committee responded that first they wanted justice. Mencken promptly answered, "That is the last thing you are going to get. What is your next point?"

In fact, Mencken's manifest fairness brought him requests to mediate public controversies, some of which he accepted. The most notable was his resolution of a boycott by the Catholic church of the *Sunpapers* because a foreign correspondent inadvisedly compared Hitler and St. Ignatius Loyola.

THE MUSICAL BALTIMOREAN

Mencken's two major concerns in life were writing and music. Writing gave him pleasure, and music was therapeutic. When the ludicrous entered into his writing his face would sometimes light up with a brief expression of amusement. Music was his decompression chamber. Thus writing and music were, to him, strong manifestations of a play impulse which is widespread in many forms of nature. His assiduous writing habits demanded interruptions and diversion, which he found on a regular basis in music.

He was an occasional concert-goer, particularly when friends were performing or the music was of special interest to him. Conradi, the concert player and Mencken's friend, gave a performance at the Peabody Conservatory in the midst of one of Baltimore's heat waves. Later, Conradi told Louis Cheslock, a faculty member at the Peabody and another friend of Mencken's, that Mencken had not come to hear him play, but to watch him sweat.

But Mencken's main delight in music was when he participated as a player, at the regular meetings of the Saturday Night Club. This organization could in no way be confused with the several principal clubs of Baltimore in Mencken's time, most notable of which were the Maryland Club and the University Club. Mencken joined the Maryland Club in 1937; for him it was a place where he could get good food and entertain guests. This had become something of a burden to him with the changing servant situation and his advancing years. That, however, was a social club. The Saturday Night Club was something else altogether.

It consisted of members who could play musical instruments. (Willie Woollcott, brother of the New York drama critic Alec Woollcott, was the exception. Mencken agreed to Willie's admission provided that he was assigned the triangle and that another member stood by him to hold his hand and strike the appropriate notes.)

The club met for many years at Albert Hildebrandt's violin shop to play music, after which it would then suspend for refreshments at the Rennert Hotel. At Hildebrandt's, Max Brödel would play the first piano and Mencken the second. With the repeal of Prohibition, the club established itself at Schellhase's Cafe and Restaurant, or, as Mencken called it, the "Kaif," then on Franklin Street and later a block away on Howard Street, where it is still in business. It was reported to have had the finest beer in Baltimore.

Mencken adored German music above all. His god was Beethoven, but he was no snob. He was also delighted when Union Square, opposite his home, was given its share of concerts in the sweltering summer months by a small peripatetic

German band which appeared in turn at neighborhood street corners and parks throughout the city to entertain the residents. (There were also Italian bands performing in various parks.) Louis Cheslock has said that the Baltimore Municipal Band also made the rounds of the city to areas such as Union Square, and Mencken and his brother August spoke of the band frequently. What they did not like was the part where the audience was urged to join in the singing of popular songs by a "leader" with a bull horn.

Baltimore's musical tastes have always been catholic, and so were Mencken's.

THE FOOD OF BALTIMORE

Mencken was not only ombibulous (his own coinage), but also omnivorous. He once remarked that in his boyhood a relative was a great nuisance in the kitchen because he disliked most foods and demanded special dishes. Mencken resolved to follow the opposite course. He had many preferences, but I never knew him to dismiss an edible preparation. From a surgical capon to "pawnhoss,"* he would exclaim with gusto over the food before him. He had a natural taste for German food, but above all he treasured the products of what he called that vast protein factory, Chesapeake Bay. Baltimore's highest compliments in this field came from Oliver Wendell Holmes, the Autocrat of the Breakfast Table, who pronounced Baltimore in 1858 the "gastronomic metropolis of the Union!" "Why don't you," he asked, "put a canvas-back duck on top of the Washington Column? Why don't you put that lady off from the Battle Monument and plant

* Similar to scrapple.

a terrapin in her place?" There is a Menckenesque touch in this proposal and a reverberation years later in Mencken's pronouncement that Chicago was the literary capital of the United States.

Mencken's hosannas to the seafood of the Bay are the loudest it has received. He knew the finest and where to get it, how to prepare it, and the accompaniments, such as Maryland beaten biscuits, that go with it. He rated as first among the public restaurants the old Hotel Rennert, manned by blacks, who served only Maryland products prepared in the Maryland manner. The chief servitor at the oyster bar wore a long black mustache, read only the London *Times*, and maintained a large bowl of the tiny live oyster crabs (found alive in oysters) which can be eaten raw, in an oyster stew or as part of a delicious bisque. Mencken was a poet of the delicacies of the Bay, and it has had no other before or since.

In the fall it was the practice of Baltimore burghers, such as Mencken's father, to suspend in the cellar a number of Virginia hams and shoulders to see them through the winter. These would sustain a family of five in comfort. Along with the hams, the householders put a supply of terrapin in the cellar, which promoted the pleasing custom at Christmas time of allowing some of the children of the neighborhood to capture terrapins and place candles on their backs for a terrapin race in the dark.

Mencken was fond of the Chincoteague oyster. The bed has now almost been fished out and oysters sold under that name are transplanted from the beds of the Rappahannock, a river farther west. After two weeks in the waters of Chincoteague Bay, they may legally be sold as the original article. So may Rappahannock oysters tied to cords and lowered into Chincoteague waters for several minutes—these are known as stringers.

Huntington Cairns

CLOSE TO HOME

One of the reasons Mencken loved Baltimore was that Baltimoreans lived in houses rather than, like New Yorkers, in apartment buildings. This gave to the city in general and its neighborhoods in particular a certain stability and feeling of permanence that one did not find in New York, Mencken claimed. As a Baltimore householder himself, he took an interest in the running of his home from the stack of wood in the backyard to the parlor on the first floor front. For this room, Mencken employed a good cabinet-maker on Howard Street, at the other end of the block from Smith's bookstore, to reproduce pieces of furniture from earlier days which he admired. He himself collected small German woodcarvings. Sarah Haardt's interest was in the Victorian period, and after his marriage to her in 1930 this interest began to take shape in the furnishing of the apartment they occupied on Cathedral Street.

Occasionally Mencken would succumb to passing health fads such as the outdoor sleeping porch, which in his case overlooked the Hollins Street backyard. The salubrious air of winter and summer was supposed to strengthen the body. Mencken found the case otherwise. He also had a septum which was off-center, with the result that one nostril was larger than the other. This was operated upon, a procedure once as fashionable as the old practice of removing the tonsils. For friends who traveled with him, the consequences were fearful. A host would now and then assign Mencken and his companion to the same room, where Mencken's snores would rattle the rooftop. Sleeping was impossible in the din, and the only remedy, as soon as Mencken was asleep, which was immediately, was to pick up one's mattress and move into the hall, protected by a tightly shut door.

Although fastidious in his personal habits, if Mencken had a tailor, neither his colleague on the *Smart Set* and *Mercury*, George Jean Nathan, nor another friend, the novelist Joseph Hergesheimer, approved of him. Mencken was known to keep an eye on the remnant counters of Baltimore's leading department stores. He was slightly color-blind but nevertheless favored bright colors, not always of harmonizing attributes. He would buy remnants and take them to a seamstress who made them into commodious pajamas, the upper and lower parts of which rarely matched.

MENCKEN AND THE HOPKINS

Johns Hopkins University and Hospital were among the chief jewels in Baltimore's crown in Mencken's time, not least because members of the Hopkins faculty to some extent entered into the social life of the city and thus added to its civilized qualities. Mencken's connections with the Hopkins Hospital were intimate and of long duration, and culminated in a series of twenty articles on the institution, published in the Baltimore *Sun* in 1937.

He maintained close relations with members of the hospital faculty and with students, particularly in the latter's amusing society meetings where he occasionally spoke. In the event illness were to incapacitate Mencken or his brother August, the two of them agreed the stricken one would immediately be transported to the hospital for treatment.

Mencken's admiration for the hospital never faltered, but he objected to the university's following the general trend of the American universities toward over-permissiveness in the curriculum. In the early 1930s Mencken compared Johns Hopkins University to the Chicago College of Paperhanging.

THE CONSTANT LOVER

In the decades after World War I, Baltimore changed—and not always for the better—to the point where there seemed at times little resemblance to the town of Mencken's youth. Nevertheless, he made the adjustment without difficulty. Even in his years as a celebrated New York critic and editor, Baltimore remained his home. The two were a combination of forces which the city had not heretofore known, and which it has not known again. His judgments were intelligent and profitable to the city. He kept his eyes upon almost all the city's activities, and he brought to their consideration an exceptional and fair intelligence which enabled him to see things in their true character. Through the years, apart from the invaluable benefactions bestowed upon the city by its merchants, Mencken probably did more for its benefit than any other person who has lived there.

He was, of course, known to the other gifted Baltimoreans of his generation, many of whom gave him support in his forays even though some were unacquainted with him. I like the remark that one of them once made to me, that Mencken was the embodiment of Frederick the Great's description of the Junkers: "They wouldn't lie and they couldn't be bought."

THE SUMMING UP

Once Mencken wheeled around in the swivel chair at his desk and peeked cautiously out of the window overlooking Union Square. He turned quickly back and said, "The sons of bitches are gaining on us."

Good Old Baltimore *appeared in the* Smart Set *for May, 1913. Mencken had been writing short pieces about Baltimore for the* Sunpapers *for years and he would continue the practice until illness forced retirement. The* Smart Set *article was his first national piece on the city and it sets forth the essence of what he had to say through the years on the subject. He never bettered it.*

◇◇◇

GOOD OLD BALTIMORE

In the life of every Baltimorean not to the manner born—that is to say, of every Baltimorean recruited from the outer darkness—there are three sharply defined stages. The first, lasting about a week, is one of surprise and delight—delight with the simple courtesy of the people, with the pink cheeks and honest hips of the girls, with the range and cheapness of the victualry, with the varied loveliness of the surrounding land and water, with the touch of Southern laziness in the air. Thus the week of introduction, of discovery, of soft sitting in the strangers' pew.

Follows now a sudden reaction—and six months of discontent. Baltimore, compared to New York or Chicago, even to Atlanta or Kalamazoo, is indubitably slow. No passion for novelty, no hot yearning for tomorrow, is in her burghers. They change their shirts but once a day—flattery!—flattery!—and their prejudices but once a generation. It is not easy to sell them new goods; it is not easy to make them sell their own goods in a new way. They show, collectively, communally, the somewhat touchy *intransigeance* of their ancient banks, their medieval public offices. Mount a soapbox and bawl your liver pills—and they will set their catchpolls on you. Give them a taste of New York brass, of Western wind music —and their smile of courtesy will freeze into a smile of amused contempt, if not into a downright sneer. Naturally enough, the confident newcomer, bounding full tilt into this barbed psychic barrier, feels that he is grossly ill used. The Baltimoreans—think of it!—actually laugh at his pedagogy, revile his high flights of commercial sapience, fling back at him his offers to lift them up! Boors, blockheads, fossils! And so the victim, leaking blood from his metaphysical wounds, sees himself a martyr, pines for home and mother, and issues a proclamation of damnation. Whence arises, beloved, the perennial news that the cobblestones of Baltimore are rough, that the harbor of Baltimore is no compote of roses, that the oysters of Baltimore are going off, that the folk of Baltimore suffer the slings and arrows of *arteriosclerosis.*

Six months of that scorn, that fever, that rebellion. And then, one day, if the gods be kind enough to keep him so long, the rebel finds himself walking down Charles Street hill, from the Cardinal's house toward Lexington Street. It is five o'clock of a fine afternoon—an afternoon, let us say, in Indian summer. A caressing softness is in the air; the dusk is stealing down; lights begin to show discreetly, far back in prim, dim shops. Suddenly a sense of the snugness, the coziness, the delightful intimacy of it all strikes and fills the wayfarer. Suddenly he glows and mellows. Suddenly his heart opens, like a clam reached by the tide. Where else in all Christendom is there another town with so familiar and alluring a promenade? Where else are there so many pretty girls to the square yard? Where else do they bowl along so boldly and yet so properly, halting here to gabble with acquaintances and block the narrow sidewalk, and there to hail other acquaintances across the narrow driveway?

Baltimoreans, filled with strange juices at Merchants' and

Manufacturers' Association banquets, talk magnificently of widening Charles Street, of making it a Fifth Avenue, a Boulevard des Italiens, a Piccadilly. But so far they have never actually come to it—and let us all send up a prayer that they never will. To widen Charles Street would be like giving Serpolette the waist of Brünnhilde—an act of defilement and indecency. The whole enchantment of that incomparable lane lies in its very narrowness, its cheek-by-jowlness, its insidious friendliness.

And in the same elements lies the appeal of Baltimore. The old town will not give you the time of your life; it is not a brazen hussy among cities, blinding you with its xanthous curls, kicking up its legs, inviting you to exquisite deviltries. Not at all. It is, if the truth must come out, a Perfect Lady. But for all its resultant narrowness, its niceness, its air of merely playing at being a city, it has, at bottom, the one quality which, in cities as in women, shames and survives all the rest. And that is the impalpable, indefinable, irresistible quality of charm.

Here, of course, I whisper no secret; some news of this has got about. Even the fellow who denounces Baltimore most bitterly—the baffled seller of green goods, the scorned and rail-ridden ballyhoo man—is willing, once his torn cartilages have begun to knit, to grant the old town some measure of that bewitchment, or at least to admit that others feel it and justly praise it. He will tell you that, whatever the hunkerousness, the archaic conservatism of the Baltimoreans, they know, at all events, how to cook victuals—in particular, how to cook terrapin *à la* Maryland. Again, he will admit the subtle allurement, almost as powerful as the lure of money, of a city with an ancient cathedral upon its central hill—the only North American city in which it was possible, until very lately, to see a prince of the Holy Church, red-hatted, lean and otherworldly, walking among his people.

So far, indeed, the pre-eminence of Baltimore is an axiom, a part of the American tradition. It is, by unanimous consent, the gastronomical capital of the New World, and it is also, by unanimous consent, the one genuine cathedral city of our fair republic. Other cities, of course, have cathedrals, too—out in the West, I believe, they are run up by the half-dozen—but only in Baltimore is there the authentic cathedral atmosphere. Only in Baltimore is there any reflection of that ecclesiastical efflorescence which gives enchantment to such Old World towns as Seville and Padua, Moscow and Milan. Only in Baltimore is it possible to imagine a procession of monks winding down a main-traveled road, holding up the taxicabs and the trolley cars, and striking newsboys dumb with reverence.

Such is the Baltimore picture that fills the public eye—a scene of banqueting and devotion. Unluckily for romance, there is not much truth in either part of it. The diamond back terrapin, true enough, is native to the Chesapeake marshes, and the see of Baltimore, true enough, is to Catholic America what the see of Rome is to all Christendom; but when you have said that you have said your say. The fact is that the terrapin, once so plentiful that it was fed to the hogs and blackamoors, has long since faded into a golden mist. It is a fowl consumed in Baltimore, as elsewhere, only at long intervals, and as an act of extraordinary debauchery. I have heard tales of ancient gourmets at the Maryland Club, obese, opulent and baggy under the eyes, who eat it daily, or, at any rate, four times a week.

But such virtuosi, in the very nature of things, must be rare. The average Baltimorean is held back from that licentiousness by what the Socialists call economic pressure. He eschews the terrapin for the same reason that he eschews yachting, polygamy and the collection of ceramics. Of the six hundred thousand folk in the town, I venture to say that three hundred thousand have never even seen a genuine diamond back, that four hundred thousand haven't the slightest notion how the reptile is cooked, and that five hundred thousand have never tasted it, nor even smelled it. Conservative figures, indeed. Let other figures support them. *Imprimis,* it is an unimaginable indecorum, if not a downright impossibility, to eat a rasher of terrapin without using champagne to wash the little bones out of the tonsils—and champagne costs four dollars a bottle. *Zum zweiten,* an ordinary helping of terrapin—not a whole *meal* of terrapin, understand, nor a whole terrapin, but an ordinary, six-ounce helping, made up, let us say, of two schnitzels from the flank, a hip, a neck, two claws and three yellow eggs—costs three dollars in the kitchen and from three fifty to four dollars on the table! So an eminent Baltimore chef told me once, dining with me, off duty, in a spaghetti joint.

"But I have eaten diamond back at two fifty," I protested.

"Ah!" said he, and lifted his diabolic brows.

"Then it wasn't genuine terrapin?" I asked in surprise.

"The good God knows!"

"But isn't it just possible that it *was?*"

"Everything is possible."

More red wine loosed his tongue, and the tale that he told was of hair raising effect upon a passionate eater—a tale of vulgar mud turtles with diamonds photographed upon their backs, of boiled squirrel helping the sophistication, of terrapin eggs manufactured in the laboratory.

"But certainly not at the ——— Hotel!"

A shrug of the shoulders.

"Or at the ———!"

Two shrugs—and the faintest ghost of a snicker.

"But the possibility of detection—the scandal—the riot!"

A frank chuckle, and then:

"In Baltimore there are eighteen men only who know terrapin from—not terrapin. In the United States, thirty-seven."

Alas, the story of the diamond back is not the whole story! Baltimore victualry is afflicted in these days, not merely by a malady of the heart, but by a general paralysis and decay of the entire organism—a sort of progressive coma, working inward from the extremities. That it was once unique, ineffable, almost heavenly—so much we must assume unless we assume alternatively that all the old-time travelers were liars. For you can't open a dusty "Journal of a Tour in the United States of North America," *circa* 1820, without finding a glowing chapter upon the romantic eating to be had in Baltimore taverns. From the beginning of the century down to the Civil War each successive tourist grew lyric in its praises. That was the Golden Age of Maryland cookery. Then it was that the black mammy of sweet memory, turbaned and oleose, reared her culinary Taj Mahals and attained to her immortality. Then it was that cornbread soared the interstellar spaces and the corn flitter (*not* fritter) was born.

But the black mammy of that arcadian day was too exquisite, too sensitive an artist to last. (The rose is a fragile flower. The sunset flames—and is gone.) Her daughter, squeezed into corsets, failed of her technique and her imagination. The seventies saw the rise of false ideals, of spurious tools and materials—saleratus, self-rising buckwheat, oleomargarine, Chicago lard, the embalmed egg, the carbolated ham, the gas stove. Today the destruction is complete. The native Baltimore cook, granddaughter to kitchen Sapphos and Angelica Kauffmanns, is now a frank mechanic, almost bad enough to belong to a union—a frowzy, scented houri in the more preposterous gauds of yesteryear, her veins full of wood alcohol and cocaine, her mind addled by the intrigues of Moorish high society, her supreme achievement a passable boiled egg, a fairish kidney stew or a wholly third rate pot of sprouts.

And if cooking in the home thus goes to the devil in Baltimore, cooking in the public inns departs even further from its old high character and particularity. In sober truth, it has almost ceased to exist—that is to say, as a native art. The Baltimore hotel chef of today shows his honorable discharges from the Waldorf-Astoria, the Auditorium Annex, the Ponce de Leon. He is simply a journeyman cook, a single member of the undistinguished world brotherhood; and the things he dishes up in Baltimore are exactly the same things he was taught to dish up in New York, or Chicago, or wherever it was that he escaped from the scullery. Good food, I do not deny, but not of Baltimore, Baltimorean. Demand of him a plate of lye hominy in the Talbot County manner, with honest hog meat at its core—and he will fall in a swoon. Ask him for soft crabs—and he will send them to the table in cracker dust! Talk to him of chitlings—and you will talk to a corpse. The largest oyster he has ever heard of is about the size of a watch. The largest genuine Maryland oyster—the veritable bivalve of the Chesapeake, still to be had at oyster roasts down the river and at street stands along the wharves—is as large as your open hand. A magnificent, matchless reptile! Hard to swallow? Dangerous? Perhaps to the novice, the dastard. But to the veteran of the raw bar, the man of trained and lusty esophagus, a thing of prolonged and kaleidoscopic flavors, a slow slipping saturnalia, a delirium of joy!

Here, it may be, I go too far. Not, of course, in celebrating the Chesapeake oyster, but in denouncing the Baltimore hotels. Let me at once ameliorate the indictment by admitting exceptions. There are hotel cooks in Baltimore, I freely grant, who have absorbed a lingering secret or two from the native air—not many, but still a few. At one hotel, for example, you will find, amid a welter of *à la*'s, the authentic soft crab of Maryland, cooked at the open fire, pronged to a sliver of country bacon—and *without* cracker dust! At another, perhaps, a very decent plate of jowl and sprouts. At a third, pawnhoss in season, fresh from the woodland sausage vats of Frederick County—and fried properly in slender shingles. At a fourth, Ann' 'Ran'el strawberries with their arteries still pulsing. At a fifth, genuine Patuxent sweet potatoes, candied in their own sugar. And always, in the background, there is that last truly Baltimore hotel—sole survivor of the glorious dynasty of Guy's and Barnum's—wherein, at the lunch bar down in the cellar, the oyster potpie is still a poem and a passion, a dream and an intoxication, a burst of sunlight and a concord of sweet sounds.

Oh, the mellowness of it! Oh, the yellowness of it! A rich, a nourishing, an exquisite dish! A pearl of victualry, believe me, and not for swine. The man who appreciates and understands it, who penetrates to the depths of its perfection, who feels and is moved by those nuances which transfigure it and sublimate it and so lift it above all other potpies under the sun—that man is of the lineage of Brillat-Savarin, and no mere footman of metabolism. But the oyster pie, however ravishing, is yet but transitory—here today and gone tomorrow, a mirage as much as a miracle—for no cultured Baltimorean will eat an oyster, dead or alive, if the mercury in the tube be above thirty-two degrees Fahrenheit.

Thus experience speaks. A thawed oyster is, at best, a dubious oyster, and may be a downright homicidal oyster. Visitors gobble the bivalve far into May and June, and then bulge the hospitals and morgues; the native, save drink masters him, is more cautious. But even if the oyster pie is thus a fleeting guest, there yet remains crab soup, its cousin and rival. I mean here, of course, not the vulgar crab soup of the barrooms, full of claws and tomato skins and with a shinbone as its base, but crab bisque, of white meat, country butter and rich cream all compact. You can find it, from May to October, just where the oyster pie blooms and glows from November to March, and that is, to give away the secret at last, in the lower eating room of the Rennert Hotel. There Maryland cookery lives out the palsied evening of its days. There the oyster pie, crab soup, boiled tongue and spinach, turkey wings with oyster sauce, early York cabbage, Charles County ham and a few other such doddering thoroughbreds make their last gallant stand against the filet mignon, the Wiener schnitzel and all the rest of the exotic *à la's*. When the old Carrollton went up in smoke, in 1904, the planked shad, as planks and shad were known to Lord Fairfax and Charles Carroll, vanished from the earth. And when, in the course of human events, the Rennert gives way to some obscene skyscraper, the last genuine oyster potpie will say good-bye.

Sic transit gloria—and whatever the bad Latin is for eating with the heart. Baltimore, of course, yet offers decent food to the stranger within her gates, but it is food he knows at home and is tired of. The native idiocrasy, the local color, save as I have indicated, are gone. One must have a guide to find a plate of indubitable hog and hominy; even so noble a dish as crab creole, a Louisiana invention raised to the stars by Maryland crabs and Maryland genius, now hides at Joyce's, an eating house remote from the white lights of the town. And for Chesapeake oysters of adult growth, the visitor must go, as I have said, down the river, a hazardous journey in winter, or brave the stenches and shanghaiers of the docks.

So, too, with the legendary processions of monks, to which we now come back after a long excursion into victualry. One looks for them in the American Rome—one finds them only after a hard search. Go out to Paca Street and peep through the portcullis of St. Mary's Seminary, *alma mater* of unnumbered bishops (and perhaps of some pope of day after tomorrow), and one may see sedate scholastics treading the shady walks, digesting their Angelic Doctor and their fast day mackerel; go out to St. Joseph's, on the Frederick Road, and one may see paunchy Passionists pottering about their grapevines—learned and venerable men; drop down Maiden Choice Lane to St. Mary's Industrial School, and one may happen upon half a dozen young Xaverians, their cassocks flapping about their legs, helping their boys at market gardening or baseball. But of ecclesiasticism in any genuine and general sense, Baltimore is bare. No Neapolitan love of processions and ceremonials, no liking for following the crozier and bowing low to the passing holy image, no feeling for the poetry and beauty of religious show seems to be left in her people. Those of them who cling to the old faith have taken away from it, I think, much that is of its essence and more that is of its spell. They go to church on Sundays; they are faithful, they are reverent, they are pious. But the old romance has gone out of their piety.

Thus the effect of the American air, of a diverse and enticing life, of the so-called enlightenment. But is that really an enlightenment which reduces gilt and scarlet to drab and gray? Alas, I am pagan enough, if not Catholic enough, to doubt it—pagan enough to lament that the pomp and circumstance visible in the ancient cathedral on a high day have so little echo in the town on all days. But whatever the pity, there is the fact. The American Rome sets no feast of crosses and banners for the pilgrim's eye; he may wander its streets for days, and yet fall upon no single hint that Holy Church has here her Western sentry post. The truth is, in brief, that the Romanism of Baltimore has a lot more of tradition in it than of reality. To speak of it, to assume it, to posit it with delight or with horror, has become a sort of convention, like the habit of calling Broadway gay. But go behind that convention to things as they are, and you will make the rather startling discovery that Baltimore, for all its primacy, is scarcely a Catholic town at all, but a stronghold of dour and dismal Puritanism—a town in which faith has lost inner beauty as well as outer ceremonial, and joy has gone with beauty. I mean, of course, joy in the Greek sense, the joy rooted in innocence, the joy of a Neapolitan procession. The Baltimore of today is not innocent. Its curse, indeed, is its conscience, an extraordinarily alert and sensitive organ. And to attend and poke that conscience, to keep alive the notion that all that is joyful must be sinful and all that is good must give pain, there are hordes of male vestals in chokers and white cravats, virtuosi of virtue, moralists clerical and moralists lay, hounds of happiness, specialists in constructive and esoteric sin.

Few things that stir the blood of man and lift him out of his wallow of lost hopes are permitted by the laws of Maryland. It is unlawful in Baltimore to throw confetti on New Year's Eve; it is unlawful, without elaborate permissive process, for a harpist to accompany flute music on the public street; it is a crime to sell chewing gum on Sunday, or to play tennis, or to have one's chin shaved, or to give a concert—or to go hawking! Fact! The Blue Laws were passed in 1723, and go back to the hell fire harangues of Cotton Mather, but every effort to mitigate and modernize them is opposed with truly savage violence. Under them, the impresario who had an orchestra play the nine symphonies of Beethoven on nine successive Sunday afternoons would be liable to a minimum fine of $25,550 and 220 days in jail.

Remember, I said "minimum." The maximum would be $127,600 and fifteen months—and Baltimore judges, being elected officers, sometimes woo the parsons in their sentences. No wonder the festive drummer, finding himself in Baltimore on a Saturday night, flees in hot haste. Even if Washington, but forty miles away, be his furthest bourne, he may at least divert himself there, on the ensuing Sunday, with moving pictures. But not in Baltimore. Baltimore fears such Babylonish lecheries. Baltimore sees the flickering film as something unspeakably secular and demoniacal. On week days it may be tolerated, as a concession to Adam's fall. But on the Sabbath it must rest.

Yet, for all that brummagem goody-goodiness, that bogus virtue, that elaborate hocus-pocus of chemical purity, that grotesque conspiracy against beauty and festivity and joy, there remains the indubitable charm of the old town. Stay there only long enough and it will infallibly descend upon you and consume you, and you will remain a Baltimorean, in spirit if not in bodily presence, to the end of your days. And it is not merely the charm of the picturesque, nor of the South, nor of the ancient, nor of the celebrated and honorable—though Baltimore delights the painter, and stands sentry for the South, and looks back to the seventeenth century, and has given the nation not only heroes but also poets to sing them. The roots and sources of that charm, in truth, go deeper than that.

Trace them down and you will come at last, I believe, to certain genuine peculiarities, to certain qualities which may not be so conveniently ticketed, to certain traits and combinations of traits which, shading into one another, give the net effect of uncommon and attractive individuality, of something not remote from true distinction. The authentic Baltimorean, the Baltimorean of Baltimoreans born and ever filled with that fact, the Baltimorean lifted above all brute contact and combat with the native blacks and the invading Goths and Huns—in brief, the Baltimorean whose home you must enter if you would really know Baltimore—is a fellow who touches civilization at more places, perhaps, than any other American. There is a simplicity about him which speaks of long habituation to his own opinions, his own dignities, his own class. In a country so largely dynamic and so little static that few of its people ever seem (or are) quite at home in their own homes, he represents a more settled and a more stately order. There yet hangs about him some of the repose, the air, the fine superiority of the Colonial planter, despite the pianola in his parlor and his daily journey to a skyscraper. One sees as the setting of his ultimate dream, not a gilded palace and a regiment of servitors, not the bent necks of multitudes and a brass band playing "Hail to the Chief!" but only his own vine and fig tree and the good red sun of Maryland beating down.

I speak, of course, of the civilized, the cultured, the mellowed, the well rooted Baltimorean, not of the mere mob man living in Baltimore. This Baltimorean makes up, putting the test as low as you will, but a small minority of Baltimore's people, and yet no long acquaintance with him is necessary to show you that whatever is essentially Baltimorean in the town is the reflection of his philosophy and his personality. The black, nearly a hundred thousand strong, is a mere cipher. Indirectly, as I shall presently show, he has greatly influenced the communal life, but directly he is as little to be considered as the cab horses. And the swarming foreigner, with his outlandish customs and his remoteness from the stream of tradition is also as negligible. Go down into Albemarle or President streets, and you are as far from Mt. Vernon Place or Peabody Heights or Harlem Park or Walbrook or Roland Park or any other genuine part of Baltimore as you are from the North Pole.

And yet it is precisely this vast body of *servi* and *ignobiles*, once all black, but of late grown disconcertingly yellow and white, that must be blamed for most of the austerity of Baltimore, and by secondary effect, for that peculiar hominess which is always marked as the distinguishing quality of the town. It was the darkey who inspired, in the years long past, many of the draconian statutes which yet linger upon the books, and many of the stern habits and self-restraints which reinforce them. Even today it is common to hear a Baltimorean say in defense of a given prohibition, not that he himself is opposed to the antithetical privilege, or thinks it, in itself, immoral or demoralizing, but that it would be unwise to let the nigger taste it. And if not the nigger, then the foreigner newly come. So, for example, with the Blue Laws above mentioned. The Baltimorean's fear of a more humane Sunday is not a fear that it would imperil his own soul, but a fear that the Lithuanian and the Sicilian, aided and abetted by the native Ethiop, would make of it a debauch. And so he clings to his ancient rigors.

To what has all of this brought us? To the fact, in brief, that the conditions of the Baltimorean's life have thrown him upon himself, that they have forced him to cultivate those social qualities which center particularly about the home and are inseparable from the home. It is a New Yorker's tendency, once he attains to ease, to make his home merely one of the hotels at which he stops. In the end, perhaps, it becomes the least of these hotels: desiring to show special favor to a guest, he will hesitate between his club, a favorite grillroom and his own hearth. The training and traditions of the Baltimorean all pull in a different direction. He cannot quite rid himself of the notion that, until a newcomer has stretched comfortably in his dining room, and admired the children and the family portraits, and examined the old water pitcher brought from England in 1735, and petted the cat, and fingered the old books in the library upstairs, and praised the bad biscuits of black Gwendolyn in the kitchen, with her high heel shoes, her eminence in the Grand United Order of Nazarenes and her fond hopes of wedding a *colorado maduro* barrister—that, until all this ceremonial has been gone through, he and the newcomer are yet strangers. Down to ten or twelve years ago, I believe, it was still considered a bit indecent for a Baltimore gentleman to take his own wife to a hotel for supper after the theater. That was not asceticism, but mere habit. The social tradition of the town had no concern with public places.

The Baltimoreans had so devised their chief joys, for years and years, that the home was the background of every one. And something of that old disposition still lingers.

A quaint town! A singular people! And yet the charm is there! You will miss the prodigal gaiety of New York—the multitude of theaters, the lavishness of entertaining, the elaborate organization of the business of pleasure. Baltimore has, between November and April, but ten performances of grand opera on a metropolitan scale. For her six hundred thousand people there are but three first class theaters. In the whole town there is not a single restaurant, not merely a hotel dining room, worth mentioning to your friends. And yet—and yet—it is not dull, it is not a prison—at least not to the Baltimoreans—at least not to those who get the Baltimore point of view.

What if the Carusos and Farrars pipe their lays but ten times a year? So much greater the joy in hearing them when they come! What if the theaters be but three? Washington, down the trolley line, has but two. And three are sufficient to house all the plays really worth seeing. Baltimore misses, perhaps, a few that Broadway enjoys—but more that Broadway suffers. And who wants to gobble the *à la*'s in a gilded and public hell when a Smithfield ham is on the sideboard at home, with beer on ice to wash it down, and a box of smuggled cigars in the lower drawer of the old secretary—and the hour invites to a neighborly palaver with Smith and Benson and Old Taylor, while the ladies exchange fashions and scandals, novel plots and obstetrics in the parlor? What fool would be in New York tonight, dodging the taxicabs, blinded by the whiskey signs, robbed by the waiters? Who would leave Baltimore, once Baltimore has taken him to her arms?

from the Smart Set, *May 1913, pp. 107–114.*

◇◇◇

800,000

I

The old Baltimore is gone, and there is no use mourning it. It was infinitely charming while it lasted, but it belongs to the past. Today the town grows more and more like Philadelphia, St. Louis, Detroit, Kansas City, Cincinnati, Buffalo, Akron, Birmingham. The same windy and humorless Babbitts run it, and the same dull hordes of slaves infest it. "Milk from contented cows!" Whoever devised that slogan was a satirist and a sociologist.

Someday, I hope, a history of Baltimore will be written—not a mere chronicle, but a history. When it is done there must be a chapter on the role played by immigrants from Virginia in the period between the end of the Civil War and the Great Fire of 1904. Not many Baltimoreans of today seem to remember what we owe to them. They brought in, first of all, a talent for civilized living, a spacious and amiable view of the world. They brought in, second and even more important, a really enlightened public spirit, as far above the puerile back-scratching of Rotary as the patriotism of Washington was above that of a professional war veteran.

Baltimore was hard hit by the Civil War, but its recovery, once there was peace, was almost instantaneous. A great deal of money was made here before Grant got into the White House, and more followed thereafter. Most of it went, not into the hands of the old-time Baltimoreans—for the war had ruined and paralyzed two-thirds of them—but into those of the new class of adventurers—what would be called, today, captains of industry. They put up new factories, opened new lines of trade, and got rich. And with their riches they got power.

They used that power as men of money use it at all times and everywhere. Baltimore became enormously corrupt. The game was to put up a complaisant and unsuspecting figurehead as mayor—say the perennial Ferdinand C. Latrobe or some honorary pallbearer from Hopkins Place—and then carry on intensive operations under cover of his respectability. The City Hall was full of grafters and the whole public service became a joke. Even the judges on the bench were on the nether side of suspicion.

II

This went on from the days of Honest Josh Vansant to 1895, a period of twenty years. Rumbles of discontent were heard from the start, but it took a long and desperate fight to bring about reforms. The combination that faced the reformers seemed almost unbeatable. On the one side were the professional politicians, first led by William Pinkney Whyte and then by Gorman and Rasin. On the other side were the stuffed shirts of Hopkins Place, contented so long as they were well taken care of, avid of petty privileges and honors, and ready to denounce and help put down any show of "radicalism."

Curiously enough, it was lawyers who finally broke up this combination—some of them, like Severn Teakle Wallis, good ones, and others, like Charles J. Bonaparte, bad ones. They sweated and schemed for twenty years, and then, in 1895, they were successful. First they made Aleneus Hooper mayor, and after that (forgetting the interlude of Malster) they put in Thomas G. Hayes. Baltimore has had some bad mayors since then, but on the whole its government has been honest, and even efficient. Nothing like the villainy of Rasin's time was seen under Mahon and Kelly. They were bad enough, God knows, but their badness was on a small scale, and what is more, it was undefended. Big Business had been expelled from statecraft.

What seems to be forgotten is the part played by Virginians in this revolution. They were mainly fugitives from the war and most of them landed in Baltimore without a cent. But they were men with a sound tradition behind them, they had a natural talent for public affairs, and they were instinctively opposed to the "good business man" point of view. No one will ever measure the value of their services to this town. They furnished volunteers for every assault upon the old Babbitt *cum* Muldoon combination, and when it was overthrown at last and the work of reorganization and rehabilitation had to be faced, they were ready with the needed skill and devotion.

III

If there were any gratitude stirring there would be monuments in Baltimore today to Hayes, to Richard M. Venable and to Joseph Packard, to name but three out of a large company. Some of that company came into conspicuous public notice in their day; others remained modestly in the background. They all had in common a genuine capacity for the public service, and they all had the highest and rarest sort of integrity. No one ever accused Packard of self-seeking: the charge would have been ridiculous on its face. Nor Venable. And even Hayes, though he had political ambitions and was bitterly disappointed when he failed to become Governor, was essentially unselfish, and never made a dollar out of politics.

I wish I could add that Baltimore's debt to these Virginians was matched by its debt to as many Marylanders of their class, but the facts only too plainly run the other way. On the whole, the people of the counties have not helped the progress of the city, but hindered it. This, I believe, is especially true of the Eastern Shoremen. Their chief gift to Baltimore, so far, has been I. Freeman Rasin, the worst corruptionist ever heard of in these parts. For the rest, they have sent in only third raters—the fanatical and preposterous Amos W. W. Woodcock, the hollow P. L. Goldsborough and others of that kind. All the Eastern Shore Governors since the Civil War have been duds.

The causes of this difference between the Shore and Virginia are mysterious, for the Shore was originally settled mainly by Virginians. To this day, indeed, it is the most Southern part of Maryland, both in its way of living and its ways of thought. It still houses the remains of a charming and relatively civilized gentry. But its politicians, with few exceptions, are low down, and those it exports to Baltimore seldom get above the Goldsborough level. In the other part of Maryland are the Methodist parsons more powerful. In some of the counties no one can get into office without their consent.

IV

With the Virginians all dead, and along with them the native Marylanders who joined them in delivering Baltimore, the town seems likely to return to the troubles which afflicted it after the Civil War. There is a plain movement back to the old corruption. The City Council, which, under Venable and Skipwith Wilmer, became almost intelligent, grows steadily more stupid, and there is a great dearth of first-rate men in the rest of the city government. Such stupidity, in politics as in more useful enterprises, is always the forerunner of something worse.

At the moment, as everyone knows, there is chaos in the city Democracy, and various ambitious leaders, most of them plainly fourth-rate, fight for the baton of Mahon, Kelly and Rasin. They will probably keep on fighting until they bring the party to disaster, and then the strongest among them, or some newcomer not yet in sight, will seize and rehabilitate the wreck. My guess is that, whoever he is, he will be pretty bad. For the town, with its hordes of new citizens, is ripe for Tammanizing. In ten years it will be riper still. And in twenty years we'll be back where we were in 1885.

It is highly unlikely that Big Business will make any resistance to this process. It never does. It was very friendly to Rasin in his day, and played into his hands whenever he needed what was called a perfumer. There were very few bankers or business men in the old Reform League, and those few were of the more cautious party. The hard slugging was done by the lawyers. In that remote era lawyers were still professional men, and many of them showed idealistic tendencies. But today they are mainly no more than slaves of Big Business, and their idealism, such as it is, is taken out on golf.

In business itself there is a change, and it seems to be for the worse. The old-time Babbitts, whatever their faults, were at least actual Baltimoreans, and so they were responsive to the traditions of the town, and took a high pride in their citizenship. Their successors are chiefly strangers. In so far as they apprehend the Baltimore tradition at all they are opposed to it. The town, to them, seems old-fashioned, poky, dull, and more than a little ridiculous. They aspire to put it on the level of Chicago. Well, they will probably get their wish. But what good that will be to the rest of us is more than I can make out.

from Baltimore Evening Sun, *July 21, 1930.*

Mencken *and the* ENGLISH LANGUAGE

Alistair Cooke

When Mencken published the parent volume of *The American Language*, he unwittingly gave a fillip to the sagging chauvinism of his countrymen in the collapse of the Coolidge prosperity. He seemed to be saying that even if the economy, which had been vaunted throughout the 1920s as a uniquely self-sustaining system, had gone the way of all other previous economies, it was time to assert that the United States had developed, in three hundred years, a language that was not a variant dialect of the mother tongue but a separate offshoot more inventive and vigorous than its parent.

Alistair Cooke has reported on America for the *Manchester Guardian* and the British Broadcasting Corporation since the 1930s. He is the editor of *The Vintage Mencken* and has included a profile of Mencken in his book *Six Men*.

This assertion was, of course, hotly rejected in England, most notably in a review of *The American Language* by Sir Arthur Quiller-Couch ("Q"), who adduced the whole body of English literature in order to maintain that American literature was a provincial appendage and that its most distinguished *littérateurs* proved the primacy of the English language by being well within the mainstream of the English of England. "Q" specially cited James Russell Lowell and Washington Irving, two of the very men Mencken himself had named as "de-Americanized Americans," to the extent that they practiced "ease and decorum . . . a sort of timorous flaccidity" in an Anglophile idiom far removed from that of their countrymen. But in *The American Language*, Mencken did not defend his new thesis (about the strong viability of American) by quoting—so far as I can discover—any of the new vernacular writers who had come up since he unloosed his first blast against the genteel tradition in 1920. It is curious that he should have admitted to *The American Language* barely a mention of Sinclair Lewis, James M. Cain, James T. Farrell, Theodore Dreiser, or the other new young realists that he had encouraged and launched in the *Smart Set* and the *American Mercury*.

But there was no contradiction between his bemoaning the "marshmallow gentility" of American literature in 1920 and his apparent salute in 1930 to the arrival of a native literature independent of the literary Establishment of England. The strictures of "Q" and the other English critics were based in a misunderstanding of Mencken's thesis, which was about *language*, not the literature that might one day grow from it. The whole of *The American Language* is a prolonged demonstration of the fact that the Americans, in a three-hundred-year experience of a new landscape, new crops, new climates, a new society, and the melding of many immigrant languages and ways of life, had developed institutions, foods, habits, relationships that coined thousands of new nouns, adjectives, and—in their speech—even new syntactical forms. It was, in fact, a new dialect at least as different from British English as the language of Brazil is different from that of Portugal or the Spanish of Mexico from that of Spain. But Mencken pushed his argument too far in his frequent assertions that American English was altogether more robust and virile than the English of England.

Thirty years later, certainly by 1960 at the latest, he would have been absolutely correct in claiming that there was an independent literature, whose written style and emotional tone were recognizable as nothing but American. With Hemingway, the vernacular innovations of Mark Twain had been carried forward to transform written English narrative as drastically as John Dryden had simplified the language of English criticism almost three hundred years before. Mencken could then have cited Hemingway, O'Hara, Jerome Weidman, J. D. Salinger, Norman Mailer, Joseph Heller, and a dozen others who, in fiction anyway, could not possibly have been mistaken for Englishmen. Yet it is an interesting irony that Mencken thought very little of Hemingway and undoubtedly would have thought as little, or less, of the others who could have vindicated his earlier lamentations.

But, we have to say that the language of American *criticism* did not noticeably depart from standard English until it developed, as a humorous form, in the hands of such as Tom Wolfe, Florence King, and John Leonard, practicing a vernacular satirical idiom that would have been incomprehensible to Mencken.

The truth is that till the day he died, Mencken's own style, while it may be more pungent and outrageous than that of his English contemporaries, is hardly different in any particular of vocabulary, syntax, or cadence from that of the prevailing English models. Indeed, it often struck his English contemporaries as being rather behind their time, a powerful and verbose variation on the invective style of Bernard Shaw.

Consider, for instance, the language of Mencken's first and most famous blast at the condition of American literature in his 1920 essay "The National Letters," published in the second series of *Prejudices*. He begins by wistfully recalling Emerson's celebrated speech "The American Scholar," given in 1837, which "brought him into instant notice at home, partly as man of letters but more importantly as seer and prophet, and the fame thus founded has endured without much diminution, at all events in New England, to this day." After mentioning the seconding enthusiasms of Poe and Whitman, Mencken asks how this prophecy had turned out:

> Now for the answering fact. How has the issue replied to these visionaries? It has replied in a way that is manifestly to the discomfiture of Emerson as a prophet, to the dismay of Poe as a pessimist disarmed by transient optimism, and to the utter collapse of Whitman. We have, as everyone knows, produced no such "new and greater literatus order" as that announced by old Walt. We have given a gaping world no books that "radiate," and surely none intelligibly comparable to stars and constellations. We have achieved no prodigies of the first class, and very few of the second class, and not many of the third and fourth classes. Our literature, despite several false starts that promised much, is chiefly remarkable, now as always, for its respectable mediocrity. Its typical great man, in our own time, has been Howells, as its typical great man a generation ago was Lowell, and two generations ago, Irving. Viewed largely, its salient character appears as a sort of timorous flaccidity, an amiable hollowness. In bulk it grows more and more formidable, in ease and decorum it makes undoubted progress, and on

the side of mere technic, of the bald capacity to write, it shows an ever-widening competence. But when one proceeds from such agencies and externals to the intrinsic substance, to the creative passion within, that substance quickly reveals itself as thin and watery, and that passion fades to something almost puerile. In all that mass of suave and often highly diverting writing there is no visible movement toward a distinguished and singular excellence, a signal national quality, a ripe and stimulating flavor, or indeed, toward any other describable goal. What one sees is simply a general irresolution, a pervasive superficiality. There is no sober grappling with fundamentals, but only a shy sporting on the surface; there is not even any serious approach, such as Whitman dreamed of, to the special experiences and emergencies of the American people. . . . On the side of letters, the aesthetic side, we present to the world at large . . . Knights of the Pythias, Presbyterians, standard model Ph.D.'s, readers of the *Saturday Evening Post*, admirers of Richard Harding Davis and O. Henry, devotees of Hamilton Wright Mabie's "white list" of books, members of the Y.M.C.A. or the Drama League, weepers at chautauquas, wearers of badges, 100 percent patriots, children of God. . . .

The current scene is surely depressing enough. What one observes is a literature in three layers, and each inordinately doughy and uninspiring—each almost without flavor or savor. It is hard to say, with much critical plausibility, which layer deserves to be called the upper, but for decorum's sake the choice may be fixed upon that which meets the approval of the reigning Lessings. This is the layer of the novels of the late Howells, Judge Grant, Alice Brown and the rest of the dwindling survivors of New England Kultur, of the brittle, academic poetry of

> Woodberry and the elder Johnson, of the tea-party essays of Crothers, Miss Repplier and company, and of the solemn, highly judicial, coroner's inquest criticism of More, Brownell, [Irving] Babbitt and their imitators. Here we have manner, undoubtedly. The thing is correctly done; it is never crude or gross; there is in it a faint perfume of college-town society. But when this highly refined and attenuated manner is allowed for, what remains is next to nothing. One never remembers a character in the novels of these aloof and de-Americanized Americans; one never encounters an idea in their essays; one never carries away a line out of their poetry. It is literature as an academic exercise for talented grammarians, almost as a genteel recreation for ladies and gentlemen of fashion.*

Apart from the mention of such institutions as the Knights of Pythias and the *Saturday Evening Post*, there is practically nothing here to indicate that we are reading an American, and not an English, critic. "Technic" for technique and "toward" for towards are tiny giveaways. "When one proceeds from such agencies and externals" could be Emerson. The verbosity, which English critics complained of when Mencken was published in England in the 1920s, takes the form of an accumulation of almost tautological adjectives. Shaw, for instance, could never have written: "In all that mass of suave and often highly diverting writing there is no visible movement toward a distinguished and singular excellence, a signal national quality, a ripe and stimulating flavor." He would most likely have pared it down to: "In all that mass of often highly diverting writing there is no sign of a distinctive American character."

* *Prejudices: Second Series* (Alfred A. Knopf, 1920).

Mencken was in his fortieth year when he wrote this passage. And in a year or two he would be in his early prime. I doubt he would ever again write anything so sustained which failed to give off a single vivid analogy, or some outlandishly funny simile, or some other hint that we were in the presence of an original. Toward the end of his life, he had this to say about his early apprenticeship: "My early writing was pretty bad, and it always makes me uncomfortable, on looking into an old clipping-book, to remember that this or that piece was regarded as well done at the time it was written . . . my model in those days was the old New York *Sun*, and especially its editorial page. This model was both good and bad—good because it taught me that good sense was at the bottom of all good writing, but bad because it showed a considerable artificiality of style, and made me overestimate the value of smart phrases."

He is talking, of course, of his earliest newspaper writing. But the same, and more, may be said about his early books, on Nietzsche and Shaw. For a time, his prose, whenever it was concerned with ideas rather than with reported events, was an earnest, almost a sweating, parody of iconoclasts both dead and alive that he particularly admired: Macaulay, Shaw, Nietzsche, worst of all Ambrose Bierce. A great deal of his first volume of *Prejudices* (1916) is heavy going. Of course, it has already achieved command of a diverse and thoroughly disciplined vocabulary and it has great driving force. But it is the energy of a railway engine and not yet that of a racehorse spanking along down the stretch. It cries for drastic editing. It didn't get it only, I suppose, because Mencken was obviously superior to his rivals in invective writing.

It will be obvious by now what this essay is about and what it is not. I am not discussing Mencken's incomparable three volumes on *The American Language* but his handling of the

English language: what it was that made him the first master craftsman of American journalism in the twentieth century; what makes him still, in a word, inimitable.

The key to his originality lies, I think, not in his chronological growth, in the time when pieces were written, so much as in the sort of piece he was writing. Compare, for example, the passage I have just quoted from "The National Letters" with his overnight obituary of William Jennings Bryan written in 1925:

> Has it been duly marked by historians that William Jennings Bryan's last secular act on this globe of sin was to catch flies? A curious detail, and not without its sardonic overtones. He was the most sedulous fly-catcher in American history, and in many ways the most successful. His quarry, of course, was not *Musca domestica* but *Homo neandertalensis*. For forty years he tracked it with coo and bellow, up and down the rustic backways of the Republic. Wherever the flambeaux of Chautauqua smoked and guttered, and the bilge of idealism ran in the veins, and Baptist pastors dammed the brooks with the sanctified, and men gathered who were weary and heavy laden, and their wives who were full of Peruna and fecund as the shad (*Alosa sapidissima*), there the indefatigable Jennings set up his traps and spread his bait. He knew every country town in the South and West, and he could crowd the most remote of them to suffocation by simply winding his horn. The city proletariat, transiently flustered by him in 1896, quickly penetrated his buncombe and would have no more of him; the cockney gallery jeered him at every Democratic national convention for twenty-five years. But out where the grass grows high, and the horned cattle dream away the lazy

afternoons, and men still fear the powers and principalities of the air—out there between the corn-rows he held his old puissance to the end. There was no need of beaters to drive in his game. The news that he was coming was enough. For miles the flivver dust would choke the roads. And when he rose at the end of the day to discharge his Message there would be such breathless attention, such a rapt and enchanted ecstasy, such a sweet rustle of amens as the world had not known since Johann fell to Herod's ax.

There was something peculiarly fitting in the fact that his last days were spent in a one-horse Tennessee village, beating off the flies and gnats, and that death found him there. The man felt at home in such simple Christian scenes. He liked people who sweated freely, and were not debauched by the refinements of the toilet. Making his progress up and down the main street of Dayton, surrounded by gaping primates from the upland valleys of the Cumberland Range, his coat laid aside, his bare arms and hairy chest shining damply, his bald head sprinkled with dust—so accoutred and on display, he was obviously happy. He liked getting up early in the morning, to the tune of cocks crowing on the dunghill. He liked the heavy victuals of the farmhouse kitchen. He liked country lawyers, country pastors, all country people. . . . In the presence of city folks he was palpably uneasy. . . . But the yokels never laughed at him. To them he was not the huntsman but the prophet, and toward the end, as he gradually forsook mundane politics for more ghostly concerns, they began to elevate him in their hierarchy. When he died he was the peer of Abraham. His old enemy, Wilson, aspiring to the same white and shining robe, came down with a thump. But Bryan made the grade. His place in Tennessee hagiography is secure. If

> the village barber saved any of his hair, then it is currently curing gall-stones down there today.*

This is as highly wrought as his lament for the National Letters, and I imagine that a few years later he would have shed such sophomoric jocosities as *Musca domestica* (for housefly) and *Homo neandertalensis* (for Neanderthal man). But it is alive with metaphors and images that could have been written by nobody but Mencken: "with coo and bellow," "the bilge of idealism," "wives . . . fecund as the shad," "winding his horn," "the cockney gallery," "debauched by the refinements of the toilet," "cocks crowing on the dunghill." And his picture of an Old Testament primitive is wonderfully reinforced by such Biblical echoes as "the powers and principalities of the air" and "since Johann fell to Herod's ax."

The main thing to notice is that this was a piece written in haste to a deadline. It was a condition that may have left Mencken no time to suppress or moderate the strain of cruelty in him, but it testifies to a characteristic of the best journalists: the heat of the deadline fires their truest talents, galvanizes their wits, as the leisure of a plotted essay can never do. As another example, compare any Mencken piece about Puritanism in the abstract with a reporter's piece on a murderer who, Mencken's instinct told him, was "A Good Man Gone Wrong." It is his review of the confessional, published *post mortem*, of Henry Judd Gray, a corset salesman who helped his mistress, Ruth Brown Snyder, to kill her husband by hacking him to death. They confessed and were executed on January 11th, 1928. A year later, Gray's book appeared.

> The present book was composed in his last days, and appears with the imprimatur of his devoted sister. From

* *Prejudices: Fifth Series* (Alfred A. Knopf, 1926).

end to end of it he protests pathetically that he was, at heart, a good man. I believe him. The fact, indeed, is spread all over his singularly naive and touching record. . . . It was his very virtue, festering within him, that brought him to his appalling doom. Another and more wicked man, caught in the net of La Snyder, would have wriggled out and gone on his way, scarcely pausing to thank God for the fun and the escape. But once poor Judd had yielded to her brummagem seductions, he was done for and he knew it. Touched by sin, he shriveled like a worm on a hot stove. From the first exchange of wayward glances to the final agony in the chair the way was straight and inevitable. . . .

What finished the man was not his banal adultery with his suburban sweetie, but his swift and overwhelming conviction that it was mortal sin. The adultery itself was simply in bad taste: it was, perhaps, something to be ashamed of, as stealing a poor taxi-driver's false teeth would be something to be ashamed of, but it was no more. Elks and Shriners do worse every day, and suffer only transient qualms. But to Gray, with his Presbyterian upbringing and his idealistic view of the corset business, the slip was a catastrophe, a calamity. He left his tawdry partner in a daze, marveling that there could be so much wickedness in the world, and no belch of fire from Hell to stop it. Thereafter his demoralization proceeded from step to step as inexorably and as beautifully as a case of Bright's disease. . . . In his eyes the step from adultery to murder was as natural and inevitable as the step from the cocktail shaker to the gutter in the eyes of a Methodist bishop. He was rather astonished, indeed, that he didn't beat his wife and embezzle his employers' funds. Once the conviction of sin had seized him he was ready to go the whole hog. He went, as a matter of record, some-

> what beyond it. His crime was of the peculiarly brutal and atrocious kind that only good men commit. . . . It was sufficient for him that he was full of sin, that God had it in for him, that he was hopelessly damned. His crime, in fact, was a sort of public ratification of his damnation. It was his way of confessing. . . . He went to the chair fully expecting to be in Hell in twenty seconds.
>
> It seems to me that his history is a human document of immense interest and value, and that it deserves a great deal more serious study than it will probably get. Its moral is plain. Sin is a dangerous toy in the hands of the virtuous. It should be left to the congenitally sinful, who know when to play with it and when to let it alone. Run a boy through a Presbyterian Sunday-school and you must police him carefully all the rest of his life, for once he slips he is ready for anything.*

In the result, this, too, is nothing but a thesis. But it was not spun out of the air on some comfortable afternoon when Mencken thought he ought to address himself to a lecture on Puritanism or the nonconformist conscience. It was triggered by an event, and when he had his mind on the sharp memory of it, or his eyes on a living exemplar before him, the generalizations are truer, less contrived, and the reasoning very much to the point.

I can imagine, for another instance, Mencken sitting down some time to deplore the vulgarity, the sentimentality and the narcissism of the motion-picture industry. He expressed his loathing of what we now call show business in many an acid aside. But nothing he wrote on the subject has the force, the persuasiveness and—I might add—the touching simplicity, of

* *The American Mercury*, Feb. 1929.

his account of a dinner with Rudolph Valentino a week or so before the latter's fatal illness.

> . . . I had never met him before, nor seen him on the screen; the meeting was at his instance, and, when it was proposed, vaguely puzzled me. But soon its purpose became clear enough. Valentino was in trouble and wanted advice. More, he wanted advice from an elder and disinterested man, wholly removed from the movies and all their works. Something that I had written, falling under his eye, had given him the notion that I was a judicious fellow. So he requested one of his colleagues, a lady of the films, to ask me to dinner at her hotel.
>
> The night being infernally warm, we stripped off our coats, and came to terms at once. I recall that he wore suspenders of extraordinary width and thickness. On so slim a young man they seemed somehow absurd, especially on a hot Summer night. We perspired horribly for an hour, mopping our faces with our handkerchiefs, the table napkins, the corners of the tablecloth, and a couple of towels brought in by the humane waiter. Then there came a thunderstorm, and we began to breathe. The hostess, a woman as tactful as she is charming, disappeared mysteriously and left us to commune.
>
> The trouble that was agitating Valentino turned out to be very simple. The ribald New York papers were full of it, and that was what was agitating him. Some time before, out in Chicago, a wandering reporter had discovered, in the men's wash-room of a gaudy hotel, a slot-machine selling talcum-powder. That, of course, was not unusual, but the color of the talcum-powder was. It was pink. The news made the town giggle for a day, and inspired an editorial writer on the Chicago *Tribune* to compose a hot weather editorial. In it he protested

humorously against the effeminization of the American man, and laid it lightheartedly to the influence of Valentino and his sheik movies. Well, it so happened that Valentino, passing through Chicago that day on his way east from the Coast, ran full tilt into the editorial, and into a gang of reporters who wanted to know what he had to say about it. What he had to say was full of fire. Throwing off his 100% Americanism and reverting to the *mores* of his fatherland, he challenged the editorial writer to a duel, and, when no answer came, to a fist fight. His masculine honor, it appeared, had been outraged. To the hint that he was less than he, even to the extent of one half of one per cent, there could be no answer save a bath of blood.

. . . So New York laughed at Valentino. More, it ascribed his high dudgeon to mere publicity-seeking: he seemed a vulgar movie ham seeking space. The poor fellow, thus doubly beset, rose to dudgeons higher still. His Italian mind was simply unequal to the situation. . . . He protested that it was infamous. Infamous? Nothing, I argued, is infamous that is not true. A man still has inner integrity. Can he still look into the shaving-glass of a morning? Then he is still on his two legs in this world, and ready even for the Devil. We sweated a great deal, discussing these lofty matters. We seemed to get nowhere.

Suddenly it dawned upon me—I was too dull or it was too hot for me to see it sooner—that what we were talking about was really not what we were talking about at all. I began to observe Valentino more closely. A curiously naive and boyish young fellow, certainly not much beyond thirty, and with a disarming air of inexperience. To my eye, at least, not handsome, but nevertheless rather attractive. There was some obvious fineness in him;

even his clothes were not precisely those of his horrible trade. He began talking of his home, his people, his early youth. His words were simple and yet somehow very eloquent. I could still see the mime before me, but now and then, briefly and darkly, there was a flash of something else. That something else, I concluded, was what is commonly called, for want of a better name, a gentleman. In brief, Valentino's agony was the agony of a man of relatively civilized feelings thrown into a situation of intolerable vulgarity, destructive alike to his peace and to his dignity—nay, into a whole series of such situations.

It was not that trifling Chicago episode that was riding him; it was the whole grotesque futility of his life. Had he achieved, out of nothing, a vast and dizzy success? Then that success was hollow as well as vast—a colossal and preposterous nothing. Was he acclaimed by yelling multitudes? Then every time the multitudes yelled he felt himself blushing inside. . . . The thing, at the start, must have only bewildered him. But in those last days, unless I am a worse psychologist than even the professors of psychology, it was revolting him. Worse, it was making him afraid.

I incline to think that the inscrutable gods, in taking him off so soon and at a moment of fiery revolt, were very kind to him. Living, he would have tried inevitably to change his fame—if such it is to be called—into something closer to his heart's desire. That is to say, he would have gone the way of many another actor—the way of increasing pretension, of solemn artiness, of hollow hocus-pocus, deceptive only to himself. I believe he would have failed, for there was little sign of the genuine artist in him. He was essentially a highly respectable young man, which is the sort that never metamorphoses into an artist. But suppose he had succeeded? Then his tragedy,

> I believe, would have only become the more acrid and intolerable. For he would have discovered, after vast heavings and yearnings, that what he had come to was indistinguishable from what he had left. Was the fame of Beethoven any more caressing and splendid than the fame of Valentino? To you and me, of course, the question seems to answer itself. But what of Beethoven? He was heard upon the subject, *viva voce*, while he lived, and his answer survives, in all the freshness of its profane eloquence, in his music. Beethoven, too, knew what it meant to be applauded. Walking with Goethe, he heard something that was not unlike the murmur that reached Valentino through his hospital window. Beethoven walked away briskly. Valentino turned his face to the wall.
>
> Here was a young man who was living daily the dream of millions of other young men. Here was one who was catnip to women. Here was one who had wealth and fame. And here was one who was very unhappy.*

I am saying, I think, that Mencken was only a second-rate philosopher when he came to do a set piece, but that he was a wiser and a better writer as a journalist, and as such an original. Like all originals, he was a bad master. By which I mean that he is a dangerous model for authors of lesser talent. During the 1920s, American newspapers and magazines, even the *Smart Set* and the *American Mercury* themselves, were full of Mencken imitators, who imitated only the windy rhetoric, the facetious polysyllables, the verbosity. There must have been some awful undergraduate essays spawned by Mencken's fame. This, however, is the price the public has to pay for the appearance of any genuine original. It was the

* *Prejudices: Sixth Series* (Alfred A. Knopf, 1927).

same, in his day, with Dickens. And with Mark Twain. And any year after *The Rite of Spring* the concert halls were glutted with fourth-rate Stravinskys.

Throughout the 1920s Mencken reveled in his talent, but he reveled just as much, I believe, in the propagandist role that he assigned to himself, which was simplified by his worshipers into that of a Daniel come to judgment, and was twisted even more by the general public into the role of a radical public scold. The fireworks of this reputation bedazzled his public and blinded it to what was best in him as a writer. I have tried to clarify this point elsewhere (in my preface to the collection called *The Vintage Mencken*) and since I cannot say it better, I will beg pardon for quoting the gist of it again:

"What has stood the test of time and the exhaustion of the Mencken cult is not, it seems to me, his orderly essays on religion or his healthy but noisy crusade against the genteel tradition; it is his passing reflections on the sex uproar of the twenties; his reports of political conventions and the (Dayton) evolution trial; an evening with Valentino, the memory of a minor revolution in Cuba . . . indeed, much of what book-writers with one foot already in obscurity call 'transient' journalism. The one prepared indictment that keeps its clarion freshness through the years is that against the plutocracy. This may be because every time the United States is launched on a new prosperity, the plutocrats take to the bridge again to dictate our values while the country-club guests reappear to set the tone of our sea-going manners. . . . Looking over the whole range of his work today, we can see that if he was overrated in his day as a thinker . . . he was vastly underrated as a humorist with one deadly sensible eye on the behavior of the human animal. He helped along this misconception by constantly reminding people that he was 'a critic of ideas,' which was true only as the ideas were made flesh:

He was, in fact, a humorist by instinct and a superb craftsman by temperament."

Before moving on to my main contention, that he is above all an American humorist, I ought to substantiate the claim —which is implied in the above passage—that he is a better reporter of political events than a professor of political theory. For most of his working life, he had had the invaluable experience of being close to politics and politicians of every echelon and he recognized, as do few outsiders or "political scientists" (whatever they may be), the complexities of running even a small town. Of course, there are men in politics all their lives who see no more than what they want to. But out of a natural perception of the foibles of the human animal, Mencken saw and learned what is there for all to see: how rarely the excellent administrator can stir an audience, how rarely the man of eloquence has horse sense, or the courageous man good judgment, or the shrewd man imagination, or the scornful idealist either horse sense, judgment, or imagination. He came to take a baleful view of men who stormed about what things *ought* to be, in government, in economics, or in the relations between the sexes; and his hereditary conservatism allied to his impish view of human pretension released a source of shrewd humor which is most nearly typical of him and of no one else.

Here is a brief passage from Mencken's running dispatches to the Baltimore *Evening Sun* on the last two days of the Democratic Convention, at Chicago in 1932, which initiated the long reign of Franklin Roosevelt. The point I want to make is that when some political event was going through its complexities in front of him, he shucked off his ideology and his whimsical prejudices and was as watchful as a cat for the realities of what was happening and what might happen. These two dispatches are much too long to quote in full—on assignment, he wrote steadily through all hours and produced dispatches of great length and accuracy. (From my own experience of sitting through three conventions with him, I can testify that while he dangled an unlit stogey and dropped occasional asides to his colleagues, he never took his eyes off the speakers or shut his ears to the backroom plots and calculations.) If you take the trouble to compare these reports with the daily coverage of any other metropolitan daily, not to mention the news agencies, you will find here an account of how the nomination was contrived that did not become generally accepted until the memoirs of the protagonists and the passage of time confirmed its truth:

Chicago, July 2

THE NOMINATION OF F.D.R.

The great combat is ending this afternoon in the classical Democratic manner. That is to say, the victors are full of uneasiness and the vanquished are full of bile. It would be hard to find a delegate who believes seriously that Roosevelt can carry New York in November, or Massachusetts, or New Jersey, or even Illinois. All of the crucial wet States of the Northeast held out against him to the last ditch, and their representatives are damning him up hill and down dale today. Meanwhile the Southern and Middle Western delegates are going home with a tattered Bible on one shoulder and a new and shiny beer seidel on the other, and what they will have to listen to from their pastors and the ladies of the W.C.T.U. is making their hearts miss every other beat. . . .

As you all know by now, the final break to Roosevelt was brought on by the Garner men from California. Garner's friends from Texas were prepared to stick to him until Hell froze over, but in California he was only a false face for McAdoo and Hearst, and McAdoo was far more bent upon punishing Smith for the events of

1924 than he was for nominating Texas Jack, just as Hearst was more eager to block his pet abomination, Newton D. Baker, than to name any other candidate. Hearst was quite willing on Thursday to turn to Ritchie, who was satisfactory to him on all the major issues, including especially the League of Nations. In fact, negotiations with him were in full blast Thursday afternoon, with Arthur Brisbane as the intermediary. But McAdoo had other ideas, chiefly relating to his own fortunes, and he pulled Hearst along. For one thing, McAdoo had a palpable itch for the Vice-Presidency. But above all he yearned to give Smith a beating, and he saw after the third ballot that Roosevelt would be the handiest stick for the job. . . .

California comes early on the roll, so there was no long suspense. McAdoo went up to the platform to deliver the State delegation in person. He must be close to seventy by now, if not beyond it, but he is still slim, erect and graceful, and as he made his little speech and let his eye rove toward the New York delegation he looked every inch the barnstorming Iago of the old school. Eight years ago at New York he led the hosts of the Invisible Empire against the Pope, the rum demon and all the other beelzebubs of the Hookworm belt, and came so close to getting the nomination that the memory of its loss must still shiver him. The man who blocked him was Al Smith, and now he was paying Al back.

If revenge is really sweet he was sucking a colossal sugar teat, but all the same there was a beery flavor about it that must have somewhat disquieted him. For he is Georgia cracker by birth and has always followed his native pastors docilely, and it must have taken a lot of temptation to make him accept the ribald and saloonish platform. Here, indeed, revenge was working both ways, and

> if Al were a man of more humor he would have been smiling, too. . . .
>
> The failure of the opposition was the failure of Al Smith. From the moment he arrived on the ground it was apparent that he had no plan, and was animated only by his fierce hatred of Roosevelt, the cuckoo who had seized his nest. That hatred may have had logic in it, but it was impotent to organize the allies and they were knocked off in detail by the extraordinarily astute Messrs. Farley and Mullen. The first two ballots gave them some hope, but it was lost on the third, for the tide by then was plainly going Roosevelt's way. Perhaps the Al of eight or ten years ago, or even of four years ago, might have achieved the miracle that the crisis called for, but it was far beyond the technique of the golf-playing Al of today. He has ceased to be the wonder and glory of the East Side and become simply a minor figure of Park Avenue.*

I tremble slightly before attempting to analyze the technique of his humor. When it is successfully done, the analyst has identified the sequences of thought which it is the business of a humorist to short-circuit; for there is no laughter without the surprise that springs from having led the reader on from one step to another and then, without warning, leapt to an illogical end (e.g., Woody Allen's immortal contribution to the notorious "Is God Dead?" controversy: "Not only is God dead, but you can't get a dentist on the weekend").

However, all humorists—before they develop a craft—must have a character trait to work on. In Mencken, this was a gift for maintaining a sweet temper at the precise moment that his victim—especially during a public argument—was beginning to

* Baltimore *Evening Sun*, July 2, 1932.

fly off the handle. In a long brawl in print with Upton Sinclair, during which Mencken ridiculed his pretensions to the Governorship of California and then to the Presidency, Sinclair complained that a joking column Mencken had written violated freedom of speech. Mencken replied: "When you proposed to become the savior and the boss of California, and then of the United States, you invited the opinion of every citizen as to your qualifications. . . . I admit you have done more or less hollering for free speech, but how much of it did you do during the war when free speech was most in danger? You actually supported Wilson. . . . Well, so did every other Socialist . . . every one save a handful. The handful went to jail. . . . In political controversy, there is such a thing as give-and-take. If you want to speak your mind freely, you must let your opponents speak *their* mind freely, even when what they have to say collides with your vanity and violates your peculiar notions of the true, the good and the beautiful."

After this, Sinclair sulked and muttered in California, and to cheer him up Mencken promised that if he outlived Sinclair he would personally start a subscription toward erecting in his memory an equestrian statue. This only sparked another flare-up from Sinclair. He became one with the other Mencken victims. Mencken made them ridiculous and did it in good temper, as if their absurdity were subject, some other time, to mathematical proof. In other words, the secret of his best and most characteristic invective is the control of his blood pressure. In his later work, the control is invisible, and what we have, instead of ringing, if merry, denunciation, is a kind of irony so rounded that it appears to be almost a species of tribute. We forget, if we ever knew, that Mencken never ceased to work on his writing and, as he grew older, purified it very strikingly. Compare the rolling derision of his obituary on Bryan with his obituary on Coolidge written in 1933:

> He talked and lived only sunshine. There was a volcano boiling under him, but he did not know it and he was not singed. When it burst forth at last, it was Hoover who got its blast. . . . How Dr. Coolidge must have chuckled in his retirement, for he was not without humor of a sad, necrotic kind. . . . He had one really notable talent; he slept more than any other President, whether by night or by day. [This is literally true: according to the chief steward of the White House in his day, Coolidge slept on an average of eleven to fifteen hours a day.] Nero fiddled, but Coolidge only snored. And when the crash came at last and Hoover began to smoke and bubble, good Cal was safe in Northampton and still in the hay. There is sound reason for believing that this great gift of self-induced narcolepsy was at the bottom of such modest popularity as he enjoyed . . . the kind of government that he offered the country was stripped to the buff. It was government that governed hardly at all. . . . Well, there is surely something to say for that (Jeffersonian) abstinence. Counting out Harding as a cipher only, Dr. Coolidge was preceded by one World Saver and followed by two more. What enlightened American, having to choose between any of them and another Coolidge, would hesitate for an instant? There were no thrills while he reigned, but neither were there any headaches. He had no ideas, and he was not a nuisance.*

Even glanced at on the page, this looks much less dense than Mencken's earlier writing. The sentences are shorter. There are few double adjectives. The subject hits the verbs at once

* *The American Mercury*, April 1933.

without subsidiary qualifications. The mood turns easily on familiar idioms and connectives. It works up not to a peroration but a simple, blank epitaph. To my mind, it is a more memorable piece of writing than the Bryan obituary, for all its majestic drum-rolling and its funny fury.

It will be plain from this passage, I think, that a man who is honing the grammar of a phrase, and carefully steering the cadence of a sentence, is going to hit his target with more devilish precision than a man who explodes at his enemies through bloodshot prose. The calm choice of a single epithet in Mencken can persuade us into believing a palpable untruth. Witness his—frankly ridiculous—remark on why he does not believe in democracy. "No doubt," he wrote, with mock simplicity, "my distaste for democracy is . . . like every other human prejudice, due to an inner lack. In this case it is very probably my incapacity for envy. . . . In the face of another man's good fortune, I am as inert as a curb broker before Johann Sebastian Bach." In one sentence, Rockefeller's millions have been earned at the expense of an ear for music, and the stock exchange is consigned to the stupid ward of a mental hospital. All because of the cool choice of the word "inert."

When I first suggested that Mencken might, after all, turn out to be not so much a critic as a well-remembered American humorist, a man who knew him well retorted grudgingly that Mencken "certainly enjoyed being an intellectual clown, and something of a mountebank also."

Intellectual clowns are wits, and Mencken could certainly be witty. But he was also, and I maintain more remarkably, a humorist, and all humorists are professional mountebanks. They instinctively (when they are good) and deliberately (when they are bad) adopt an attitude toward the facts of life that is more naive than that of their audience. This puts the audience in a superior frame of mind, which is the proper frame for the agreeable form of compassion known as laughter. However, the laughter would remain in its pure state of pity if the humorist were really naive. He is, in fact, sharper than his audience. But the successful technique of humor demands that he should throw furtive hints of intelligence to his readers, as if they were his only allies in a world of oafs. The circuit of flattery is now complete. The audience begins by chuckling at the simpleness of the writer and goes on to laugh in triumph at the sudden discovery that they and he alone form a secret society of mockers at the great mass of men.

I will go no further with this abstract analysis, which requires that you have good examples at the back of your mind, for I well remember the unanswerable complaint that confronted Max Eastman when, long ago, he wrote a critical book with the doleful title, *Enjoyment of Laughter*. Charlie Chaplin killed the book with the remark: "People don't want to know why they laugh. They want to laugh."

So be it. Let me try to isolate under the microscope one or two examples of what I take to be a particular species of American humor. Both the simpleness that makes the audience feel superior and the shrewdness that makes the audience feel more superior still may be seen in compound in a single sentence containing an apparently fair analogy, which is instantly recognized as outrageous. James Thurber, on going before his draft board: "I failed to get into the army on account of my sight, the way grandfather failed on account of his age." We see the same screwy logic in Mencken's "I hate all sports as rabidly as a man who loves sports hates common sense." The trick lies in an extreme sensitivity to the way that simple conjunctions may be stood on their heads. At his best, nobody had it better than Churchill (the half-American statesman), whose fun lies not in a choice of bizarre or consciously amusing language but in the logical fallacy implied in a simple connective. Witness his solemnly hypocritical obituary tribute, delivered in the House of Commons, to Lord Balfour: "His aversion from the Roman Catholic faith was dour and inveterate. Otherwise, he seemed to have the personal qualifications of a perfect Pope." The key word is "otherwise." The laughter is triggered not by wit or cleverness but by a shrewd appeal to simple prejudice through the hilarious double-meanings that lie buried in the simplest vernacular grammar. I suppose the master of this form was S. J. Perelman, who passed on his rollicking playfulness with grammar and syntax to the Marx Brothers in the scripts he wrote for their early movies.

This masquerade may seem harder to discover in Mencken, because he was a practicing intellectual. He was most famous, as we have seen, for invective and the smashing of scholarly skulls. Yet in his quintessential passages (which people would have accepted from Mark Twain, because he was the national wag, whereas Mencken was the national terror) he maintains the same air of alert stupidity, the chronic baffled air of a man who doesn't see that he is missing the point. Take the essay, an early one, in which he is affecting to analyze what he calls "the lure of beauty" in woman. His pretended thesis is that men have never really looked closely at the female form. But Mencken has looked. And what does he see?

> A pure illusion . . . the female body, even at its best, is very defective in form; it has harsh curves and very clumsily distributed masses; compared to it the average milk-jug, or even cuspidor, is a thing of intelligent and gratifying design—in brief, an *objet d'art.* Below the neck by the bow and below the waist astern there are two masses that simply refuse to fit into a balanced composition. Viewed from the side, a woman presents an

> exaggerated S bisected by an imperfect straight line, and so she inevitably suggests a drunken dollar-mark.*

His most effective personal technique is one that combines an affected naiveté with the pose of a conscientious reporter of absurd events. He used this brilliantly at presidential conventions, where he employed a portentous vocabulary on people who, in life, took themselves portentously but whom Mencken turns into comic characters. It is a more sophisticated variation on the young Dickens's reporting of the election at Eatanswill. Mencken never used it better than in his account of a revolution in Cuba that he was sent to cover in 1917. A fascinating fact about this piece, as you can confirm from any standard Latin-American history, is that in substance it is a remarkably accurate account of the revolt of the liberal José Miguel Gómez against the incumbent conservative president Menocal. An important fact for us to note is that Mencken's piece was written in retrospect, in 1943, when he was sixty-two and when, as I have tried to show, his prose style had mellowed and matured and, while still ribald—and still willing to call on its old baroque inventions for comic effects—had become more flexible and lucid.

To get the issues straight at the start Mencken resolved to interview both leaders. El Presidente said that José Miguel was a "fiend in human form who had hoped by his treasons to provoke American intervention through the New York banks." José Miguel was at the front, so Mencken saw the head of the revolutionary junta, a doctor, who said that Miguel, "though somewhat bulky for field service, was comparable to Hindenburg or Hannibal. As for Menocal, he was a fiend in human form who hoped to provoke American in-

* A *Mencken Chrestomathy* (Alfred A. Knopf, 1949).

tervention through the New York banks and thereby make his corrupt and abominable regime secure." All this, says, Mencken, "struck me as somewhat unusual, though as a newspaper reporter I was supposed to be incapable of surprise." Next, he wanted to see the war and it was arranged that a fleet of Fords should take Mencken and his colleagues as close to the front as prudence allowed. "The trip," he says, "was never made, for at the precise moment the order for it was being issued, a dashing colonel in Santa Clara was leading his men in a grand assault upon José Miguel, and after ten minutes of terrific fire and deafening yells, the Cuban Hindenburg hoisted his shirt upon the tip of his sword and surrendered. He did not have to take his shirt off for the purpose: it was already hanging upon a guava bush, for he had been preparing for a siesta in his hammock . . . The palace press agents spit on their hands when they heard the news and turned out a series of communiqués perhaps unsurpassed in the history of war. Their hot, lascivious rhetoric was still flowing three or four days later."

All that remained for the correspondents was to witness and report the execution of José Miguel, and to their surprise the permission was granted. "He was to be turned off, it appeared, at 6 a.m. promptly, so we were asked to be at the gate of La Cabaña an hour earlier. Most of us were on hand, but the sentry on watch refused to let us in, and after half an hour's wrangle a young officer came out and said that the execution had been postponed until the next day. But the next day it was put off again, and again the next, and after three or four days no more colleagues showed up at the gate. It was then announced by the palace literati that President Menocal had commuted the sentence to solitary confinement for life in a dungeon (on the Cayos de las Doce Leguas) off the south coast, where the mosquitoes were as large as bullfrogs, along with confiscation of all the culprit's property, whether real, personal or mixed, and the perpetual loss of his civil rights, such as they were.

"But even this turned out to be only tall talk, for President Menocal was a very humane man, and pretty soon he reduced José Miguel's sentence to fifty years, and then to fifteen, and then to six, and then to two. Soon after that he wiped out the jugging altogether and substituted a fine—first of $1,000,000, then of $250,000, and then of $50,000. The common belief was that José Miguel was enormously rich, but this was found to be an exaggeration. When I left Cuba he was still protesting that the last and lowest fine was far beyond his means, and in the end, I believe, he was let off with the confiscation of his yacht, a small craft then laid up with engine trouble."

So what we have unveiled at the end is a humorist in the classic American tradition, about halfway between Mark Twain and Woody Allen. Aside from his tribute to the lasting effect on him of *Huckleberry Finn*, Mencken has left us almost nothing about the writers who excited him to imitation, apart from his aforementioned early apeings of Shaw and Nietzsche and Bierce. But on the last page of the last book he published (*Minority Report*) he has something revealing to say about an early idol, to whom he reverted in later life:

> I am still convinced that the prose of Thomas Henry Huxley was the best produced by an Englishman in the Nineteenth Century. He always put clarity first. . . . [His prose] was as far ahead of that of Macaulay as that of Macaulay was ahead of the ornate quasi-Latin of the later Eighteenth Century. No matter how difficult the theme he dealt with, Huxley was always crystal clear. He even made metaphysics intelligible, and, what is more, charming. . . . The imbeciles who have printed acres of

> comment on my books have seldom noticed the chief character of my style. It is that I write with almost scientific precision—that my meaning is never obscure. The ignorant have often complained that my vocabulary is beyond them, but that is simply because my ideas cover a wider range than theirs do. Once they have consulted the dictionary they always know exactly what I intend to say. I am as far as any writer can get from the muffled sonoritics of, say, John Dewey.*

No doubt what I have been doing all along is rationalizing a personal preference for classic English over the baroque English of the early Mencken crusades. And, of course, Mencken's fame was rightly grounded in the vigor, and often the noble indignation, he brought to unpopular causes. Otherwise, he would never have earned the best of the tributes paid to him when he died: that editorial in the Catholic *Commonweal* which applauded his courage and services to human decency, embraced him as a brother, and ended with the touching line: "And so, my dear Mencken, I think you are on the side of the angels."

But I have been considering him mainly as a prose stylist, and there is enough in his own pronouncement of T. H. Huxley as a model, and the abundant witness of his later work (his autobiographical masterpiece, *Happy Days*, especially) to show that Mencken himself moved toward a similar ideal of what he took to be good writing.

* *Minority Report* (Alfred A. Knopf, 1956).

The COMFORTABLE BOURGEOIS

The Thought of H. L. MENCKEN

Charles A. Fecher

I

In *Minority Report*, that collection of miscellaneous notes and aphorisms which was the very last thing he prepared for publication himself (and which, lost and forgotten after his 1948 stroke, appeared only posthumously in 1956), H. L. Mencken wrote:

> Converting me to anything is probably a psychological impossibility. At all events, it has never been achieved by anyone, though I have been exposed more than once to the missionary technic of very talented virtuosi. I can't

Charles A. Fecher, a native Baltimorean, works for the Roman Catholic Archdiocese of Baltimore. He is the author of *Mencken: A Study of His Thought*.

> recall ever changing my mind about any capital matter. My general body of fundamental ideas is the same today as it was in the days when I first began to ponder.*

This lifelong immutability of his thought was remarked on by many people besides himself. To a friend and colleague like Hamilton Owens, it signified that Mencken had been able to avoid the painful intellectual experience, so common to most of us, of being forced to discard one set of beliefs because they had proved false or inadequate and then grope about for a new set to take their place. To critics or outright enemies, it constituted proof positive that he was narrow-minded and prejudiced, closed to any point of view that did not happen to coincide with his own, and had never gone through the normal processes of maturing.

Both sides, however, friendly and unfriendly, have invariably failed to note two other things. The first is the almost complete consistency of his thought, the way that those "fundamental ideas" tie in with each other and flow from one another with inexorable logic. Most of us, too, feel no embarrassment about holding opinions that are inherently quite irreconcilable—for example, up until a few years ago it was perfectly possible for an American Catholic, *as an American*, to defend the constitutional guarantees of freedom of speech and the press, and simultaneously, *as a Catholic*, defend with equal fervor the right of the Church to censor books and silence heterodox opinion. In a democratic society it is commonplace to maintain that all persons have equal rights, and yet to feel, too, that Jews, or blacks, or women, or some other group, do not deserve to have quite the same rights as the majority.

Mencken was guilty of no such contradictions. It goes with-

* *Minority Report* (Alfred A. Knopf, 1956).

out saying, of course, that any man who wrote as voluminously as he did, and on such an infinite range of subjects, can occasionally be trapped in some inconsistencies of detail. It is even possible to come across them at what one might call a "middle level"—thus, in the field of literary criticism he was quite open to experimentation and new forms in the novel, but utterly closed to the same kind of development in poetry. He thought that the Puritan attitude toward sex was irrational and nonsensical, but held to a level of sexual morality that could only be termed puritanical. And yet these things do not really affect the basic unity of his thought.

From his high regard for scientific achievement his skeptical attitude toward religion naturally follows. His opinions on religion lead directly to what might be called, if in his case it did not sound so dreadfully formal, his "philosophy of man." His view of human nature is the foundation for his contemptuous dismissal of democracy, and for all his beliefs about government and politics. And so it goes. The total number of his fundamental ideas may have been small, but the very same thing can be said about the builders of the most complex philosophical "systems," and his hold together as coherently as most of theirs do.

The second point usually overlooked is that all of this was quite in accord with the predominant *Weltanschauung* of his time and place in history. In other words, he mirrored his age. The whole late nineteenth century took a dim view of religion; so did he. In spite of that fact, it was intensely respectable; so, as I have indicated, was he. It had little confidence in the great Truths enunciated by the philosophers of the past; he had no more. But it held to an unquestioning faith in the ability of science to add to the store of human knowledge and enhance the quality of life; and so, most profoundly, did he.

I am not suggesting, of course, that Mencken was in agreement with, or a spokesman for, the prevailing ideas of the society about him. That is precisely what he was not, and any claim that he was would have evoked in him, to whom indignation was so foreign, the most violent indignation. But no man grows up in a vacuum, and all of us are shaped to some degree at least by the ideas that we imbibe in our youth. Aristotle was thus shaped, and so was St. Paul, and so, centuries later, were Voltaire and Nietzsche. And it follows that the same thing was just as true of Mencken.

II

That society looked upon itself as the heir to more than two hundred years of intellectual enlightenment and scientific progress. The discoveries of astronomy that had begun with Copernicus and Galileo and continued unbroken ever since had made it very clear that the earth, far from being the fixed center around which the rest of the universe turns admiringly, is rather only a very insignificant satellite of a very minor sun. Newton had established the seemingly immutable laws by which that universe is governed. Anton van Leeuwenhoek's microscope had revealed the existence of a world as infinitely small as the heavens are infinitely vast. And so recently as 1859, Charles Darwin had done to the human race what Galileo had done to the earth: in his epochal *Origin of Species* he demonstrated with an overwhelming mass of evidence that man is not the unique lord of creation but has evolved from lower forms of life, and that he still bears in his body the marks of that humble origin.

All these things might well have shaken mankind's belief in itself—and there is no doubt that on many fronts they did—but parallel advances in physiology and medicine had also had the effect of giving that body better health, greater strength, and longer life. The whole series of extremely practical inventions that ushered in the Industrial Revolution enabled people to live with an ease and a comfort hitherto undreamed of. We of today may perhaps smile at those primitive comforts, but it remains a fact that as the nineteenth century drew to its close and the twentieth dawned, people had every reason to suppose that scientific progress was a law of nature and human perfection was its ultimate goal.

Yet a price had to be paid for these achievements—and philosophy and religion were the departments of knowledge called upon to pay it. Each new discovery seemed to chop away at what had hitherto been their exclusive preserves. Once philosophy had been the "queen of the sciences," engaged in the pursuit and establishment of Truth; now it appeared that there was no such thing as Truth, but only facts to be ascertained and verified. Once religion had called for faith in an omnipotent God who knew about the fall of every sparrow, and who rewarded men for their good deeds and punished them for their wicked ones; now the universe could be explained quite easily without such a being. The nineteenth century turned away from God not because it could not believe in Him, but simply because it did not need Him.

This was the world-view that H. L. Mencken accepted as unquestioningly as he ever accepted anything at all. The point hardly needs to be labored that Mencken was not a scientist in any sense of the word, and certainly he had small confidence in the inevitability of human perfection. But he never doubted for a moment that the scientific answers to questions were infinitely more rational and convincing than philosophical or religious ones. "To me," he wrote,

> the scientific point of view is completely satisfying, and it has been so long as I can remember. Not once in this

> life have I ever been inclined to seek a rock and a refuge elsewhere. It leaves a good many dark spots in the universe, to be sure, but not a hundredth time as many as theology. We may trust it, soon or late, to throw light upon many of them, and those that remain dark will be beyond illumination by any other agency. It also fails on occasion to console, but so does theology; indeed, I am convinced that man, in the last analysis, is intrinsically inconsolable.*

Philosophy, quite the contrary, was "moonshine and wind-music," and that branch of it which is known as metaphysics had not only never made any contribution to human knowledge but had actually impeded it. "Half of it," he assured Theodore Dreiser, "is a tremendous laboring of the obvious, and the other half is speculation that has very little relation to the known facts."† Scientists built upon the work of their predecessors, and scientific knowledge was a patient accumulation of the labors of all of them; philosophers were everywhere in rivalry with one another, and no two of them agreed. "Philosophy consists very largely," he held, "of one philosopher arguing that all others are jackasses. He usually proves it, and I should add that he also usually proves that he is one himself."‡

Religion was in even worse case—if only because, while philosophy was the ivory-tower pursuit of a handful of pedants, religion touched the lives of almost everyone. He always used to insist, no doubt quite sincerely, that his attitude toward it was one of "amiable skepticism"; he had been born without a believing mind himself and so could not accept any of its tenets, but he had no quarrel with those who did. He was

* *Ibid.*

† Letter of April 19, 1939, to Dreiser, in *Letters of H. L. Mencken*, ed. Guy J. Forgue (Alfred A. Knopf, 1961).

‡ *Minority Report.*

even willing to admit that, the initial tenets being granted, all the rest followed consistently enough. Nevertheless, there are times when the amiability shows very definite signs of straining.

"Religion," he declared, "is fundamentally opposed to everything I hold in veneration—courage, clear thinking, honesty, fairness, and, above all, love of the truth. In brief, it is a fraud."* Faith was "an illogical belief in the occurrence of the improbable," and the man of faith was not a mere ass—he was actually ill. The decline in religious belief since the Renaissance was a very definite and encouraging sign of human progress, and "the time must inevitably come," he thought,

> when mankind shall surmount the imbecility of religion, as it has surmounted the imbecility of religion's ally, magic. It is impossible to imagine this world being really civilized so long as so much nonsense survives. In even its highest forms religion embraces concepts that run counter to all common sense. It can be defended only by making assumptions and adopting rules of logic that are never heard of in any other field of human thinking.†

In his approach to the world's religions he managed to achieve absolute impartiality—Hinduism had "absolutely nothing to offer a civilized white man," Buddhism was "complete hooey," the Judaic Law was full of "general irrationality." But in a society at least putatively Christian it was, of course, his assaults on Christianity that earned him his greatest fame—or notoriety. He believed that it leaned upon supernaturalism and the irrational to a much greater extent than any of its

* From the autobiographical notes supplied by Mencken in 1925 to Isaac Goldberg for the latter's book *The Man Mencken*, and housed in the H. L. Mencken Room, Enoch Pratt Free Library, Baltimore.

† *Minority Report*.

competitors, and what Christians were called upon to believe would, if put in the form of an affidavit, "be such shocking nonsense that even bishops and archbishops would laugh at it."* All that saved it was its gorgeous poetry; but poetry was only a denial of facts and a sonorous statement of the obviously not true. His contemporaries, shocked beyond bearing by such forthrightness, promptly labeled him as Antichrist.

And yet despite all this, it remains a fact that in his private life he was a model of the solid virtues inculcated by Christianity. For poverty and obedience he probably had no more use than most believers have ever had, but his views on chastity—though grounded on quite other premises—were startlingly similar to those preached by the Church. He was convinced that ordinary monogamy and family life provided the best possible solution to the demands of sex. His own marriage, if tragically brief, was romantically happy. He had a very deep sense of family ties—for years, despite fantastic offers, he refused to take a job that would require living in New York, not only because he hated the city but also, and more importantly, because he could not bring himself to leave his mother in Baltimore; and his relations to his home, his brothers and sister, and later his niece and her family, were unusually close all his life long.

Like many of his contemporaries—though again for different reasons—he placed an extremely high value on sobriety and characterized himself as a "somewhat cagey drinker." He was prudent in money matters, and never permitted himself to be in debt. He prided himself on the orderly neatness of his rooms, his personal effects, and his papers. It was his ironclad rule to answer every letter to him on the day that the postman left it at his door, and he stubbornly maintained that this was nothing more than a common courtesy owed to the

* *Treatise on the Gods* (Alfred A. Knopf, 1946).

sender. He treasured friendships, and his kindness and consideration toward all with whom he came in contact were proverbial. And he always held that "the most steadily attractive of all human qualities" was the plain virtue of competence: the plumber who, efficiently and with the least cost to his customer, could open up a clogged drain was infinitely superior to the English professor who had little knowledge of his subject and less ability to impart it to others.

Altogether he was as typical, in his way, of the world about him as any business executive, or bartender, or even—God help us all!—member of the Elks or the Knights of Pythias. "I was born a larva," he wrote late in life,

> of the comfortable and complacent bourgeoisie, though I was quite unaware of the fact until I was along in my teens, and had begun to read indignant books. To belong to that great order of mankind is vaguely discreditable today, but I still maintain my dues-paying membership in it, and continue to believe that it was and is authentically human, and therefore worthy of the attention of philosophers, at least to the extent that the Mayans, Hittites, Kallikuks and so on are worthy of it.*

III

What, then, made him different? If he believed that society to be authentically human, and always maintained his dues-paying membership in it, why did he spend a lifetime hurling at it the most outrageous insults it has ever had to bear and bringing down on his own head its hatred and obloquy in return?

* *Happy Days* (Alfred A. Knopf, 1940).

Both during his lifetime and since, it has been commonplace to say of Mencken that he was the archfoe of sham and hypocrisy. This is true, and it is likewise true that the era provided him with a great deal of sham and hypocrisy to be the foe of. But such a statement actually says very little: it tells only how he felt about the values he saw around him, and nothing about his own set of values or why he believed them to be better.

If the nineteenth century had abandoned any serious belief in religion, it had substituted for it a fierce and intransigent morality that was religious only in name and by a distortion of the term. This morality, which carried over into the twentieth century and came up to at least the period between the two World Wars, was preached and enforced by Christian churches, but it was Mencken's view that the churches themselves were about as far from Christ as it would be possible to get. From his gentle, tolerant, and forgiving spirit as portrayed in the New Testament, they had gone back to the harsh and vengeful Yahweh of the Old. The name for this morality was "Puritanism." It was "the haunting fear that someone, somewhere, may be happy"; its most implicit conviction was that "every human act must be either right or wrong, and that 99 percent of them are wrong," and its aim was to play policeman to the world and require all persons to be good by its standards.

Mencken would have no part of such a morality; to it he opposed his own highly personal concept of "honor." The moral man abstained from such things as murder, theft, adultery, trespass, and false witness because he was afraid that somebody might be looking; the man of honor abstained from them too, but because they went contrary to what he regarded as elementary human decency. The moral man lived in fear of hell; the man of honor cared precisely nothing about hell and its terrors, and indeed regarded them as part of an outmoded mythology, but he lived no differently because he was free of such superstitions. The moral man would lie whenever it was necessary to save his own skin; the man of honor would lie only to save the good name and happiness of someone else. And this did not mean, of course, that the man of honor did not occasionally fall beneath his own standards—he did, but he picked himself up and went on, whereas the moral man always looked about frantically for somebody else on whom to cast the blame.

"Honor," Mencken contended, "is the morality of superior men."

And it is at this point that the things that made him different begin to come into view. For if he was guided in his conduct by a sense of honor, and if honor is the morality of superior men, then it had to follow that he was superior. It also had to follow that others—namely, the "moral" men—were inferior. This is precisely the conclusion that he drew. He may not have arrived at it through the steps of a syllogism, but he believed it fully, it was the foundation for his whole ethical, social, and political philosophy, and he did not hesitate to extract from it every latent implication it was capable of holding.

Expressed in psychological terms, this dichotomy separated mankind into "the intelligent minority" and the "vast herd of human blanks." (For the latter group he coined the term "booboisie," which became his own most notable contribution to the language.) In terms of inherent gifts and ability, it clearly meant that "there are men who are naturally intelligent and can learn, and there are men who are naturally stupid and cannot."* In terms of usefulness to the race, it meant that "the safeguarding and development of civilization are and always have been in the exclusive care of a very small

* *Notes on Democracy* (Alfred A. Knopf, 1926).

minority of human beings of each generation, and that the rest of the human race consists wholly of deadheads."*

But it was, needless to say, in the field of politics that Mencken made the most fertile applications of this distinction, and from beginning to end it was the sole basis for all his scathing denunciations of democracy. For democracy rests on the proposition that all men are equal, and if the foregoing statements are true then obviously any belief in the equality of men becomes the sheerest nonsense. The lines are drawn in precisely the same way and the same truths hold, but they are expressed now in the language of political theory: there is a small aristocracy, not of birth or blood or money, but of nature, and it is to this enlightened and clear-seeing minority that mankind is indebted for all the social, cultural, and intellectual progress it has ever made. On the other hand there is the "mob," ignorant, envious of its betters, fearful of change, suspicious of new ideas but ready to believe everything that is palpably untrue, and swayed by the bawling and promises of that most contemptible of all figures, the democratic politician.

"The average citizen of a democracy," Mencken maintained, "is a goose-stepping ignoramus and poltroon. . . . The average democratic politician, of whatever party, is a scoundrel and a swine."†

This is a harsh philosophy. In a nation dedicated to the principle that no man is better than any other, it does not exactly make for popularity. He who holds it may be set down, not unreasonably, as an intellectual snob, and the distance between him and his fellows becomes very great. Lastly, if there is such a thing as a "superior" man, the burden upon him must be a heavy one, since against all the ignorance

* *Prejudices: Fourth Series* (Alfred A. Knopf, 1924).
† Baltimore *Evening Sun*, Dec. 27, 1921.

and resentment and resistance of the "mob" he is obliged to struggle for enlightenment, decency, honesty, and truth. One can hardly blame him if, sometimes, the sham and hypocrisy seem an easier way to live than his own demanding code of honor.

Yet it was the philosophy that Mencken held to through seventy-five years of life, with a firmness of conviction and a singleness of purpose that are unequaled in literary history. If it did not make him popular, he cared precisely nothing for popularity. If it put a distance between him and his fellows, there is no evidence that the fact worried him. He never concealed his belief in the validity of the distinction, he never apologized for it, and it seemed to him to be the most obvious of all scientifically observable facts.

It stayed the first principle of his "general body of fundamental ideas," and all the talented virtuosi of the world never converted him to any other way of thinking.

IV

But there is not the slightest bit of evidence, either, that Mencken ever acted superior to anybody. All the available testimony runs in the opposite direction. It speaks of his unfailing amiability and courtesy to everyone. He mingled as easily with the employees in the pressroom of the *Sunpapers* as he did with the dignitaries who made up the company's board of directors. He bought candy for the black children who lived in the alley behind Hollins Street as readily as he took a bottle of fine wine to the home of a friend. He may not have suffered fools gladly—no man in his position does—but he never turned them off; "he is a foe of democracy," George Jean Nathan once wrote, "and politely sees every person, however asinine, who comes to call on him."

Neither did the harshness of the philosophy make him for one moment cold, or dour, or misanthropic. No man ever enjoyed himself more. The humor that runs through his work ran through his life, and inevitably communicated itself to others. He might take the dimmest possible view of human nature, but the spectacle of it never failed to delight him. He resolutely refused to join what he called "the race of viewers-with-alarm": "I have had too good a time of it in this world," he insisted, "to go down that chute."

Is there in all this an inconsistency, a contradiction between the theory and its application to reality? There may very well be, but the fact should not worry us any more than it ever worried him. The very respectable bourgeois citizen who lived in Hollins Street, formed by generations of equally respectable German ancestors and by the conventional morality of nineteenth-century Baltimore, may have been different, but he was not outlandish. He may have been caustic, but he was never venomous. He loved to shock but he would not have dreamed of hurting. He was a gentleman.

◇◇◇

ON METAPHYSICIANS

In the Summer of the year, when the weather on my estates in the Maryland jungles is too hot for serious mental activity, I always give over a couple of weeks to a re-reading of the so-called philosophical classics, with a glance or two at the latest compositions of the extant philosophers. It is a far from agreeable job, and I undertake it sadly, as a surgeon, after an untoward and fatal hemorrhage, brushes up on anatomy; there is, somewhere down in my recesses, an obscure conviction that I owe a duty to my customers, who look to me to flatter them with occasional dark references to Aristotle, Spinoza and the categorical imperative. Out of the business, despite its high austerity, I always carry away the feeling that I have had a hell of a time. That is, I carry away the feeling that the art and mystery of philosophy, as it is practiced in the world by professional philosophers, is largely moonshine and wind-music—or, to borrow Henry Ford's searching term, bunk.

Is this anarchy and atheism? Has Russian gold got to me at last? Am I in training for the abattoir of the Department of Justice? In stay of execution I can only point to the philosophy books themselves. For three millenniums their authors have been searching the world and its suburbs for the truth—and they have yet to agree upon so much as the rules of the search. Since the dawn of time they have been trying to get order and method into the thinking of *Homo sapiens*—and *Homo sapiens*, when he thinks at all, is still a brother to the lowly ass (*Equus africanus*), even to the ears and the bray. I include the philosophers themselves, unanimously and especially. True enough, one arises now and then who somehow manages to be charming and even plausible. I point to Plato, to Nietzsche, to Schopenhauer. But it is always as poet or politician, not as philosopher. The genuine professional, sticking to his gloomy speculations, is as dull as a table of logarithms. What man in human history ever wrote worse than Kant? Was it, perhaps, Hegel? My own candidate, if I were pushed, would be found among the so-called Critical Realists of today. They achieve the truly astounding feat of writing worse than the New Thoughters, whom they also resemble otherwise—nay, even worse than the late Warren Gamaliel Harding.

What reduces all philosophers to incoherence and folly, soon or late, is the lure of the absolute. It tortures them as the dream of Law Enforcement tortures Prohibitionists. Now and then, when they forget it transiently, they grow relatively rational and even ingratiating, but in the long run they always resume their chase of it, and that chase carries them inevitably into the intellectual Bad Lands. For the absolute, of course, is a mere banshee, a concept without substance or reality. No such thing exists. When, by logical devices, it is triumphantly established, the feat is exactly on all fours with that of the mathematician who proved that twice two was double once two. Who believes in Kant's categorical imperatives today? Certainly not any student of psychology who has got beyond the first page of his horn-book. There is, in fact, no idea in any man that may be found certainly in all men. Only the philosophers seem to cling to the doctrine that there is. Functioning as theologians, for example, they still argue for the immortality of the soul on the ground that a yearning for immortal life is in all of us. But that is simply nonsense. I know scores of men in whom no such yearning is apparent, either outwardly or in their consciousness. I have seen such men die, and they passed into what they held to be oblivion without showing the slightest sign of wishing that it was something else. All the other absolutes, whether theological, ethical or philosophical in the strict sense, are likewise chimeras. On inspection it always turns out that they are no more the same to all men than a woman A or a cocktail B is the same to all men. They are even different to the same man at different times. I cherished ethical postulates at the age of twenty-one that seem puerile to me today, and today I am cherishing postulates that would have shocked me then. *Quod est veritas?* Simply something that seems to me to be so—now, and to me. It has no more objective character than the sweet and dreadful passion of love. It is as tenderly personal and private as a gallstone.

The common sense of mankind, which is immensely superior to the anaemic, camphor-smelling wisdom of philosophers, long ago revolted against the quest of the absolute. Men found back in Mousterian days that it got them nowhere, but left them, intellectually speaking, with one leg up and one leg down. So they began to set up arbitrary values, if only to get some peace. Religion is a series of such arbitrary values. Most of them are dubious, and many of them are palpably false, but the experience of the race has shown that, for certain types of mind and in certain situations, they work. So they are accepted as, if not quite true, then as true enough, and the gloomy business of rectifying them, when they need it, is turned over to theologians, who are enemies of mankind anyhow, and thus deserve and get no sympathy when they suffer. Arbitrary values of the same sort are made use of every day in all the fields of human speculation and activity. They are brilliantly visible in the field of politics and government. Here they are rammed into children in the little red schoolhouse, and questioning them later in life becomes a crime against the Holy Ghost. Is it therefore to be assumed that they are true? Not at all. Many of them are so transparently dubious that even patriots, preparing to mumble them, have to make ready for it by closing their eyes and taking long breaths. But they at least work. They at least get some semblance of order into the complicated and dangerous business of living together in society. They at least relieve the mind. And so they are cherished.

Unfortunately, human existence is not static but dynamic, and in consequence the axioms that work well today tend to work less well tomorrow. Now and then, as the social organization changes, certain ancient and honorable ones have to be abandoned. This is always a perilous business, and usually it is accomplished only by a letting of blood. The fact is not without its significance. In the long run, I believe, it will be found that (as the Behaviorists argue even now) human ideas come out of the liver far more often than they come out of the soul, and that changing them is a job for surgeons rather than for metaphysicians. The thought leads at once to a constructive suggestion, and in the exalted field of pedagogy. What is the present aim of education, as the professors thereof expound it? To make good citizens. And what is a good citizen? Simply one who never says, does or thinks anything that is unusual. Schools are maintained in order to bring this uniformity up to the highest possible point. A school is a hopper into which children are heaved while they are still young and tender; therein they are pressed into certain standard shapes and covered from head to heels into certain standard rubber-stamps. Unluckily, it is a very inefficient machine. Many children, though squeezed diligently, do not take the standard shapes. Others have hides so oily that the most indelible of rubber-stamps is washed from them by the first rain, or even blown from them by the first wind.

It is my notion that surgery will one day find a remedy for this unpleasant and dangerous state of affairs. It will first perfect means of detecting such aberrant children in their early youth, and then it will devise means of curing them. The child who laughs when the Bill of Rights is read will not be stood in a corner and deprived of chewing-gum, as now; it will be sent to the operating-table, and the offending convolution, or gland, or tumor, or whatever it is will be cut out. While it is lying open all other suspicious excrescences will be removed, and so it will be returned to the classroom a normal 100% American. This scheme, if it turns out to be practicable, will add a great deal to the happiness of the American people. It will not only protect those of us who are naturally respectable from the menace of strange and disturbing ideas; it will also relieve the present agonies of those who cherish them. For the search for imaginary absolutes—*i.e.*, for the truth, that ghost—is not pleasant, as poets allege, but intensely painful. There is no record in human history of a happy philosopher; they exist only in romantic legend. Many of them have committed suicide; practically all of them have turned their children out of doors and beaten their wives. And no wonder! If you want to find out how a philosopher feels when he is engaged in the practice of his profession, go to the nearest zoo and watch a chimpanzee at the wearying and hopeless job of chasing fleas. Both suffer damnably, and neither can win.

from Prejudices: Sixth Series (*Alfred A. Knopf, 1927*).

◇◇◇

SABBATH MEDITATION

My essential trouble, I sometimes suspect, is that I am quite devoid of what are called spiritual gifts. That is to say, I am incapable of religious experience, in any true sense. Religious ceremonials often interest me aesthetically, and not infrequently they amuse me otherwise, but I get absolutely no stimulation out of them, no sense of exaltation, no mystical *katharsis*. In that department I am as anesthetic as a church organist, an archbishop or an altar boy. When I am low in spirits and full of misery, I never feel any impulse to seek help, or even mere consolation, from supernatural powers. Thus the generality of religious persons remain mysterious to me, and vaguely offensive, as I am unquestionably offensive to them. I can no more understand a man praying than I can understand him carrying a rabbit's foot to bring him luck. This lack of understanding is a cause of enmities, and I believe that they are sound ones. I dislike any man who is pious, and all such men that I know dislike me.

I am anything but a militant atheist and haven't the slightest objection to church-going, so long as it is honest. I have gone to church myself more than once, honestly seeking to experience the great inward kick that religious persons speak of. But not even at St. Peter's in Rome have I sensed the least trace of it. The most I ever feel at the most solemn moment of the most pretentious religious ceremonial is a sensuous delight in the beauty of it—a delight exactly like that which comes over me when I hear, say, "Tristan und Isolde" or Brahms' fourth symphony. The effect of such music, in fact, is much keener than the effect of the liturgy. Brahms moves me far more powerfully than the holy saints.

As I say, this deficiency is a handicap in a world peopled, in the overwhelming main, by men who are inherently religious. It sets me apart from my fellows and makes it difficult for me to understand many of their ideas and not a few of their acts. I see them responding constantly and robustly to impulses that to me are quite inexplicable. Worse, it causes these folks to misunderstand me, and often to do me serious injustice. They cannot rid themselves of the notion that, because I am anesthetic to the ideas which move them most profoundly, I am, in some vague but nevertheless certain way, a man of aberrant morals, and hence one to be kept at a distance. I have never met a religious man who did not reveal this suspicion. No matter how earnestly he tried to grasp my point of view, he always ended by making an alarmed sort of retreat. All religions, in fact, teach that dissent is a sin; most of them make it the blackest of all sins, and all of them punish it severely whenever they have the power. It is impossible for a religious man to rid himself of the notion that such punishments are just. He simply cannot imagine a civilized rule of conduct that is not based upon the fear of God.

Let me add that my failing is in the fundamental religious impulse, not in mere theological credulity. I am not kept out of the church by an inability to believe the current dogmas. In point of fact, a good many of them seem to me to be reasonable enough, and I probably dissent from most of them a good deal less violently than many men who are assiduous devotees. Among my curious experiences, years ago, was that of convincing an ardent Catholic who balked at the dogma of papal infallibility. He was a very faithful son of the church and his inability to accept it greatly distressed him. I proved to him, at least to his satisfaction, that there was nothing intrinsically absurd in it—that if the dogmas he already accepted were true, then this one was probably true also. Some time later, when this man was on his death-bed, I visited him and he thanked me simply and with apparent sincerity for resolving his old doubt. But even he was unable to comprehend my own lack of religion. His last words to me were a pious hope that I would give over my lamentable contumacy to God and lead a better life. He died firmly convinced that I was headed for Hell, and, what is more, that I deserved it.

from A Mencken Chrestomathy (*Alfred A. Knopf,* 1949).

◇◇◇

THE STATE OF RELIGION TODAY

1

The modern era was brought in, not by the Reformation, but by the Renaissance, which preceded it in time and greatly exceeded it in scope and dignity. The Renaissance was a reversion to the spacious paganism of Greece and Rome; as someone has well said, it was a *bouleversement* of all the principles of Christianity. Its test for ideas was not the authority behind them but the probability in them. It was immensely curious, ingenious, skeptical and daring—in brief, everything that Christianity was not. Unfortunately, its intuitions ran far ahead of its knowledge, and so, while it left all enlightened men convinced that Christian theology was a farrago of absurdities, all it had to offer in place of that theology was a series of bold surmises. What was needed was a body of exact facts, explaining the cosmos and man's place in it in rational terms. The task of accumulating those facts fell upon the Seventeenth Century, and the light began to dawn toward its close. One by one the basic mysteries yielded to a long line of extraordinarily brilliant and venturesome men—Bacon, Galileo, Newton, Leibniz, Harvey and Leeuwenhoek among them. The universe ceased to be Yahweh's plaything and became a mechanism like any other, responding to the same immutable laws. The world dwindled to the estate of what A. J. Balfour called "one of the meanest of planets." Man became an animal—the noblest of them all, but still an animal. Heaven and Hell sank to the level of old wives' tales, and there was a vast collapse of Trinities, Virgin Births, Atonements and other such pious phantasms. The Seventeenth Century, and especially the latter half thereof, saw greater progress than had been made in the twenty centuries preceding—almost as much, indeed, as was destined to be made in the Nineteenth and Twentieth.

But it had run out before the fact began to be generally understood, and so the century following reaped the harvest. It was in that century, the Eighteenth, that Christian theology finally disappeared from the intellectual baggage of all really civilized men. On both sides of the Reformation fence the Christian church fought for its life, and nearly everywhere it had the support of the universities, which is to say, of official learning, which is to say, of organized ignorance. But the new thing called science was now really free, even from the control of the learned, so it kept on advancing steadily, and presently the reluctant universities had to take it in. By the middle of the century what Nietzsche was later to call a transvaluation of all values was in full blast. Nothing sacred was spared —not even the classical spirit that had been the chief attainment of the Renaissance—and of the ideas and attitudes that were attacked not many survived. It was no longer necessary to give even lip service to the old preposterous certainties, whether theological or political, aesthetic or philosophical. In France Voltaire, Rousseau and Diderot were making a bonfire of all the ancient Christian superstitions; in England Gibbon was preparing to revive the long dormant art of history and Adam Smith was laying the foundations of the new science of economics; in Germany Kant was pondering an ethical scheme that would give the Great Commandment a rational basis and a new dignity; everywhere knowledge of the visible world was widening day by day.

The Seventeenth Century had made the basic discoveries, but it was in the Eighteenth that they began to have practical effects upon the everyday life of civilized peoples. The old gloomy dread of *post mortem* penalties and retributions was thrown off, and Western man set out to enjoy himself in a world that grew ever more pleasant. It must have been a charming day to live in. For as skepticism spread everywhere, the urbanity that is its hallmark spread with it, the upper classes improved vastly in manners and dignity, and even the lower orders showed a ponderable advance in that direction. Set free from the fears that had been hag-riding it for nearly two thousand years, the race began to give thought to the amenities, to rational comforts and luxuries, to the cultivation of leisure, to the game of ideas. The arts, liberated at last from the dark influence of theology, sought beauty for its own sake, and found it everywhere. The sciences, leaping forward from the bases established during the century preceding, threw off a long series of practical inventions, most of them conducive to the ease and security of mankind, and some of them working revolutions in its daily life. It was in this era, throughout Western Europe and also in America, that man's most useful and durable possession, the house he dwells in, ceased to be a magnified kennel and became a genuine home, beautiful in itself and filled with sightly furniture. Pestilences diminished, the supply of food became more abundant and varied, the transport of men and goods improved, and even war itself was tamed by new decencies. At no time in history, either before or since, have men and women lived more delightfully, or better deserved to be called civilized.

Unhappily, life became more complicated as it grew more refined, and in the end the Golden Age blew up, as Golden Ages always do soon or late. The new inventions were simply too much for the old aristocracy—a race of military banditti sadly deficient in the enterprise and resourcefulness needed to utilize them. They were also, of course, too much for the lower orders, which lacked altogether the qualities needed to master the machine, and so became its slaves. Its control fell to a new category of entrepreneurs, flowing out of the commercial middle class come down from medieval times, but reinforced by occasional recruits from above and below. These entrepreneurs rapidly collared most of the free wealth of Christendom, and were soon reaching out for power. The revolution that followed was too complex to be summarized hurriedly: its causes and events are debated in whole libraries of books, most of them worthless. Suffice it to say here that the middle class got what it set out to get, but at the cost of launching a ferocious—and well grounded—*jacquerie* below it. The lower orders, once promised a fair share in the new comfort and urbanity, had been thrust into a gehenna where they quickly came to resemble dumb brutes, and meanwhile they were tantalized by lofty talk about the inalienable rights of man. The result, as everyone knows, was a cataclysm. The mob, led by political demagogues on the one hand and theological fanatics on the other, rose against the new civilization and tried to destroy it. The control of the state, seized by the middle class, quickly passed to lower and lower levels, and the popular religion surged up from its sewers and polluted every rank of society save the highest. This vast reaction went further in England than anywhere else. The Eighteenth Century, rocking to its gory end there, saw the whole programme of progress challenged by the twin superstitions of democracy and evangelical Christianity, and the Nineteenth took over a burden of stupidity and folly that the so-called Anglo-Saxon race, on both sides of the Atlantic, is still struggling hopelessly to throw off.

2

In the field of religion, however, the reaction was probably a great deal less catastrophic than it looked at the time, even in England and America. Its proportions were exaggerated beyond the reality by the support it got from the new sect of demagogues, eager for office and willing to do anything, say anything and believe anything in order to get it. In the Eighteenth Century the rulers of the Western World, being secure in their places, could afford to comport themselves as relatively civilized men. Specifically, they could afford to give their countenance and support to the skepticism that was its chief hallmark. I point to Frederick the Great in Prussia, to the gay and mocking oligarchies that ruled France and England, and to such scoffers as Franklin and Jefferson in the nascent United States. A statesman in those days was not necessarily a rogue and an ignoramus: he might, if he would, associate openly with philosophers, artists and men of science, and not infrequently he made some show of qualifying under one or another of those headings himself. Frederick, when he craved society at Potsdam, sent for Voltaire and Johann Sebastian Bach, not for the Eighteenth Century equivalents of radio crooners and movie stars. Franklin was himself a scientist of the first contemporary chop, and amused himself, not with Elks and golf-players, but with savants and charming women. Jefferson, like Franklin, would have passed as a civilized man at the courts of Pericles, Lorenzo de' Medici or Pius II. But with the spread of the democratic pestilence all this was changed. The rulers of the peripheral Christian lands, menaced by the rising of the *Chandala*, began to take their orders from below, and their ideas therewith, and it came to be the chief duty of a statesman to find out and carry out the mandates of persons to whom information was a stranger and thought a pain. On the political level this new polity produced a cancerous proliferation of demagogy in all its forms, with the results now visible everywhere on earth. And on the theological level—to confine examples to the American Republic, the envy and despair of all other nations—it gave us such indecencies as comstockery, Prohibition, and the laws against the teaching of evolution as a biological fact.

But these reversions to the childish certainties of the Ages of Faith were, after all, only diseases of civilization, and it is not to be forgotten that they by no means affected all men in Christendom, nor the best men, and that the underlying course of events continues against them, so that we may yet hope that, in the long run, they will be cured. The rise of Methodism, on the American frontier, was acompanied by the rise of Unitarianism in New England, with a collapse of the old Puritan theology. That theology, to be sure, did not vanish altogether: it was simply transferred to the receding West and South, and still survives in their more barbaric enclaves; moreover, what remained of it on its old stamping-ground was taken over eagerly by an invading horde of moron Catholics, swarming in from Ireland and French Canada. But the main current of intellectual progress has left it behind, and if a current president of Harvard were to preach the theology of Increase Mather he would be locked up as a lunatic, though he is still free (and expected) to merchant the prevailing political balderdash. Save among politicians, it is no longer necessary for any educated American to profess belief in Thirteenth Century ideas. The rise of biology, the great event of the Nineteenth Century, is responsible for that change, and especially the appearance and acceptance of the Darwinian hypothesis of organic evolution. Darwin, to be sure, did not answer any of the basic riddles of existence, but he at least showed that the theological answers were rubbish, and he thereby completed the revolutionary work of Galileo, Newton, Leibniz, Harvey and Leeuwenhoek. Today no really civilized man or woman believes in the cosmogony of Genesis, nor in the reality of Hell, nor in any of the other ancient imbecilities that still entertain the mob. What survives under the name of Christianity, above the stratum of that mob, is no more than a sort of Humanism, with hardly more supernaturalism in it than you will find in mathematics or political economy.

In other words, civilized man has become his own god. When difficulties confront him he no longer blames them upon the inscrutable enmity of remote and ineffable powers; he blames them upon his own ignorance and incompetence. And when he sets out to remedy that ignorance and to remove that incompetence he does not look to any such powers for light and leading; he puts his whole trust in his own enterprise and ingenuity. Not infrequently he overestimates his capacities and comes to grief, but his failures, at worst, are much fewer than the failures of his fathers. Does pestilence, on occasion, still baffle his medicine? Then it is surely less often than the pestilences of old baffled sacrifice and prayer. Does war remain to shame him before the bees, and wasteful and witless government to make him blush when he contemplates the ants? Then war at its most furious is still less cruel than Hell, and the harshest statutes ever devised by man have more equity and benevolence in them than the irrational and appalling jurisprudence of the Christian God.

Today every such man knows that the laws which prevail in the universe, whatever their origin in some remote and incomprehensible First Purpose, manifest themselves in complete impersonality, and that no representation to any superhuman Power, however imagined, can change their operation in the slightest. He knows that when they seem arbitrary and irrational it is not because omnipotent and inscrutable Presences are playing with them, as a child might play with building blocks; but because the human race is yet too ignorant to penetrate to their true workings. The whole history of progress, as the modern mind sees it, is a history of such penetrations. They have come slowly, and, as time appears to transient and ardent man, at weary intervals, but nevertheless one has followed another pretty regularly, and since the beginning of the Seventeenth Century they have been coming ever faster and faster. Each in its turn has narrowed the dominion and prerogative of the gods. There was a time when a man laid low by disease sent for a priest and made a votive offering; now he goes to a physician who is an agnostic by definition. There was a time when it took a miracle to fling him through the air; now he proceeds by airplane. There was a time when he bore all his burdens with resignation, fearing to offend the gods that sent them; now he rises in indignation and tries to throw them off. There is no longer any resignation among enlightened men; there is only a resolute patience, fortified by almost endless ingenuity. The problems that remain bristle with difficulties, and every time one of them is solved another confronts the seekers, but there is no doubt any more that even the most vexatious of them will probably yield, soon or late, some part of its secret.

from Treatise on the Gods (*Alfred A. Knopf*, 1930).

◇◇◇

THE ORIGIN OF MORALITY

In the world that we now live in the moral sense seems to be universally dispersed, at all events among normal persons beyond infancy. No traveler has ever discovered a tribe which failed to show it. There are peoples so primitive that their religion is hard to distinguish from a mere fear of the dark, but there is none so low that it lacks a moral system, elaborate and unyielding. Nor is that system often challenged, at least on the lower cultural levels, by those who lie under it. The rebellious individual may evade it on occasion, but he seldom denies its general validity. To find any such denial on a serious scale one must return to Christendom, where a bold and impatient re-examination of the traditional ethical dogma has followed the collapse of the old belief in revelation. But even in Christendom the most formidable critics of the orthodox system are still, as a rule, profoundly moral men, and the reform they propose is not at all an abandonment of moral imperatives, but simply a substitution of what they believe to be good ones for what they believe to be bad ones. This has been true of every important iconoclast from Hobbes to Lenin, and it was preeminently true of the arch-iconoclast Nietzsche. His furious attack upon the Christian ideal of humility and abnegation has caused Christian critics to denounce him as an advocate of the most brutal egoism, but in point of fact, he proposed only the introduction of a new and more heroic form of renunciation, based upon abounding strength rather than upon hopeless weakness; and in his maxim "Be hard!" there was just as much sacrifice of immediate gratification to ultimate good as you will find in any of the *principia* of Jesus.

The difference between moral systems is thus very slight, and if it were not for the constant pressure from proponents of virtues that have no roots in ordinary human needs, and hence appeal only to narrow and abnormal classes of men, it would be slighter still. All of the really basic varieties of moral good have been esteemed as such since the memory of mankind runneth not to the contrary, and all of the basic wickednesses have been reprehended. The Second Commandment preached by Jesus (Mark XII, 31) was preached by the Gautama Buddha six centuries before Him, and it must have been hoary with age when the Gautama Buddha made it the center of his system. Similarly, the Ten Commandments of Exodus and Deuteronomy were probably thousands of years old when the Jewish scribes first reduced them to writing. Finally, and in the same way, the Greeks lifted their concept of wisdom as the supreme good out of the stream of time, and if we think of them today as its inventors, it is only because we are more familiar with their ethical speculations than we are with those of more ancient peoples.

The five fundamental prohibitions of the Decalogue—those leveled at murder, theft, trespass, adultery and false witness—are to be found in every moral system ever heard of, and seem to be almost universally supported by human opinion. This support, of course, does not mean that they are observed with anything properly describable as pedantic strictness; on the contrary, they are evaded on occasion, both by savages and by civilized men, and some of them are evaded very often. In the United States, for example, the situations in which killing a fellow human being is held to be innocent are considerably more numerous than those in which it is held to be criminal, and even in England, the most moral of great nations, there are probably almost as many. So with adultery. So, again, with theft, trespass and false witness. Theft and trespass shade by imperceptible gradations into transactions that could not be incommoded without imperiling the whole fabric of society, and bearing false witness is so easy to condone that bishops are sometimes among its most zealous practitioners. But despite this vagueness of moral outline and this tolerance of the erring the fact remains that all normal and well-disposed men, whether civilized or uncivilized, hold it to be axiomatic that murder, theft, trespass, adultery and false witness, in their cruder and plainer forms, are anti-social and immoral enterprises, and no one argues seriously, save maybe in time of war, when all the customary moral sanctions are abandoned, that they should be countenanced. When they are perpetrated in a naked manner, without any concession to the ancient and ineradicable feeling against them, they are viewed with abhorrence, and the guilty are severely punished.

from Treatise on Right and Wrong (*Alfred A. Knopf, 1934*).

◇◇◇

THE ESSENCE OF DEMOCRACY

The elements in democracy that are sound in logic and of genuine cultural value may be very briefly listed. They are:

1. Equality before the law.
2. The limitation of government.
3. Free speech.

All the rest of the democratic dogma is, at best, dubious, and at worst palpable nonsense. No professional whooper-up of democracy, so far as I know, is in favor of the three things

I have listed. Every time democratic enthusiasm rises to orgiastic heights violent attempts are made to put down all of them.

from Minority Report (*Alfred A. Knopf*, 1956).

◇◇◇

LAST WORDS

One of the merits of democracy is quite obvious: it is, perhaps, the most charming form of government ever devised by man. The reason is not far to seek. It is based upon propositions that are palpably not true—and what is not true, as everyone knows, is always immensely more fascinating and satisfying to the vast majority of men than what is true. Truth has a harshness that alarms them, and an air of finality that collides with their incurable romanticism. They turn, in all the great emergencies of life, to the ancient promises, transparently false but immensely comforting, and of all those ancient promises there is none more comforting than the one to the effect that the lowly shall inherit the earth. It is at the bottom of the dominant religious system of the modern world, and it is at the bottom of the dominant political system. Democracy gives it a certain appearance of objective and demonstrable truth. The mob man, functioning as citizen, gets a feeling that he is really important to the world—that he is genuinely running things. Out of his maudlin herding after rogues and mountebanks there comes to him a sense of vast and mysterious power—which is what makes archbishops, police sergeants and other such magnificoes happy. And out of it there comes, too, a conviction that he is somehow wise, that his views are taken seriously by his betters—which is what makes United States Senators, fortune-tellers and Young Intellectuals happy. Finally, there comes out of it a glowing consciousness of a high duty triumphantly done—which is what makes hangmen and husbands happy.

All these forms of happiness, of course, are illusory. They don't last. The democrat, leaping into the air to flap his wings and praise God, is forever coming down with a thump. The seeds of his disaster, as I have shown, lie in his own stupidity: he can never get rid of the naive delusion—so beautifully Christian!—that happiness is something to be got by taking it away from the other fellow. But there are seeds, too, in the very nature of things: a promise, after all, is only a promise, even when it is supported by divine revelation, and the chances against its fulfilment may be put into a depressing mathematical formula. Here the irony that lies under all human aspiration shows itself: the quest for happiness, as always, brings only *un*happiness in the end. But saying that is merely saying that the true charm of democracy is not for the democrat but for the spectator. That spectator, it seems to me, is favored with a show of the first cut and caliber. Try to imagine anything more heroically absurd! What grotesque false pretenses! What a parade of obvious imbecilities! What a welter of fraud! But is fraud unamusing? Then I retire forthwith as a psychologist. The fraud of democracy, I contend, is more amusing than any other—more amusing even, and by miles, than the fraud of religion. Go into your praying-chamber and give sober thought to any of the more characteristic democratic inventions. Or to any of the typical democratic prophets. If you don't come out paled and palsied by mirth then you will not laugh on the Last Day itself, when Presbyterians step out of the grave like chicks from the egg, and wings blossom from their scapulae, and they leap into interstellar space with roars of joy.

I have spoken hitherto of the possibility that democracy may be a self-limiting disease, like measles. It is, perhaps, something more: it is self-devouring. One cannot observe it objectively without being impressed by its curious distrust of itself—its apparently ineradicable tendency to abandon its whole philosophy at the first sign of strain. I need not point to what happens invariably in democratic states when the national safety is menaced. All the great tribunes of democracy, on such occasions, convert themselves, by a process as simple as taking a deep breath, into despots of an almost fabulous ferocity. Nor is this process confined to times of alarm and terror: it is going on day in and day out. Democracy always seems bent upon killing the thing it theoretically loves. All its axioms resolve themselves into thundering paradoxes, many amounting to downright contradictions in terms. The mob is competent to rule the rest of us—but it must be rigorously policed itself. There is a government, not of men, but of laws—but men are set upon benches to decide finally what the law is and may be. The highest function of the citizen is to serve the state—but the first assumption that meets him, when he essays to discharge it, is an assumption of his disingenuousness and dishonor. Is that assumption commonly sound? Then the farce only grows the more glorious.

I confess, for my part, that it greatly delights me. I enjoy democracy immensely. It is incomparably idiotic, and hence incomparably amusing. Does it exalt dunderheads, cowards, trimmers, frauds, cads? Then the pain of seeing them go up is balanced and obliterated by the joy of seeing them come down. Is it inordinately wasteful, extravagant, dishonest? Then so is every other form of government: all alike are enemies to decent men. Is rascality at the very heart of it? Well, we have borne that rascality since 1776, and continue to survive. In the long run, it may turn out that rascality is necessary to human government, and even to civilization itself —that civilization, at bottom, is nothing but a colossal swindle. I do not know: I report only that when the suckers are running well the spectacle is infinitely exhilarating. But I am, it may be, a somewhat malicious man: my sympathies, even when it comes to suckers, tend to be coy. What I can't make out is how any man can believe in democracy who feels for and with them, and is pained when they are debauched and made a show of. How can any man be a democrat who is sincerely a democrat?

from Notes on Democracy (*Alfred A. Knopf, 1926*).

◇◇◇

THE ICONOCLAST

The iconoclast proves enough when he proves by his blasphemy that this or that idol is defectively convincing—that at least *one* visitor to the shrine is left full of doubts. The liberation of the human mind has been best furthered by gay fellows who heaved dead cats into sanctuaries and then went roistering down the highways of the world, proving to all men that doubt, after all, was safe—that the god in the sanctuary was a fraud. One horse-laugh is worth ten thousand syllogisms.

from A Mencken Chrestomathy.

Mencken, POLITICS, *and* POLITICIANS

Malcolm Moos

The history of Mencken on politics is shot through with a paradox as clear as a vein in marble: for the great majority of politicians he had, as an observer, the utmost contempt; and yet he liked them personally. As a critic of the American political scene, he professed little or no faith in a system so heavily populated with buffoons and charlatans, whose apotheosis was most nearly reached in the carnival capers of their quadrennial conventions; yet it is possible, even probable, that he took more joy in writing about politics in general and political conventions in particular than in any other writing that

---

Malcolm Moos has taught at many universities and is the former president of the University of Minnesota. He served as a special assistant to President Dwight D. Eisenhower. He has written several books on American politics and higher education, including one on Mencken, A *Carnival of Buncombe*.

he did—and it can be argued that he wrote better about politics than about anything else.

For proof of the first statement, it is not necessary to quote him at length. "A good politician," he said, "[is] as unthinkable as an honest burglar, and the fundamental miscalculation of the electorate lies in making the assumption that some politicians are better than others." (Elsewhere he was not quite so absolute: "Good men not infrequently get into politics, but they seldom last long enough to come to any stature or influence.") And yet, "I like politicians much better than I like professors," he also confessed. "They sweat more freely and are much more amusing."

Neither of those statements is uncharacteristic of Mencken, as both his life and the preponderance of his writings attest. Yet it is also true that he was not a hypocrite, and the apparent contradiction is easily reconciled. A man of enormous intelligence and perception, and for a time the leading critic in the country, in personality he was the opposite of the stuffy superiority that is the popular image of a critic. No Edmund Wilson type, nor a snob either intellectually or socially, Mencken actually had many of the characteristics of the politicians he derided and enjoyed. While he loved to dethrone the politician and de-mystify political rites in his own explosive prose, both in work habits and in character he embodied the essential traits for success in politics, had he ever entertained such an outlandish fantasy.

His mastery of detail and genuine kindness to people are legend. His solicitude for children, the ill, and the elderly are equally well known. And the letters that bounded from his geriatric corona were eagerly prized as collector's items. Whatever his personal devils, to the world he was an extrovert—a jovial, good companion. He could talk as endlessly as a politician but much better than most. And while he believed himself mentally superior to almost everyone, he was as proud of his solid bourgeois heritage as any politician who calls himself "a man of the people"; and proud of his—in many cases—bourgeois tastes, too. If the weekly meetings of the Saturday Night Club began with Mencken and his friends playing Beethoven, they invariably ended up with beer in the back room of Schellhase's, not so unlike any other "night out with the boys."

So Mencken's simultaneous love and disdain for politicians is easily explained: He was wise enough to see through them, and realistic enough to acknowledge his affinity for them. But why should this great critic, this man who, as Alistair Cooke has said, was at one time as famous in America as Bernard Shaw was in England, want to spend so much of his time writing about the inanities and idiocies of American politics? Certainly he didn't expect to change anything, for he didn't expect politicians to have enough sense either to accept his opinions or to be able to do anything about it if they did. He thought, in fact, that insofar as the system worked at all, it lurched along rather in spite of the politicians than because of them. As he once wrote, with considerable muzzle velocity, but playfully as well: "There are the leaders. . . . On the lower levels one encounters men so dreadful that it would be painful to describe them realistically. Nevertheless the government goes on. There is some disorder, but not enough to be uncomfortable. A certain amount of money is wasted, but not enough to bankrupt us. The laws are dishonest and idiotic, but it is easy to imagine worse. How are we to account for this? I can conjure up but two plausible theories. One is to the effect that this country is actually under the protection of God, as many clergymen allege every fourth of July. The other is that the hated and reviled bureaucracy must be a great deal more competent than it looks."

Yet for several reasons politics was the ideal subject for

Mencken. For one, politics was more alive than literature. For another, writing about it gave him a far wider audience than literary criticism. He believed that "we live, not in a literary age, but in a fiercely political age." That is no doubt why, after World War I, his interest in political issues overtook his concern with literary criticism, and he could write to Louis Untermeyer, "You will escape from literary criticism, too, as I am trying to do." Even when in 1923 Alfred Knopf, George Jean Nathan, and Mencken launched the *American Mercury*, which was to become the Bible of college students primarily for its literary aspects, Mencken announced his intention to "shake up the animals in politics." Clearly he became enchanted with the riptide of American politics and reveled in the fumes of controversy. As his old musician friend Louis Cheslock notes, H. L., like Beethoven, "was a disturber of complacency."

Another reason for Mencken's overriding interest in politics was his joyous pursuit of the effervescence of American speech. *The American Language: Supplement One* devotes seventy-five pages to political terms, outdistancing by far the other sections of this volume as he traces the paternity of such vernacular words and phrases as "back and fill," "bolters," "fat cats," and "Locofocos," and defines politics as the art of "who gets what, when and how."

But more important, probably, the nature of his interest in politics was precisely the reason why, though he liked it, he could never have been a politician: "I am a writer, and shall remain so until the last chapter." Not only a writer but a humorist, one who acknowledged his debt to Mark Twain above all others, and whose style has often been compared to Twain's. As such, Mencken epitomized Shaw's description of good critics, that they "tickle those whom they shock."

Or as Walter Lippmann put it, Mencken was "splendidly and contagiously alive. He calls you a swine and an imbecile, and he increases your will to live." As a humorist, Mencken possessed one of the most boisterous and exuberant prose styles in the history of American letters, and achieved many of his most telling effects through the device of exaggeration. What better subjects to practice his skills on, then, than the boisterous and exuberant antics, the exaggerated prose and promises, of the American politicians of his day? In fact he gave the clue to his lifelong devotion to political writing in a statement in which he purported to define the only real use of politics: "Has the art of politics no apparent utility? Does it appear to be unqualifiedly ratty, raffish, sordid, obscene and lowdown, and its salient virtuosi a gang of unmitigated scoundrels? Then let us not forget its high capacity to soothe and tickle the midriff, its incomparable services as a maker of entertainment." Although his criticism had its serious side, Mencken was above all, like the politicians he loved to write about, a "maker of entertainment." The difference was that with Mencken the entertainment was intended.

It was this quality of the entertainer that made him so good at reporting national political conventions—"that travesty of popular institutions" as an unkind critic once put it.

H. L. was not a Frank Kent, surgically probing the shifting tides of delegate pledges, the switch hitters, the trade-offs, the supermarket rumors of concession from withdrawing candidates, the seductive but frothy promises of deliverable votes. Mencken captured the conventions with all the iridescence of street theater. In his valedictory, the Progressive Party convention of 1948, which nominated Henry Wallace, "the ladies were chiefly bulky, unlovely, precisely like Republican and Democratic ladies, but they did not run to the same gaudy and preposterous frocks and hats." And Wallace had "acquired such a semi-celestial character that if when he is nominated he suddenly sprouts wings and begins flapping around the hall no one will be surprised."

At the 1920 Republican convention in Chicago he shrugged off those deploring the lack of enthusiasm among delegates, judged by earlier standards, with the question "How could you wring anything properly describable as enthusiasm out of delegates whose carburetors were filled with lakewater?" Prohibition was upon the land. To an English journalist sitting in the gallery and bored with the preliminary pontificating at the 1924 Democratic convention he snapped: "Just wait. Those are Democrats down there." That was the convention that picked its candidate on the 103rd ballot.

A convention was for Mencken a simmering casserole, and he savored all the ingredients. It is impossible not to think of him to this day, as we look at television and watch delegates swarming about, some with hair frozen like dollops of ice cream on the tops of their heads, scrambling for all the world like homeroom teachers getting ready for the Christmas party. A convention, he wrote, is "vulgar, ugly, stupid and tedious," and yet at times "a show so gaudy and hilarious, so melodramatic and obscene, so unimaginably exhilarating and preposterous that one lives a gorgeous year in an hour."

For all his rich insights into the eccentric orbits of politics, however, Mencken left poor marks as a political weathercock. His classic miscall occurred at the 1924 Democratic marathon in Madison Square Garden. As the convention moved near the 100th ballot in steaming heat, Mencken struck off the following lead for his story to the *Sun:* "Everything is uncertain in this convention but one thing: John W. Davis will never be nominated." Told a few seconds after he had filed his story that Davis *had* been nominated, Mencken was stunned, recovered quickly, and snapped back, "Why, that's incredible! I've already sent off a story that it's impossible." Then as an afterthought he added, "I wonder if those idiots in Baltimore will know enough to strike out the negative."

In late October of 1928 he conceded Hoover's defeat and

declared that Al Smith would have the Solid South behind him. Al lost Virginia, Florida, North Carolina, Tennessee, and Texas, along with the election, although across the nation he won more votes than any previous Democratic presidential candidate.

Again in 1931, as the Depression deepened, he said Hoover was as certain of re-election as two and two make four. Still later he insisted that in 1932 Hoover could even lose New York with its 45 electoral votes "and be as safe as a cop in a speakeasy." In 1948, he had lots of company in picking Dewey as the winner, but cheerfully shrugged off the thumping upset as "a mathematical impossibility demanding a coroner's inquiry."

The winner of the 1932 election, Franklin Delano Roosevelt, was one of perhaps only two national political figures with whom Mencken, demolition expert that he was, was guilty of overkill. The other was William Jennings Bryan. The day after Bryan died, Mencken flayed him in the Baltimore *Evening Sun* as "a charlatan, a mountebank, a zany without sense or dignity. A poor clod . . . deluded by a childish theology, full of an almost pathological hatred of all learning, all human dignity, all beauty, all fine and noble things."

H. L. actually voted for F.D.R. in 1932 (though he complained that his voice was too "tenorish"), but he quickly became disenchanted. Roosevelt's concept of government, he gibed, was a "milch cow with 125,000,000 teats," and his appeals "were not addressed to the cortex but to the midriff." Mencken also lamented that the objective of the New Deal was to provide everyone with "free mayonnaise mixers." Back from the 1936 convention, he exploded: "What a God-awful world it is. I hear of nothing but death and disaster. The only man who continues to be lucky seems to be Franklin Delano Roosevelt, and I am in hopes that God will turn upon him anon." By 1944 he had mellowed a little, but the hook was still carefully honed in a letter to Sara Mayfield: "I voted for Roosevelt and with the greatest of pleasure. The country richly deserves him, and during the next four years I hope and pray it will get a sufficient dose of him." Asked in his last interview if he disliked F.D.R. as much as he said, or if it was just to rile up his readers, he shot back: "Every bit of it. In my book that man was an unmitigated S.O.B. in his public life and an S.O.B. in his private life."

There is an implied contradiction here that superficial readers of Mencken have often pointed out. True, both Bryan and Roosevelt ("Roosevelt Minor" as Mencken referred to F.D.R., to distinguish him from Teddy, "Roosevelt Major") can be viewed as populists of sorts. But it was Mencken the social liberal, who got himself arrested for selling the *Mercury* in Boston when it was banned there, who castigated Bryan, champion of the fundamentalists, in the 1925 essay quoted above, written just after the Scopes trial. The Mencken of the 1930s, on the other hand, was seen as a conservative when he railed against the New Deal social legislation of F.D.R.

After the onset of the Depression, Mencken the merry muckraker plummeted from his position as idol of the iconoclastic literati with the speed of a man sliding down the stock market charts. In part it was the style, likened to the noise of a snorting volcano combined with the language of the lunch counter. The copy that spilled from the arthritic portable still crackled in the 1930s, but it got a different reception, in a nation undergoing the harrowing experiences of the Depression, from that accorded the rebel of the Roaring Twenties.

And the disillusionment was reinforced by the apparent change in Mencken's point of view. The liberal of the 1920s, it seemed, had suddenly turned into the reactionary of the 1930s, and it was excusable for his readers to believe that he had deserted not only their ideas but his own as well. He received a lot of shelling in subsequent years from the political left, most of it mere name-calling. He was dubbed "a Tory who hates the Soviet Union" and "a Nordic Chauvinist who fears and hates the yellow race," and his style was dismissed as "the writing of a clown."

In reality, though, what happened was that the times changed and he would not or could not change with them. His thinking was entirely—it may well have been much too—consistent; for Mencken was a classical liberal in the eighteenth-century mold who believed sincerely that he governs best who governs least. Mencken was not at all inconsistent, from his own point of view, in thinking that a government which tries to structure the economy along Keynesian lines is as evil as a government which tries to ban books or prohibit the teaching of evolution. His oft-repeated diatribes against the democratic system resulted in his being called an autocrat and even a fascist, but in reality he was suspicious of all government because the cornerstone of his political beliefs was liberty. "I believe in only one thing, and that is human liberty," he wrote. "I believe that all government is evil, and that all government must make war on liberty, and that the democratic form is as bad as other forms." From time to time he poured praise on regencies, oligarchies and monarchies, but it was with tongue in cheek. At bottom, democracy for Mencken, in company with Churchill, was the worst form of government except for the others. He was a "consistent libertarian" as Murray Rothbard of *The Economist* reminds us, and he was immovably so.

Never to be minimized, in searching for the sources of Mencken's political thought, is the setting in which he grew up. It was Maryland, the Free State, the colony that brought religious toleration to the Catholics; and Baltimore, which was spawning the first great graduate school in the United States, Johns Hopkins University, under its first president, the remarkable educator Daniel Coit Gilman. It also had one of the most intellectual and liberal prelates the nation has produced, Cardinal Gibbons. The spirit of freedom of thought and inquiry was bound to rub off on a mind as inquisitive as Mencken's.

A self-proclaimed atheist, Mencken was a great admirer of Cardinal Gibbons, but this made him no apologist for the Catholic church or for any religious meddling in politics. Weighing the Catholic problem in assessing Al Smith's 1928 presidential contest, he said: "Worst of all, the great ecclesiastical organization of which he is a humble satellite may do something so inept and preposterous that his chances, and those of every Catholic, will go down to zero for another generation. Moreover, the last possibility is not to be dismissed as remote. The Catholic hierarchy is not overburdened with men of wisdom and discretion." There was, he said, no leader "comparable to Archbishop Ireland" (of St. Paul, Minnesota, who urged that the Catholic church not establish parochial schools because they would be a divisive factor in the emerging American culture and would one day be prohibitive for the Church to finance), "and none remotely comparable to Cardinal Gibbons."

"Can you imagine Cardinal Gibbons," he continued, "calling in police to rough up a meeting of birth control fanatics as was done by certain eminent ecclesiastical dignitaries in New York a couple of years ago—to the scandal of the Church and the mirth of the town?" Here, as H. L. looked down the gun barrel of history, his aim was hardly out of date if one contemplates the "hit list" being prepared by anti-abortion groups for the next congressional elections.

Like his attitude toward church and state, his attitude toward race and state reflects his basic political ideas. Mencken has often been called a racist, and from some of his utterances the conclusion seems inescapable. It must be remembered however that he was a product of his time and place, and it is as well to be reminded that he was genuinely appalled at some of the prohibitions against blacks which existed then.

In 1935, when the Board of Regents of the University of Maryland wanted to deny the admission of a Negro (Donald G. Murray, a graduate of Amherst) to the law school because it would violate the "separate schools policy of Maryland," Mencken called the objection "absurd. Law school students should not be divided into hostile camps over the color of their skins," he argued. (Murray filed suit and was admitted.) A decade or so later, Mencken was outraged when a group of black and white progressives were arrested in Baltimore's Druid Hill Park for scheduling an interracial tennis match. On what authority, he challenged, could the Park Board prohibit the game? Neither common sense nor decency could uphold such a ruling. So long as the contestants did not disturb the peace, citizens had an inalienable right to compete in games of skill. Public parks, he added, are supported by funds contributed by both blacks and whites. "Why should the law set up distinctions and discriminations which the persons directly affected themselves reject?" The rule, he charged, was both "irrational and nefarious," and in the same breath he reproached the Park Board for the idiocy of the rule permitting black and white golfers to play the links only on alternate days.

Mencken was nothing short of disgusted by a lynching on Maryland's Eastern Shore. In December 1931, he fired off a brace of articles to the *Evening Sun*, denouncing the slinking refusal of law enforcement authorities to apprehend and punish those guilty of such unconscionable outrages. He was immediately threatened with lynching if he ever trespassed on the Eastern Shore. But he strode ahead, and had some influence in the passage of the Costigan-Warner Bill of 1934, drafted to shift jurisdiction from state to federal courts when state authorities dragged their feet in apprehending or punishing lynchers.

Mencken, of course, was gone before the civil disobedience campaigns for the civil rights of blacks and other minorities, in the 1960s, as well as the youthquake that erupted over the Vietnam war and disenchantment with higher education. He was hesitant, however, about integrating public schools. It was not the right time, and youngsters should not be expected to "rise above the prevailing mores." The contradictions of his position on matters of race and rights have been put forth fairly by two Baltimoreans, Nancy Barrick and Ernest Brown, a public school teacher and a surgeon: "Mencken grappled with the movement for Negro civil rights such as it was before World War II in as sophisticated fashion as anyone of his day. In principle he upheld civil rights as guaranteed by the constitution. Yet, he was uncertain. While he appeared to know and give much thought to integration, free speech, and civil disobedience, the image of the Negro as a completely free and equal citizen made him uneasy. He seemed somewhat encumbered by the superstitions promoted by white supremacists, by the lack of opportunity to see Negroes perform in meaningful situations, and by what appeared to him to be the practicalities of racial desegregation. . . . He did not deny the Negro his rights (as interpreted by Mencken), but he did not see that forced segregation in any situation is, of itself, an enemy of the civil rights he held so dear."

Mencken's attitudes toward racial questions and the government reflect in part his serious reservations about what the structural political inventions of society might do to advance the common good. Basically he felt what might emerge from mental exercises debating such measures was bound to be pretty low-grade ore. "This great pox of civilization, alas," he wrote, "I believe to be incurable, and so I propose no new quackery for its treatment. I am against dosing it and I am against killing it." But on one occasion this impatience with the nostrums of reform was shattered by a thunderclap. This time he had no thought of tinkering or patching with spare parts surgery. He pounced forward like a bulldozer, knocking aside one sacred cow after another. On April 12, 1937, H. L. confounded and stunned the citizenry of the Free State when the *Sun* published the full text of his "Proposed New Constitution for the State of Maryland."

Undoubtedly, much of what Mencken proposed, here as elsewhere, was done with tongue in cheek—although political scientists were not amused. Professor Glenn of the University of Virginia Law School dubbed it, unjustly, "an honest effort to combine personal liberty and fascism." Mencken's constitution sought sweeping rollbacks of administrative agencies, a traditional element of all large-scale reorganization plans. But he advocated going much further. His reform of the governorship caused critics to blink in disbelief—a ten-year unbroken term for governors, as compared to only five for legislators. He also proposed that the legislature be cropped to fifteen members and that no one be allowed to serve who had held either a federal or a state job during the previous five years. In certain of his recommendations, H. L. delighted in shooting off Roman candles with ideas so flaky they were bound to make staid constitutionalists grow pale. Sterilization was an eminently reasonable way to dispose of the "unfit," and he called for a constitutional limit on marriage to two to a person. Elsewhere he advocated creating a grand inquest—a group of outstanding citizens to monitor the conduct of government—an idea that prompted one member of the Maryland House of Delegates to quote Judge Learned Hand's vow that he would never make public servants accountable to a "bevy of guardian angels."

Some ingredients of Mencken's constitution were banished to the back burner without debate. Two of his biggest war whoops, however, bear careful re-examination in light of the tide of events: his advocacy of a unicameral legislature and eclipse of the two-party system.

He prepared his charter, of course, before the Supreme Court decision mandating one man–one vote, commanding both houses of state legislatures to be apportioned strictly in accordance with population—a decision which surely torpedoes the rationale for bicameralism. But Mencken correctly perceived the frailties of bicameralism among the states—the same witnesses testifying before both houses, the already tedious, tortuous and increasingly complex calendars, and the compelling need for constitutional surgery. The returns are not yet all in from Nebraska, which adopted unicameralism in 1934; however, although political scientists may disagree, the performance of the Nebraska legislature has been a muscular one, and its track record should encourage other states to follow.

The recommendation that all state and regional elections be conducted without partisan designation was hardly a new proposal—it was long championed by early reform leagues for municipal and local elections; but Mencken called for extending political celibacy statewide. Again Nebraska comes to mind, having combined nonpartisan elections with its unicameral legislature in 1934. George Norris, father of the unicameral and non-partisan legislature in Nebraska, in summing up the first session of the Nebraska legislature in 1938, declared that the supreme purpose of such an institution was the "divorce of the legislative proceedings of the state entirely from party promises, party pledges, party deceptions, and party intrigues." In a longhand letter to this writer the same year, he dismissed as "bunk" the notion that party responsibility is "always necessary for good work in a legislature," urging that rank partisanship was one of the greatest evils in municipal and legislative offices. More telling, and more substantiated by subsequent experience, was his argument that where legislatures are elected by partisan designation, "most of the time of the session is taken up in the game of politics."

How to sum up the total Mencken? The most characteristic traits to be found throughout his writings and his life are his consistent emphasis on style, his love of the great American show, and his unflagging, ever-billowing humor. In explaining Theodore Roosevelt's success story, Mencken well described his own: "Life fascinated him and he knew how to make it fascinating to others." As for the ability to expound a coherent body of thought, at least in the domain of political theory, it might be fair to say that Mencken was highly capable of *thoughts* rather than *thought*. He himself acknowledged that he was extremely skeptical of finding hard-and-fast truths in the arena of political ideas. In this arena, as in that of political action, he was fundamentally an observer and critic, which is perhaps why his writings on political theorists were as likely to center on their writing styles as on their ideas.

When he dismissed Thorstein Veblen's economics as "smacking of socialism and water," it was partly ideological dissent, but there was an even sharper stab at the social theorist's constipated style. "If," he wrote, "one tunneled under his great moraines and stalagmites of words, dug down under his vast kitchen-midden of discordant and raucous polysyllables, blew up the hard thick shell of his almost theological manner, all one found was a mass of platitudes." That he was not just wearing ideological blinkers in the case of Veblen seems clear from the admiration he held for other contemporaries with whose ideas he was not smitten. Liberals and Socialists were prime targets, but he liked Upton Sinclair and corresponded with him extensively even though he felt that much of his thinking was madcap stuff, and said so. He also admired Norman Thomas, four-time Socialist candidate for the presidency. Only a month before Mencken's stroke in 1948, an article appeared in Baltimore under the headline "MENCKEN THANKS THOMAS: RARE HULLABALLOO BY REALLY INTELLIGENT MAN." And Edwin Castagna, former director of Baltimore's Enoch Pratt Free Library, has written that while Mencken would find John Kenneth Galbraith's ideas unacceptable and even ridiculous, he would applaud Galbraith's expressive, lucid style.

In his deep distrust of the enthronement of power, Mencken seems to sympathize with the Chinese proverb that the great man is a public misfortune; he was sensitive to a widening continental divide in American belief between those who hold that the fundamental purpose of government is to improve men and women and those who hold that its true purpose is only to restrain them, to prevent them from destroying themselves. In the latter corner he gave his testimony according to the lights that he followed.

◇◇◇

THE POLITICIAN

Half the sorrows of the world, I suppose, are caused by making false assumptions. . . . One that corrupts all [the thinking of the American people] about the great business of politics and vastly augments their discontent and unhappiness [is] the assumption that politicians are divided into two classes, and that one of those classes is made up of good ones. I need not argue, I hope, that this assumption is almost universally held among us. Our whole politics, indeed, is based upon it and has been based upon it since the earliest days. What is any political campaign save a concerted effort to turn out a set of politicians who are admittedly bad and put in a set who are thought to be better? The former assumption, I believe, is always sound; the latter is just as certainly false. For if experience teaches us anything at all it teaches us this: that a good politician, under democracy, is quite as unthinkable as an honest burglar. His very existence, indeed, is a standing subversion of the public good in every rational sense. He is not one who serves the common weal; he is simply one who preys upon the commonwealth. It is to the interest of all the rest of us to hold down his powers to an irreducible minimum, and to reduce his compensation to nothing; it is to his interest to augment his powers at all hazards, and to make his compensation all the traffic will bear. To argue that these aims are identical is to argue palpable nonsense. The politician, at his ideal best, never even remotely approximated in practice, is a necessary evil; at his worst he is an almost intolerable nuisance.

What I contend is simply that he would be measurably less a nuisance if we got rid of our old false assumptions about him, and regarded him in the cold light of fact. At once, I believe, two-thirds of his obnoxiousness would vanish. He would remain a nuisance, but he would cease to be a swindler; the injury of having to pay freight on him would cease to be complicated by the insult of being rooked. It is the insult and not the injury that makes the deeper wounds, and causes the greater permanent damage to the national psyche. All of us have been trained, since infancy, in putting up with necessary evils, plainly recognized *as* evils. We know, for example, that the young of the human species commonly smell badly; that garbage men, bootblacks and messenger boys commonly smell worse. These facts are not agreeable, but they remain tolerable because they are universally assumed—because there is no sense of having been tricked and cozened in their perennial discovery. But try to imagine how distressing fatherhood would become if prospective fathers were all taught that the human infant radiates an aroma like the rose—if the truth came constantly as a surprise! Each fresh victim of the deception would feel that he had been basely swindled—that his own child was somehow bogus. Not infrequently, I suppose, he would be tempted to make away with it in some quiet manner, and have another—only to be shocked again. That procedure would be idiotic, admittedly, yet it is exactly the one we follow in politics. At each election we vote in a new set of politicians, insanely assuming that they are better than the set turned out. And at each election we are, as they say in the Motherland, done in.

Of late the fraud has become so gross that the plain people begin to show a great restlessness under it. Like animals in a cage, they trot from one corner to another, endlessly seeking a way out. If the Democrats win one year, it is a pretty sure sign that they will lose the next year. State after state becomes doubtful, pivotal, skittish; even the solid South begins to break. In the cities it is still worse. An evil circle is formed. First the poor taxpayers, robbed by the politicians of one great party and then by those of the other, turn to a group of freelance rogues in the middle ground—non-partisan candidates, Liberals, reformers or whatnot: the name is unimportant. Then, flayed and pillaged by these gentry as they never were by the old-time professionals, they go back in despair to the latter, and are flayed and pillaged again. Back to Bach! Back to Tammany! Tammany reigns in New York because the Mitchel outfit was found to be intolerable—in other words, because the reformers were found to be even worse than the professionals. Is the fact surprising? Why should it be? Reformers and professionals are alike politicians in search of jobs; both are trying to bilk the taxpayers. Neither ever has any other motive. If any genuinely honest and altruistic politician had come to the surface in America in my time I'd have heard of him, for I have always frequented newspaper offices, and in a newspaper office the news of such a marvel would cause a dreadful tumult. I can recall no such tumult. The unanimous opinion of all the journalists that I know, excluding a few Liberals who are obviously somewhat balmy—they all believed, for example, that the late war would end war—is that, since the days of the national Thors and Wotans, no politician who was not out for himself, and for himself alone, has ever drawn the breath of life in the United States.

The gradual disintegration of Liberalism among us, in fact, offers an excellent proof of the truth of my thesis. The Liberals have come to grief by fooling their customers, not merely once too often, but a hundred times too often. Over and over again they have trotted out some new hero, usually from the great open spaces, only to see him taken in the immemorial malpractices within ten days. Their graveyard, indeed, is filled with cracked and upset headstones, many covered with ribald pencilings. Every time there is a scandal in the grand manner the Liberals lose almost as many general officers as either the Democrats or Republicans. Of late, racked beyond endurance by such catastrophes at home, they have gone abroad for their principal heroes; losing humor as well as hope, they now ask us to venerate such astounding paladins as the Hon. Béla Kun, a gentleman who, in any American state, would not only be in the calaboose, but actually in the death-house. But this absurdity is only an offshoot of a deeper one. Their primary error lies in making the false assumption that some politicians are better than others. This error they share with the whole American people.

I propose that it be renounced, and contend that its renunciation would greatly rationalize and improve our politics. I do not argue that there would be any improvement in our politicians; on the contrary, I believe that they would remain substantially as they are today, and perhaps grow even worse. But what I do argue is that recognizing them frankly for what they are would instantly and automatically dissipate the indignation caused by their present abominations, and that the disappearance of this indignation would promote the public contentment and happiness. Under my scheme there would be no more false assumptions and no more false hopes, and hence no more painful surprises, no more bitter resentment of fraud, no more despair. Politicians, in so far as they remained necessary, would be kept at work—but not with any insane notion that they were archangels. Their rascality would be assumed and discounted, as the rascality of the police is now assumed and discounted. Machinery would be gradually developed to limit it and counteract it. In the end, it might be utilized in some publicly profitable manner, as the insensitiveness to filth of garbage men is now utilized, as the reverence of the clergy for capitalism is now utilized. The result, perhaps, would be a world no better than the present one, but it would at least be a world more intelligent.

In all this I sincerely hope that no one will mistake me for one who shares the indignation I have spoken of—that is, for one who believes that politicians can be made good, and cherishes a fond scheme for making them so. I believe nothing of the sort. On the contrary, I am convinced that the art and mystery they practice is essentially and incurably anti-social—that they must remain irreconcilable enemies of the common weal until the end of the time. But I maintain that this fact, in itself, is not a bar to their employment. There are, under Christian civilization, many necessary offices that demand the possession of anti-social talents. A professional soldier, regarded realistically, is much worse than a professional politician, for he is a professional murderer and kidnaper, whereas the politician is only a professional sharper and sneak-thief. A clergyman, too, begins to shrink and shrivel on analysis; the work he does in the world is basically almost indistinguishable from that of an astrologer, a witch-doctor or a fortune-teller. He pretends falsely that he can get sinners out of hell, and collects money from them on that promise, tacit or express. If he had to go before a jury with that pretension it would probably go hard with him. But we do not send him before a jury; we grant him his hocus-pocus on the ground that it is necessary to his office, and that his office is necessary to civilization, so-called. I pass over the journalist delicately; the time has not come to turn state's evidence. Suffice it to say that he, too, would probably wither under a stiff cross-examination. If he is no murderer, like the soldier, then he is at least a sharper and swindler, like the politician.

What I plead for, if I may borrow a term in disrepute, is simply *Realpolitik*, *i.e.*, realism in politics. I can imagine a political campaign purged of all the current false assumptions and false pretenses—a campaign in which, on election day, the voters went to the polls clearly informed that the choice before them was not between an angel and a devil, a good man and a bad man, an altruist and a go-getter, but between two frank go-getters, the one, perhaps, excelling at beautiful and nonsensical words and the other at silent and prehensile deeds

—the one a chautauqua orator and the other a porch-climber. There would be, in that choice, something candid, free and exhilarating. Buncombe would be adjourned. The voter would make his selection in the full knowledge of all the facts, as he makes his selection between two heads of cabbage, or two evening papers, or two brands of chewing tobacco. Today he chooses his rulers as he buys bootleg whiskey, never knowing precisely what he is getting, only certain that it is not what it pretends to be. The Scotch may turn out to be wood alcohol or it may turn out to be gasoline; in either case it is not Scotch. How much better if it were plainly labeled, for wood alcohol and gasoline both have their uses—higher uses, indeed, than Scotch. The danger is that the swindled and poisoned consumer, despairing of ever avoiding them when he doesn't want them, may prohibit them even when he does want them, and actually enforce his own prohibition. The danger is that the hopeless voter, forever victimized by his false assumption about politicians, may in the end gather such ferocious indignation that he will abolish them teetotally and at one insane swoop, and so cause government by the people, for the people and with the people to perish from this earth.

from Prejudices: Fourth Series (*Alfred A. Knopf, 1924*).

◇◇◇

THE LAST GASP

Tomorrow the dirty job. I shall be on my knees all night, praying for strength to vote for Gamaliel. What ass first let loose the doctrine that the suffrage is a high boon and voting a noble privilege? Looking back over 19 years I can recall few times when I voted with anything approaching exhilaration—maybe the two times I voted for the late Major-General Roosevelt, a fellow who always delighted me—the mountebank inordinate and almost fabulous, the great *reductio ad absurdum* of democracy, and even of civilization.

from Baltimore Evening Sun, *November 1, 1920.*

GAMALIELESE

On the question of the logical content of Dr. Harding's harangue of last Friday I do not presume to have views. The matter has been debated at great length by the editorial writers of the Republic, all of them experts in logic; moreover, I confess to being prejudiced. When a man arises publicly to argue that the United States entered the late war because of a "concern for preserved civilization," I can only snicker in a superior way and wonder why he isn't holding down the chair of history in some American university. When he says that the United States has "never sought territorial aggrandizement through force," the snicker arises to the virulence of a chuckle, and I turn to the first volume of General Grant's memoirs. And when, gaining momentum, he gravely informs the boobery that "ours is a constitutional freedom where the popular will is supreme, and minorities are sacredly protected," then I abandon myself to a mirth that transcends, perhaps, the seemly, and send picture postcards of A. Mitchell Palmer and the Atlanta Penitentiary to all of my enemies who happen to be Socialists.

But when it comes to the style of a great man's discourse, I can speak with a great deal less prejudice, and maybe with somewhat more competence, for I have earned most of my livelihood for twenty years past by translating the bad English of a multitude of authors into measurably better English. Thus qualified professionally, I rise to pay my small tribute to Dr. Harding. Setting aside a college professor or two and half a dozen dipsomaniacal newspaper reporters, he takes the first place in my Valhalla of literati. That is to say, he writes the worst English that I have ever encountered. It reminds me of a string of wet sponges; it reminds me of tattered washing on the line; it reminds me of stale bean-soup, of college yells, of dogs barking idiotically through endless nights. It is so bad that a sort of grandeur creeps into it. It drags itself out of the dark abysm (I was about to write abscess!) of pish, and crawls insanely up the topmost pinnacle of posh. It is rumble and bumble. It is flap and doodle. It is balder and dash. . . .

The whole inaugural address reeked with just such nonsense. The thing started off with an error in English in its very first sentence—the confusion of pronouns in the *one-he* combination, so beloved of bad newspaper reporters. It bristled with words misused: *Civic* for *civil*, *luring* for *alluring*, *womanhood* for *women*, *referendum* for *reference*, even *task* for *problem*. "The *task* is to be *solved*"—what could be worse? Yet I find it twice. "The expressed views of world opinion"—what irritating tautology! "The expressed conscience of progress"—what on earth does it mean? "This is not selfishness, it is sanctity"—what intelligible idea do you get out of that? "I know that Congress and the administration will favor every wise government policy to aid the resumption and encourage continued progress"—the resumption of what? "Service is the supreme *commitment* of life"—*ach, du heiliger!*

But is such bosh out of place in a stump speech? Obviously not. It is precisely and thoroughly in place in a stump speech. A tight fabric of ideas would weary and exasperate the audience; what it wants is simply a loud burble of words, a procession of phrases that roar, a series of whoops. This is what it got in the inaugural address of the Hon. Warren Gamaliel Harding. And this is what it will get for four long years—unless God sends a miracle and the corruptible puts on incorruption. . . . Almost I long for the sweeter song, the rubber-stamps of more familiar design, the gentler and more seemly bosh of the late Woodrow.

from Baltimore Evening Sun, *March 7, 1921.*

THE CLOWNS MARCH IN

At first blush, the Republican National Convention at Cleveland next week promises to be a very dull show, for the Hon. Mr. Coolidge will be nominated without serious opposition and there are no issues of enough vitality to make a fight over the platform. The whole proceedings, in fact, will be largely formal. Some dreadful mountebank in a long-tailed coat will open them with a windy speech; then another mountebank will repeat the same rubbish in other words;

then a half dozen windjammers will hymn good Cal as a combination of Pericles, Frederick the Great, Washington, Lincoln, Roosevelt and John the Baptist; then there will be an hour or two of idiotic whooping, and then the boys will go home. The LaFollette heretics, if they are heard of at all, will not be heard of for long; they will be shoved aside even more swiftly than they were shoved aside when Harding was nominated. And the battle for the Vice-Presidency will not be fought out in the hall, but somewhere in one of the hotels, behind locked doors and over a jug or two of bootleg Scotch.

A stupid business, indeed. Nevertheless, not without its charms to connoisseurs of the obscene. What, in truth, could more beautifully display the essential dishonesty and imbecility of the entire democratic process. Here will be assembled all the great heroes and master-minds of the majority party in the greatest free nation ever seen on earth, and the job before them will be the austere and solemn one of choosing the head of the state, the heir of Lincoln and Washington, the peer of Caesar and Charlemagne. And here, after three or four days of bombarding the welkin and calling upon God for help, they will choose unanimously a man whom they regard unanimously as a cheap and puerile fellow!

I don't think I exaggerate. Before the end of the campaign, of course, many of them will probably convince themselves that Cal is actually a man of powerful intellect and lofty character, and even, perhaps, a gentleman. But I doubt seriously that a single Republican leader of any intelligence believes it today. Do you think that Henry Cabot Lodge does? Or Smoot? Or any of the Pennsylvania bosses? Or Borah? Or Hiram Johnson? Or Moses? Or our own Weller? These men are not idiots. They have eyes in their heads. They have seen Cal at close range. . . . But they will all whoop for him in Cleveland.

In such whooping lies the very soul and essence of humor. Nothing imaginable could be more solidly mirthful. Nor will there be any lack of jocosity in the details of the farce: the imbecile paralogy of the speeches; the almost inconceivable nonsense of the platform; the low buffooneries of the Southern delegates, white and black; the swindling of the visitors by the local apostles of Service; the bootlegging and boozing; the gaudy scenes in the hall. National conventions are almost always held in uncomfortable and filthy places; the one at San Francisco, four years ago, is the only decent one I have ever heard of. The decorations are carried out by the sort of morons who arrange street fairs. The hotels are crowded to suffocation. The food is bad and expensive. Everyone present is robbed, and everyone goes home exhausted and sore.

My agents in Cleveland report that elaborate preparations are under way there to slack the thirst of the visitors, which is always powerful at national conventions. The town is very well supplied with bootleggers, and regular lines of rum ships run into it from Canadian ports. Ohio has a State Volstead act and a large force of spies and snoopers, many of them former jailbirds. These agents of the Only True Christianity, no doubt, will all concentrate in Cleveland, and dispute with the national Prohibition blacklegs for the graft. I venture the guess that bad Scotch will sell for $15 a bottle in the hotels and at the convention hall, and that more than one delegate will go home in the baggage car, a victim to methyl alcohol. . . .

The managers of the Hon. Mr. Coolidge's campaign are apparently well aware that the nomination of the Hon. Al Smith by the Democrats would plunge them into a very bitter and serious fight, and so they are trying to weaken Al by weakening Tammany Hall. One of the principal arguments used to bring the Democratic convention to New York was that Tammany would see that the delegates and alternates got enough sound drinks at reasonable prices to keep pleasantly jingled—an unbroken tradition at Democratic national conventions since the days of Andrew Jackson. Now the Coolidge managers have hurled hundreds of Prohibition agents into Manhattan, and a desperate effort is under way to make the town bone-dry. The Dogberries of the Federal bench, as usual, lend themselves willingly to the buffoonery: dozens of injunctions issue from their mills every day, and some of the principal saloons of the Broadway region are now padlocked.

But all the New Yorkers that I know are still optimistic. There are, indeed, so many saloons in the town that all the Federal judges east of the Mississippi, working in eight-hour shifts like coal miners, could not close them completely in the month remaining before the convention opens. Every time one saloon is closed two open. Meanwhile, the 12-mile treaty with England seems to have failed absolutely to discourage bootlegging from the Bahamas. On the contrary, the price of Scotch has declined steadily since it was signed, and the stuff now coming in is of very excellent quality. It is my belief that the theory that it is heavily adulterated is spread by Prohibitionists, who are certainly not noted for veracity. I have not only encountered no bad Scotch in New York for a year past; I have never heard of any. All the standard brands are obtainable in unlimited quantities, and at prices, roughly speaking, about half those of a year ago.

Moreover, very good beer is everywhere on sale, and nine-tenths of the Italian restaurants, of which there must be at least two thousand in the town, are selling cocktails and wine. Along Broadway the difficulty of concealing so bulky a drink as beer and the high tolls demanded by the Prohibition enforcement officers make the price somewhat high, but in the side streets it is now only 60 percent above what it was in the days before the Volstead act. The last time I went into a beer-house in New York, two or three weeks ago, the *Wirt* greeted me with the news that he had just reduced the price 10 cents a *Seidel*. His place was packed to the doors.

I am thus inclined to believe that the efforts of M. Coolidge's partisans to employ the Eighteenth Amendment against M. Smith will fail.

from Baltimore Evening Sun, *June 2, 1924.*

◇◇◇

POST-MORTEM

On the morning after the final adjournment of the late Democratic National Convention, as I snored in the Biltmore Hotel, dreaming of this and that, a colleague of the *Sunpaper* came in and shook me. My eyes, as I opened them, were half blinded by the flash of sunlight from his bald head. Under his union suit rolled the lovely curves of his matronly but still heroic form. His aspect was stern. Obviously, he was agog.

"What I want you to do," he said, "is to take down my words. Wake up Hyde. I want two witnesses."

I woke up Hyde, and besought him to proceed. He plunged at once into the oath laid down in the Maryland statutes: "In the presence of Almighty God, I do solemnly promise and declare"—But what? Simply that he was done with national conventions forever—that he would never attend another one in this life—that if, by any chance, I ever caught him at one or within a hundred miles of one, I should be free to knock him in the head, boil him down, and sell his bones to a dice factory.

I have never seen a more earnest man. His eyes flashed blue and awful flames. His whole hide glowed scarlet through his union suit. Had there been any hair on his head it would have bristled like the *vibrissae* of a Tom cat. In one long and indignant sentence he recited a great catalogue of hardships—meals bolted suicidally or missed altogether, nights spent in pursuing elusive and infamous politicians, hours wasted upon the writing of dispatches that were overtaken by fresh news before they could get into the *Sunpaper*, dreadful alarm and surprises at three o'clock in the morning, all the horrors of war without any of its glory. Twice he swore his oath, and then, for good measure, he damned the whole universe.

But Hyde and I were not impressed. We had heard such high talk before. We knew that the deponent was an honest man, but we also knew that he was mistaken. We knew that he would be on hand for the next great show, as he had been on hand for this one and for all others in his time—that, for all his protestations and high resolves, he could no more break himself of the convention habit than he could break himself of the habit of breakfasting on five fried eggs and two Manhattan cocktails. The fellow was doomed, as we were ourselves, and if he didn't know it, it was simply because he was not himself.

For there is something about a national convention that makes it as fascinating as a revival or a hanging. It is vulgar, it is ugly, it is stupid, it is tedious, it is hard upon both the higher cerebral centers and the *gluteus maximus*, and yet it is somehow charming. One sits through long sessions wishing heartily that all the delegates and alternates were dead and in hell—and then suddenly there comes a show so gaudy and hilarious, so melodramatic and obscene, so unimaginably exhilarating and preposterous that one lives a gorgeous year in an hour.

from Baltimore Evening Sun, *July 14, 1924.*

◇◇◇

ONWARD, CHRISTIAN SOLDIERS!

The holy war against Al in the late Confederate States seems to be breaking into two halves. On the one hand, some of the Methodist and Baptist papers begin to be extremely polite to him, and warn their customers that it is unChristian (and, what is worse, unwise) to have at opponents too hotly. On the other hand, there are journals which pile indignation upon indignation, and devote practically all of their space to philippics against Al, Raskob, Tammany, the Beer Trust and the Pope.

A good specimen of the former class is the *Southern Christian Advocate*, of Columbia, S.C.—like all the multitudinous *Christian Advocates*, a Methodist organ. In the current issue I can find but two references to Al, and both of them are quite inoffensive. Nor does Pastor E. O. Watson, the editor, print anything against the Pope. So with the *Biblical Record* (Baptist), of Raleigh, edited by Pastor Livingston Johnson. Dr. Johnson, indeed, is so moderate that he feels moved to explain his lack of ferocity. Some of his subscribers have protested against it. Says he:

> Because we have not used more vitriolic language some have thought that the editor was weakening in his posi-

tion. The writer has simply endeavored to keep a cool head, as he has two or three times advised others to do.

. . . The *Baptist Courier*, of Greenville, S.C., belongs to the other wing. It denounces Raskob as "a private chaplain [*sic*] of the papal household," and says that "without doubt he has been on his knees before the Pope." Further, it prints an article entitled "The Romish Peril," by the learned Dr. A. T. Robertson, of the Southern Baptist Theological Seminary, in which he sounds a warning that "the Pope undoubtedly longs for the wealth and power of the United States to be in his hands." He goes on:

> He will never give up that hope. He will leave no stone unturned to gain that end. . . . Rome means to get control of the United States sooner or later. Protestants may well understand that purpose.

Dr. Robertson does not mention Al, but his meaning is plain enough. Dr. C. M. Bishop, writing in the *Texas Christian Advocate*, of Dallas, Texas, goes further. He identifies Tammany and the Pope with the horrendous beasts mentioned in the Book of Revelation, and heads his article "Unclean Spirits Like Frogs." In the same journal Dr. Bob Shuler, the chief rival of Dr. Aimée Semple McPherson in Los Angeles, pursues the melancholy subject in his well-known trenchant style. .

The *Baptist Message*, of Shreveport, La., and the *Baptist and Commoner*, of Benton, Ark., are full of hot stuff against the Pope. The latter gives three and a half pages to a diatribe under the heading of "Is the Catholic Church a Christian Church?" The answer is no. The Pope, it appears, is an impostor, for "Christ said He would send the Holy Ghost into the world to direct His work." So are all priests, for Christ "called His ministers preachers and shepherds, never priests." The papal title of pontiff is pagan. The Catholic Church is "a brutal, hell-born power," and its clergy scoundrels.

> They are always to be found at the bedside of the dying to extort money for the pretense of making prayers, and on hand to extort from the widow every penny possible for the same pretense. To meet them in the street or in the church, they seem to be devout: but when you come to know them you find that they are hypocrites and filled with iniquity.

. . . *The Baptist Trumpet*, of Killeen, Texas, warns its readers that if Al is elected "the Romish system will institute persecutions again, and put the cruel, blood-stained heel upon all who refuse her authority," and points for proof to Revelation 11, 21, wherein "Rome is called by the name of Jezebel, because Jezebel was a heathenish woman, married to an Israelitish king." The *Christian Index*, of Atlanta, prints a long attack upon the Knights of Columbus by Pastor T. F. Calloway, of Thomasville, Ga., wherein he quotes Priest D. S. Phelan, editor of the *Western Watchman*, as saying on June 27, 1912, that "if the Government of the United States were at war with the church, we would say tomorrow, '*To hell with the Government of the United States!*' "

The *Baptist Progress*, of Dallas, Texas, speaks of Al politely, but is hot against the Knights of Columbus. It says that "they claim that America justly belongs to the Catholic Church because a wise Jew, Columbus, who joined Catholics, discovered America in 1492." It argues that "the devil is behind both Romanism and the liquor traffic." In the *Baptist and Commoner*, previously quoted, Pastor J. A. Scarboro says the same thing, and points to texts in Daniel and Revelation to support him. He goes on furiously:

> The devil's crowd—Catholics, political demagogues, brewers, bootleggers, prostitutes—the whole motley belly-gang are for Smith!

In the same paper Elder W. C. Benson rehearses his reasons for voting for Lord Hoover. I quote a few of them:

> To vote for Al Smith would be granting the Pope the right to dictate to this Government what it should do.
>
> A vote for Al Smith would be the sacrificing of our public schools. Rome says to hell with our public schools.
>
> To vote for Al Smith would be to say that all Protestants are now living in adultery because they were not married by a priest.
>
> To vote for Al Smith is to say our offspring are bastards. Are you ready to accept this?

And so on, and so on. I quote only a few specimens. Acres of such stuff are being printed. In some of the papers the Pope gets so much attention that he almost crowds out Prohibition. But most of them still have space to bawl out the wets. The *Wesleyan Christian Advocate*, of Atlanta, for example, denounces Governor Ritchie as one "who is not only wet, but blasphemously so." This may seem exaggerated—until one remembers that Prohibition is now an integral part of the neo-Confederate theology. To be wet down there is to be an infidel, and doomed to hell. Nothing that a wet says is honest, and nothing that a dry does is evil. The *Richmond Christian Advocate*, replying to a charge that Prohibition agents have committed more murders in the South than in the North, says complacently:

> It is a credit to these Southern States that the records show that they are trying to enforce the law, *even at the cost of human life*.

In other words, murder is a lesser crime than bootlegging! I doubt that many Southern pastors would dissent from that.

from Baltimore Evening Sun, *August 24, 1928.*

◇◇◇

IMPERIAL PURPLE

Most of the rewards of the Presidency, in these degenerate days, have come to be very trashy. The President continues, of course, to be an eminent man, but only in the sense that Jack Dempsey, Lindbergh, Babe Ruth and Henry Ford are eminent men. He sees little of the really intelligent and amusing people of the country: most of them, in fact, make it a sort of point of honor to scorn him and avoid him. His time is put in mainly with shabby politicians and other such designing fellows—in brief, with rogues and ignoramuses. When he takes a little holiday his customary companions are vermin that no fastidious man would consort with—dry Senators with panting thirsts, the proprietors of bad newspapers in worse towns, grafters preying on the suffering farmers, power and movie magnates, prehensile labor leaders, the more pliable sort of journalists, and so on. They must be pretty dreadful company. Dr. Harding, forced to entertain them, resorted to poteen as an analgesic; Dr. Coolidge loaded them aboard the

Mayflower, and then fled to his cabin, took off his vest and shirt, and went to sleep; Dr. Hoover hauls them to the Rapidan at 60 miles an hour, and back at 80 or 90.

The honors that are heaped upon a President in this one hundred and fifty-sixth year of the Republic are seldom of a kind to impress and content a civilized man. People send him turkeys, opossums, pieces of wood from the Constitution, goldfish, carved peach-kernels, models of the State capitols of Wyoming and Arkansas, and pressed flowers from the Holy Land. His predecessors before 1917 got demijohns of 12-year-old rye, baskets of champagne, and cases of Moselle and Burgundy, but them times ain't no more. Once a year some hunter in Montana or Idaho sends him 20 pounds of bear-steak, usually collect. It arrives in a high state, and has to be fed to the White House dog. He receives 20 or 30 chain-prayer letters every day, and fair copies of 40 or 50 sets of verse. Colored clergymen send him illustrated Bibles, mad-stones and boxes of lucky powders, usually accompanied by applications for appointment as collectors of customs at New Orleans, or Register of the Treasury.

His public rewards come in the form of LL.D.'s from colleges eager for the publicity—and on the same day others precisely like it are given to a champion lawn-tennis player, a banker known to be without heirs of his body, and a general in the Army. No one ever thinks to give him any other academic honor; he is never made a Litt.D., a D.D., an S.T.D., a D.D.S., or a J.U.D., but always an LL.D. Dr. Hoover, to date, has 30 or 40 such degrees. After he leaves office they will continue to fall upon him. He apparently knows as little about law as a policeman, but he is already more solidly *legum doctor* than Blackstone or Pufendorf, and the end is not yet.

The health of a President is watched very carefully, not only by the Vice-President but also by medical men detailed for the purpose by the Army or Navy. These medical men have high-sounding titles, and perform the duties of their office in full uniform, with swords on one side and stethoscopes on the other. The diet of their imperial patient is rigidly scrutinized. If he eats a few peanuts they make a pother; if he goes in for a dozen steamed hard crabs at night, washed down by what passes in Washington for malt liquor, they complain to the newspapers. Every morning they look at his tongue, take his pulse and temperature, determine his blood pressure, and examine his eye-grounds and his knee-jerks. The instant he shows the slightest sign of being upset they clap him into bed, post Marines to guard him, put him on a regimen fit for a Trappist, and issue bulletins to the newspapers.

When a President goes traveling he never goes alone, but always with a huge staff of secretaries, Secret Service agents, doctors, nurses, and newspaper reporters. Even so stingy a fellow as Dr. Coolidge had to hire two whole Pullman cars to carry his entourage. The cost, to be sure, is borne by the taxpayers, but the President has to put up with the company. As he rolls along thousands of boys rush out to put pennies on the track, and now and then one of them loses a finger or a toe, and the train has to be backed up to comfort his mother, who, it usually turns out, cannot speak English and voted for Al in 1928. When the train arrives anywhere all the town bores and scoundrels gather to greet the Chief Magistrate, and that night he has to eat a bad dinner, with only ginger-ale to wash it down, and to listen to three hours of bad speeches.

The President has less privacy than any other American. Thousands of persons have the right of access to him, beginning with the British Ambassador and running down to the secretary of the Republican county committee of Ziebach County, South Dakota. Among them are the 96 members of the United States Senate, perhaps the windiest and most tedious group of men in Christendom. If a Senator were denied admission to the White House, even though he were a Progressive, the whole Senate would rise in indignation, even though it were 80% stand-pat Republican. Such is Senatorial courtesy. And if the minister from Albania were kicked out even the French and German Ambassadors would join in protesting.

Many of these gentlemen drop in, not because they have anything to say, but simply to prove to their employers or customers that they can do it. How long they stay is only partly determined by the President himself. Dr. Coolidge used to get rid of them by falling asleep in their faces, but that device is impossible to Presidents with a more active interest in the visible world. It would not do to have them heaved out by the Secret Service men or by the White House police, or to insult and affront them otherwise, for many of them have wicked tongues. On two occasions within historic times Presidents who were irritable with such bores were reported in Washington to be patronizing the jug, and it took a lot of fine work to put down the scandal.

All day long the right hon. lord of us all sits listening solemnly to quacks who pretend to know what the farmers are thinking about in Nebraska and South Carolina, how the Swedes of Minnesota are taking the German moratorium, and how much it would cost in actual votes to let fall a word for beer and light wines. Anon a secretary rushes in with the news that some eminent movie actor or football coach has died, and the President must seize a pen and write a telegram of condolence to the widow. Once a year he is repaid by receiving a cable on his birthday from King George V. These autographs are cherished by Presidents, and they leave them, *post mortem*, to the Library of Congress.

There comes a day of public ceremonial, and a chance to

make a speech. Alas, it must be made at the annual banquet of some organization that is discovered, at the last minute, to be made up mainly of gentlemen under indictment, or at the tomb of some statesman who escaped impeachment by a hair. A million voters with IQ's below 60 have their ears glued to the radio: it takes four days' hard work to concoct a speech without a sensible word in it. Next day a dam must be opened somewhere. Four dry Senators get drunk and make a painful scene. The Presidential automobile runs over a dog. It rains.

The life seems dull and unpleasant. A bootlegger has a better time, in jail or out. Yet it must have its charms, for no man who has experienced it is ever unwilling to endure it again. On the contrary, all ex-Presidents try their level damndest to get back, even at the expense of their dignity, their sense of humor, and their immortal souls. The struggles of the late Major-General Roosevelt will be recalled by connoisseurs. He was a melancholy spectacle from the moment the White House doors closed upon him, and he passed out of this life a disappointed and even embittered man. You and I can scarcely imagine any such blow as that he suffered in 1912. It shook him profoundly, and left him a wreck.

Long ago I proposed that unsuccessful candidates for the Presidency be quietly hanged, as a matter of public sanitation and decorum. The sight of their grief must have a very evil effect upon the young. We have enough hobgoblins in America without putting up with downright ghosts. Perhaps it might be a good idea to hand over ex-Presidents to the hangman in the same way. As they complete their terms their consciences are clear, and their chances of going to Heaven are excellent. But a few years of longing and repining are enough to imperil the souls of even the most philosophical of them. I point to Dr. Coolidge. He pretends to like the insurance business, but who really believes it? Who can be unaware that his secret thoughts have to do, not with 20-year endowment policies, but with 1600 Pennsylvania Avenue? Who can fail to mark the tragedy that marks his countenance, otherwise so beautifully smooth and vacant, so virginally bare of signs? If you say that he does not suffer, then you say also that a man with *cholera morbus* does not suffer.

On second thoughts, I withdraw my suggestion. It is probably illegal, and maybe even immoral. But certainly something ought to be done. Maybe it would be a good idea to make every ex-President a Methodist bishop.

from Baltimore Evening Sun, *August 17, 1931.*

◇◇◇

THE CHOICE TOMORROW

Nevertheless, and despite all Hell's angels, I shall vote for the Hon. Mr. Landon tomorrow. To a lifelong Democrat, of course, it will be something of a wrench. But it seems to me that the choice is one that genuine Democrats are almost bound to make. On the one side are all the basic principles of their party, handed down from its first days and tried over and over again in the fires of experience; on the other side is a gallimaufry of transparent quackeries, puerile in theory and dangerous in practice. To vote Democratic this year it is necessary, by an unhappy irony, to vote for a Republican. But to vote with the party is to vote for a gang of mountebanks who are no more Democrats than a turkey buzzard is an archangel.

This exchange of principles, with the party labels unchanged, is naturally confusing, but it is certainly not so confusing that it goes unpenetrated. Plenty of Republicans who believe sincerely in a strong Federal Government are going to vote tomorrow for the Hon. Mr. Roosevelt, and plenty of Democrats who believe sincerely in the autonomy of the States and a rigid limitation of the Federal power are going to vote, as I shall, for the Hon. Mr. Landon. Whether the shift that confronts us will be permanent remains to be seen. But while it lasts it is manifestly very real, and those who let party loyalties blind them to its reality will be voting very foolishly.

The issue tends to be confused by a distrust of both Presidential candidates, inevitable under the circumstances. There are those who believe that the Hon. Mr. Roosevelt, if he is re-elected, will abandon the socialistic folderol that he has been advocating since 1933 and go back to the traditional program of his party, and there are those who believe that the Hon. Mr. Landon, if elected, will quickly turn out to be only another Harding, Hoover or McKinley. Both notions, it seems to me, represent little more than a naive sort of wishful thinking. Landon, I am convinced, will actually stay put, and so will Roosevelt. Roosevelt, to be sure, has flopped once, but he has now gone too far down his new road to turn back again.

The defense commonly made of him is that he confronted, in 1933, an unprecedented situation, and so had to resort to new and even revolutionary devices in dealing with it. There is no truth in either half of that theory. The situation that he confronted differed only quantitatively, and not at all qualitatively, from others that had been confronted in the past. And of all the devices he employed in dealing with it the only ones that really worked were those that had been tried before.

I am aware that there are many undoubtedly intelligent persons who believe otherwise. The fact, indeed, is not to be wondered at, for the intelligent, like the unintelligent, are responsive to propaganda, and all the propaganda since 1933 has been running one way. But it still remains historically true that all the major problems before the country when Hoover blew up were intrinsically simple and familiar ones, and it still remains true that those which were not tackled in tried and rational ways still remain unsolved.

All the rest was quackery pure and unadulterated. The situation of the country was exaggerated in precisely the same way that a quack doctor exaggerates the illness of his patient, and for exactly the same reason. And the showy and preposterous treatments that were whooped up had no more virtue in them, at bottom, than his pills and liniments. We then and there entered upon an era of quackery that yet afflicts and exhausts the country. We'll not get clear of it until all the quacks are thrown out.

Whether that will happen tomorrow I do not know. The probabilities, as anyone can see, are largely against it. But soon or late the business will have to be undertaken, and the longer it is delayed the more difficult it will become. For people in the mass soon grow used to anything, including even being swindled. There comes a time when the patter of the quack becomes as natural and as indubitable to their ears as the texts of Holy Writ, and when that time comes it is a dreadful job debamboozling them.

The *bona fides* of the Hon. Mr. Roosevelt was pretty generally assumed in the first days of his Presidentiad. He was, to be sure, excessively melodramatic, but observers remembered that he was a Roosevelt, and that a talent for drama was thus in his blood. Even his closing of the banks in retrospect, a highly dubious measure—was accepted without serious protest, even by bankers. The NRA, when it was first announced, seemed a plausible if somewhat violent remedy for admitted evils, and most of his other devices of those days got the same tolerant reception.

But as his administration closed its first year, and he gradually extended and elaborated his program, it began to be evident that he was going far beyond the borders of the reasonable, and that the theory underlying some of his major operations, as it was expounded by his principal agents, was becoming increasingly fantastic and absurd. Bit by bit, the purpose of restoring the country to its normal manner and ease of life was submerged in the purpose of bringing in a brummagem Utopia, fashioned in part out of the idiotic hallucinations of the cow States and in part out of the gaudy evangel of Moscow. And simultaneously, the welfare of the American people as a whole began to be forgotten in a special concern for special classes and categories of them, all of manifestly inferior status and all willing to vote for goods in hand.

In brief, the New Deal became a political racket, and that is what it is today—that and nothing more. Its chief practical business is to search out groups that can be brought into the Hon. Jim Farley's machine by grants out of the public treasury, which is to say, out of the pockets of the rest of us. To serve that lofty end the national currency has been debased, the national credit has been imperiled and a crushing burden has been put on every man who wants to pay his own way in the world and asks only to be let alone. The excuse that a grave emergency justified such pillage is now abandoned. The emergency is past, but the pillage goes on.

At tomorrow's plebiscite this grandiose and excessively dangerous tammanyizing of the country will come to judgment, with the chances, as I have said, in favor of its ratification. That it will be supported heartily by all its bencficiaries goes without saying. Every dole-bird in the country, of whatever sort, will certainly vote for it. It will get the suffrages of all the gimme pseudo-farmers in the Middle West, of all the half-witted sharecroppers in the South, of all the professional uplifters and of all the jobholders on Farley's ever-swelling roll. It will be whooped up by every politician who lives and thrives by promising to turn loose A in B's cornfield. It will have the kindly aid of all other varieties of professional messiahs, ranging from the fantoddish prophets of millenniums to the downright thieves.

Will there be enough of them to ratify it? Probably not. It will meet also some support by honest if deluded men and women. Thousands of them, I gather, are in the ranks of the labor organizations. They have been told that the New Deal saved them their jobs, which it didn't, and that it will prosper them hereafter, which it won't, and large numbers of them have believed. The actual fact is that they are not, and can never be, the beneficiaries of any such carnival of loot; they can only be its goats. In the long run the cost of the whole show will settle down upon them. In the long run every man and woman who works will have to pay for the upkeep of some Farley heeler who has been taught that working is foolish and unnecessary and even a shade immoral.

The Brain Trust brethren, of course, still promise that all the bills will be sent to the rich. Well, they were so sent in Russia, and paid in full. But when they had been paid, more money was still needed, and it is now being provided by the Russian workers. Living in filthy and miserable dens, and badly fed on poor and monotonous food, they labor under a brutal stretch-out system which yields them the equivalent of ten American dollars a month. That is what Utopia always comes to in the end.

from Baltimore Evening Sun, *November 2, 1936.*

CORONER'S INQUEST

The Hon. Mr. Roosevelt's colossal victory in last Tuesday's plebiscite gave him plenty of excuse to leap and exult, but if he is really the smart politician that he seems to be he must be entertaining certain stealthy, *pizzicato* qualms today. He now carries all the burdens of omnipotence. There is no one to say nay—that is, no one he is bound to heed. He has in his hands a blank check from and upon the American people, authorizing him to dispose of all their goods and liberties precisely as he listeth. The Congress that was elected with him will no more dare to challenge him than a pussy cat would dare to challenge a royal Bengal tiger, and even the nine old metaphysicians on Capitol Hill may be trusted to recall, if only subconsciously, that it is imprudent to spit too often into Caesar's eye.

In brief, he has become a sort of chartered libertine, and it will be interesting to note how he reacts to his franchise. The great majority of his lieges believe firmly in the Utopia that he has been preaching since 1933, and they will now expect him to bring it in at last. He can no longer make the excuse that wicked men are hindering him, nor can he plead that he is navigating unmapped waters and must proceed cautiously. He has been engaged, for nearly four years, in exploring and mapping the way, and in that work he has had the aid of a vast band of transcendental engineers of his own choice. What everyone will look for now is full steam ahead. Either we must soon see the glorious shores of Utopia or the whole argosy will be wrecked.

For a year or two past, as everyone knows, it has been making heavy weather. Not one of its greater objectives has been attained. The rich continue rich, and many millions of the poor remain on the dole. Business has improved, but it has improved a great deal more for stockmarket speculators than for honest men. The one-crop farmers continue to bellow piteously for help. Labor is still torn between sweat-shop employers on the one hand and racketeering labor leaders on the other. For all these woes and malaises the right hon. gentleman must now find something colorably resembling remedies, and with reasonable dispatch. Either he is actually a wizard and knows how to cure them, or he is the worst quack ever heard of on earth.

Against his success in this great moral enterprise stand two inconvenient facts. The first is the fact that many, and perhaps indeed most, of the woes and malaises aforesaid appear to be inherently incurable. The second is the fact that people in the mass are very mercurial, and especially the sort of people who believe in miracles. They are all with him today, but that is no assurance that they will be with him tomorrow. On the contrary, there is every reason to believe that they will turn on him, soon or late, as they have turned on all popular messiahs since the dawn of history.

from Baltimore Evening Sun, *November 9, 1936.*

The LITERARY CRITIC

William H. Nolte

Although he was for nearly two decades our most powerful and influential literary critic, having become in the early 1920s our first literary dictator, H. L. Mencken is not generally remembered for his criticism of *belles lettres*. This may seem at first blush ironic, but the fact that Mencken excelled in various other areas (one might even say in other careers) dispels the irony. In simple fact, he defies all labels; he fits no pigeonhole yet devised by the card-indexers. He is now, for example, probably better remembered for his studies of the American language than for his book criticism, even though he always insisted that he was an amateur as a linguist, who took up the study as a hobby and wrote the various editions of *The American Language* and the two enormous *Sup-*

William H. Nolte is C. Wallace Martin Professor of English at the University of South Carolina. He is the author of *H. L. Mencken, Literary Critic*, and the editor of *H. L. Mencken's Smart Set Criticism*.

plements only because no one else at the time seemed inclined to do the necessary spade work. But no one would think of labeling him a linguist or philologist—not, that is, without stating that he was much else besides. Considering the breadth of his interests, palpably evidenced in the thousands of articles written on every aspect of American culture, one must recognize the fatuity of all restrictive labels. If we must classify him at all, and the urge for classification is well nigh irresistible, then we should simply call him The American as Critic.

Besides his wide interests, there is, of course, another reason for our inability to fit him in the filing cabinets and thus make him proper material for the textbooks and hence remove him from public view. Though hard to pin down, the reason should be apparent to any discerning reader of his essays and books on whatever subject. In an "appreciation" written shortly after Mencken's death in 1956, Joseph Wood Krutch touched on the reason I have in mind when he said that though "Mencken was a spokesman, a symbol, an embodiment, and all the other things he has been called," he was above all else "a master of the written word and, unless the world changes a great deal more than seems likely, that is the only thing which will count in the long run." Men are mentioned in textbooks, Krutch wrote, because they were so right or so wrong or because they were so typical of this or that, but they are read only because they were great writers. If that seems an elementary truth, it is nonetheless one that we frequently overlook when trying to explain why this or that writer, once considered pre-eminently important, is no longer attended to. Krutch concluded his tribute by predicting that "the time will come when it will be generally recognized, as by a few it already is, that Mencken's was the best prose written in America during the twentieth century. Those who deny that fact had better confine themselves to direct attack.

They will be hard put to find a rival claimant." To my mind, no plausible claimant has yet been proposed to wear the laurel now securely fastened to his brow.

Like most critics whose work outlives them, Mencken came to the practice of literary criticism by a circuitous route, through the back door so to speak. Before joining the *Smart Set* magazine, for which he wrote his most significant criticism, Mencken had seen three books through the press: a volume of Kiplingesque verse, *Ventures into Verse*, in 1903; the first interpretation ever written of Bernard Shaw's plays, in 1905 (as a young man Mencken was avidly interested in the theater and was for a time the drama reviewer for the Baltimore *Herald* and, later, for the Baltimore *Sun*); and an explication, the first in English, of Friedrich Nietzsche's philosophy, in 1908. This last work was a popular and critical success that still warrants consideration. He had also had numerous short stories published in various of the popular magazines, and had, among other things, ghostwritten a number of widely read medical articles for a Baltimore physician named Leonard K. Hirshberg.

In the first of the 182 book articles he was to write for the *Smart Set*, covering the span from November 1908 to December 1923, Mencken set the pattern to which he adhered more or less throughout the fifteen-year period. He began his initial piece, entitled "The Good, the Bad and the Best Sellers," by endeavoring in the opening paragraphs to lure or charm his reader into following his arguments and reading his book criticism:

> Platitudes have their uses, I have no doubt, but in the fair field of imaginative literature they have a disconcerting habit of denouncing and betraying one another. Separate a single platitude from the herd, and you will find it impeccable, inviolable and inevitable; comfort-

> able, amiable and well-mannered. But then lead out another and try to drive them tandem; or three more and try to drive them four-in-hand; and you will quickly land in the hospital—your collar-bone broken, your head in a whirl and your raiment muddy and torn.

After indulging in a brief parody of an example of the platitude that can stand alone (viz., It is wrong for the rich to rob the poor) which becomes absurd when placed beside a brother platitude (viz., Only the poor are happy), he asked, apropos of his preliminary material, what platitudes have to do with the divine art of literature. And, more particularly, what they have to do with Upton Sinclair's "new romance," *The Moneychangers*. Answering his own rhetorical question, he concluded:

> Simply this: that hordes of the *bacillus platitudae* have entered Sinclair's system and are preying upon his vitals. They have already consumed his sense of humor and are now fast devouring his elemental horse sense. The first result is that he is taking himself and the world seriously, and the second result is that he is writing tracts.

And the tract, with the exception of "explanatory programs for symphony concerts," is, Mencken said, the lowest of all forms of literature. In order to write a play, a novel, a poem, or even a newspaper editorial, "one must first ensnare an idea. To write a tract one needs but leisure, a grouch and a platitude."

Lamenting the fact that Sinclair had not fulfilled his early promise, Mencken pointed to the great success of *The Jungle* as the point in Sinclair's career when "The afflatus of a divine mission began to stir him, and he sallied forth to preach his incomprehensible *jehad*." He admitted that Sinclair's picture of the Wall Street jackals was probably a true one, drawn much more unerringly than "any Presidential message or leading article yet inflicted on the public"; but he asked why the obvious needed demonstration: "Why mouth platitudes and draw the willing tear with banalities?" He asked Sinclair to "remember that an economic struggle, to make material for fiction, must be pictured, not objectively and as a mere bout between good and evil, but subjectively and as some chosen protagonist sees and experiences it." Stating one of his lasting and cardinal beliefs, Mencken insisted that the interest the reader or viewer has in a novel or drama lies, "always and inevitably, in some one man's effort to master his fate." Here Mencken might well have been thinking of, for him, the greatest of English novelists—Joseph Conrad.

Since most of the books he reviewed in the early years on the *Smart Set* had little if any intrinsic merit, Mencken had to rely upon his own skills as artist to hold his reader. With rare exceptions, the dozen or so books he reviewed, or anyhow briefly noticed, in the book articles, which frequently ran to 5,000 words, did little more than provide him with copy. That those articles are still a delight to read is thus a tribute to Mencken's artistry. This fact is all the more singular when one considers that not much criticism of even the best works of art can be returned to years later with anything approaching joy. Most of his praise went to European writers—Conrad, Galsworthy, Arnold Bennett, George Moore, Shaw, Gorki, Andreev, Max Beerbohm, Anatole France, Sudermann, Hauptmann, H. G. Wells (at least in his early career before he succumbed to the messianic virus), Havelock Ellis, Synge, and various other writers of the Irish Renaissance—to name only a few. In promoting those foreign elixirs he was following the lead of James Huneker, who had done more than any other critic before Mencken to enlighten the provincial American audience. In showing what went on abroad he was also, through implication, revealing the artistic sterility then apparent, to him at least, in the Republic.

Although he often singled out an especially popular book to satirize, Mencken spent the majority of his time in search of the few worthy books to praise. The fact that he found so few such works naturally caused his readers to accuse him of being too severe, a charge which he readily answered in a typically Menckenian fashion:

> Criticism itself, at bottom, is no more than prejudice made plausible. The judicial temperament, like moral beauty, is merely a phrase that men use to fool themselves. When I put on my hangman's gown of criticism and buckle on my celluloid sword, I make a mental oath that I will be as fair, as honest and as charitable as any judge on the bench. I succeed, like the judge, in being as fair, as honest and as charitable as any lawyer at the Bar.

Charitable he may have been, though not always to the satisfaction of those who received his charity. For example, he concluded a brief notice of a Hall Caine novel by informing his reader that the book "is magnificent, and if you like Hall Caine you won't stop to inquire if it is also art." With unfailing glee, Mencken noticed the works of Caine, who was one of the most popular novelists of his time. "Here is the tested stuff," he wrote of a novel in 1913, "the immemorial stuff, the sure stuff. And here it is with new frills, new magnetos, new sauces. A dash of mental telepathy, a pinch of white slavery, a drop or two of frenzied finance, a garnish of polar exploration—and behold, the Duchess and Augusta Evans have become Hall Caine!" A few more words and his good deed was done. More interesting than Caine's novels was Caine himself. Poker-faced, Mencken insisted that Caine's autobiography offered the reader a rare opportunity:

> Suppose you could actually look into the cerebellum of the man who mows your chin, or of the woman who dusts your office, or of your trousers presser, your ward leader, your father-in-law, or any other human blank of your acquaintance: what a host of interesting discoveries you would make! You would learn in one easy lesson why it is that sentient beings, theoretically sane, join fraternal orders, march in parades, go to political meetings, wear badges, read the poems of Ella Wheeler Wilcox and weep over the plays and novels of Hall Caine.

During those years before the founding of the *American Mercury* in 1924, by which time his interest in purely literary matters had greatly waned, Mencken kept up a running battle with the hypocrisy and sentimentality in our national letters, and with the reigning critics, mainly academicians (the schoolmarms of both sexes), who sought to discredit the realists. Incidentally, Mencken defined realism as "simply intellectual honesty in the artist"; he had little respect for what might be called photographic realism.

If Mencken's fame derived in large part from his incomparable demolition work, he should also be remembered for the support and encouragement he gave to the best writers of the period. It is but small exaggeration to say that the best American writers of the generation that came of age around 1920 either got their start in the pages of the *Smart Set*, which Mencken and Nathan edited after 1914, or were directly aided by Mencken's criticism. His long battle on behalf of Dreiser, for example, is well known. Among others, young and old, whom he supported, and in many cases published in the *Smart Set*, were E. W. Howe, Joseph Hergesheimer, James Branch Cabell, Sherwood Anderson, Sinclair Lewis, Floyd Dell, John Dos Passos, Ben Hecht, F. Scott Fitzgerald, Ruth Suckow, Willa Cather, Conrad Aiken, Edgar Lee Masters, Sara Teasdale, Weldon Johnson, Eugene O'Neill, S. N. Behrman, and Ezra Pound. Some of these figures are not much read today, but they were all important at the time.

When Mencken was complimented many years later for having discovered numerous writers of that early period, he refused to take credit for discovering anyone since, as he put it, every artist worth his salt will eventually find an audience no matter what obstacles he has to overcome. His only regret, he said, was that he hadn't helped others who might have needed help. The fact remains that the writers Mencken praised most highly are at least known today, while those he condemned are forgotten.

Mencken's telling indictment of the "moral obsession" that weighed on our literature may be found in the long essay "Puritanism as a Literary Force," published along with essays on Conrad, Dreiser, and Huneker in *A Book of Prefaces* (1917). His most important book of literary criticism, *Prefaces* was quickly thrust into the storm center of the bitterest critical war of the century. Inevitably, the reigning America First critics fell on *A Book of Prefaces* like angels on the Antichrist. Never before in America had a writer directed such a blast against an American institution. And to publish such an un-American essay just when the nation was making the world safe for democracy was more than most right-thinking men could stand. The reception of *Prefaces*—which had a small sale in 1917, but enjoyed a wide audience when reissued in 1924—is a good gauge of Mencken's popularity. During the War only a few rebels could stomach him; after the return of the conquering army, a whole generation accepted the Menckenian theses as gospel.

Mencken's most appealing quality, it seems to me, was his enthusiasm and exuberance. Delighting in the world about him, he conveyed that delight to his readers. If he viewed most things American as being generally farcical, he by no means found them dull. Though essentially pessimistic concerning man's fate, a fact that is most evident in his writings on such men as Conrad and Dreiser, Mencken never doubted the great gift of life itself. Having early on concluded that life was meaningless in that it had no cosmic purpose that man could discover—he liked to quote Sophocles' "O ye deathward-going tribes of men!/What do your lives mean except that they go to nothingness?"—he never let that mundane fact stay him from the feast. Nor did he ever indulge himself, after the fashion of the modern existentialists, in self-pity. Rather he took a heathenish delight in the world out there and in the farcical antics of the people in it. The merriest, maddest Pied Piper of them all, he infects us with that delight in the here and now. If he frequently insisted that all was lost, including honor, we knew and know better than to take him seriously, something he adamantly refused to do himself.

In a letter dated August 30, 1925, to Ernest Boyd, Mencken remarked that he never had any interest in the numerous aesthetic theories that were prevalent in 1908, when he began his work on the *Smart Set*. The "aesthetic gabble" seemed to him "to be mainly buncombe. I have, in fact, no respect for aesthetic theories. They are always blowing up. More and more I incline to the notion that every first-rate work of art, like every first-rate man, is *sui generis*. When I hear a theory I suspect a quack." This same critical atheism (or determinism) Mencken had developed at length in his "Footnote on Criticism" three years earlier. In that essay, a kind of valedictory to that part of his career which was predominantly concerned with literary criticism, he argued that the best critics were themselves artists and hence (to paraphrase his argument) less concerned with the work of art before them than with the "simple desire to function freely and beautifully, to give outward and objective form to ideas that bubble inwardly and have a fascinating lure in them, to get rid of them dramatically and make an articulate noise in the world." (For a more detailed discussion of what constitutes good criticism, one should turn to his "Criticism of Criticism of Criticism," originally published as a review of Joel Spingarn's *Creative Criticism* in the August 1917 *Smart Set* and then refurbished for the first volume of *Prejudices* in 1919.)

If Mencken almost single-handedly created a sophisticated reading public and did more than anyone else in paving the way for the literature that came into being in the 1920s, he performed that service as a ribald advocate of free expression in the arts, and as a saucy debunker of the moralistic aesthetic of the Genteel Tradition. No one ever performed the serious business of transvaluating values in a more devil-may-care fashion than Mencken. Those who missed reading the *early* literary criticism missed reading the best that he was ever to write and the best that was written by an American of his day.

◇◇◇

CRITICISM OF CRITICISM OF CRITICISM

Every now and then, a sense of the futility of their daily endeavors falling suddenly upon them, the critics of Christendom turn to a somewhat sour and depressing consideration of the nature and objects of their own craft. That is to say, they turn to criticizing criticism. What is it in plain words? What is its aim, exactly stated in legal terms? How far can it go? What good can it do? What is its normal effect upon the artist and the work of art?

Such a spell of self-searching has been in progress for several years past, and the critics of various countries have contributed theories of more or less lucidity and plausibility to the discussion. Their views of their own art, it appears, are quite as divergent as their views of the arts they more commonly deal with. One group argues, partly by direct statement and partly by attacking all other groups, that the one defensible purpose of the critic is to encourage the virtuous and oppose the sinful —in brief, to police the fine arts and so hold them in tune with the moral order of the world. Another group, repudiating this constabulary function, argues hotly that the arts have nothing to do with morality whatsoever—that their concern is solely with pure beauty. A third group holds that the chief aspect of a work of art, particularly in the field of literature, is its aspect as psychological document—that if it doesn't help men to know themselves it is nothing. A fourth group reduces the thing to an exact science, and sets up standards that resemble algebraic formulae—this is the group of metrists, of contrapuntists and of those who gabble of light-waves. And so, in order, follow groups five, six, seven, eight, nine, ten, each with its theory and its proofs.

Against the whole corps, moral and aesthetic, psychological and algebraic, stands Major J. E. Spingarn, U.S.A. Major Spingarn lately served formal notice upon me that he had abandoned the life of the academic grove for that of the armed array, and so I give him his military title, but at the time he wrote his "Creative Criticism" he was a professor in Columbia University, and I still find myself thinking of him, not as a soldier extraordinarily literate, but as a professor in rebellion. For his notions, whatever one may say in opposition to them, are at least magnificently unprofessorial—they fly violently in the face of the principles that distinguish the largest and most influential group of campus critics. As witness: "To say that poetry is moral or immoral is as meaningless as to say that an equilateral triangle is moral and an isosceles triangle immoral." Or, worse: "It is only conceivable in a world in which dinner-table conversation runs after this fashion: 'This cauliflower would be good if it had only been prepared in accordance with international law.' " One imagines, on hearing such atheism flying about, the amazed indignation of Prof. Dr. William Lyon Phelps, with his discovery that Joseph Conrad preaches "the axiom of the moral law"; the "Hey, what's that!" of Prof. W. C. Brownell, the Amherst Aristotle, with his eloquent plea for standards as iron-clad as the Westminster Confession; the loud, patriotic alarm of the gifted Prof. Dr. Stuart P. Sherman, of Iowa, with his maxim that Puritanism is the official philosophy of America, and that all who dispute it are enemy aliens and should be deported. Major Spingarn, in truth, here performs a treason most horrible upon the reverend order he once adorned, and having achieved it, he straightway performs another and then another. That is to say, he tackles all the antagonistic groups of orthodox critics *seriatim,* and knocks them about unanimously—first the aforesaid agents of the sweet and pious; then the advocates of unities, meters, all rigid formulae; then the experts in imaginary psychology; then the historical comparers, pigeonholers and makers of categories; finally, the professors of pure aesthetic. One and all, they take their places upon his operating table, and one and all they are stripped and anatomized.

But what is the anarchistic ex-professor's own theory?—for a professor must have a theory, as a dog must have fleas. In brief, what he offers is a doctrine borrowed from the Italian, Benedetto Croce, and by Croce filched from Goethe—a doctrine anything but new in the world, even in Goethe's time, but nevertheless long buried in forgetfulness—to wit, the doctrine that it is the critic's first and only duty, as Carlyle once put it, to find out "what the poet's aim really and truly was, how the task he had to do stood before his eye, and how far, with such materials as were afforded him, he has fulfilled it." For poet, read artist, or, if literature is in question, substitute the Germanic word *Dichter*—that is, the artist in words, the creator of beautiful letters, whether in verse or in prose. Ibsen always called himself a *Digter,* not a *Dramatiker* or *Skuespiller.* So, I daresay, did Shakespeare. . . . Well, what is this generalized poet trying to do? asks Major Spingarn, and how has he done it? That, and no more, is the critic's quest. The morality of the work does not concern him. It is not his business to determine whether it heeds Aristotle or flouts Aristotle. He passes no judgment on its rhyme scheme, its length and breadth, its iambics, its politics, its patriotism, its piety, its psychological exactness, its good taste. He may note these things, but he may not protest about them—he may not complain if the thing criticized fails to fit into a pigeon-hole. Every sonnet, every drama, every novel is *sui generis;* it must stand on its own bottom; it must be judged by its own inherent intentions. "Poets," says Major Spingarn, "do not really write epics, pastorals, lyrics, however much they may be deceived by these false abstractions; they express *themselves, and this expression is their only form.* There are not, therefore, only three or ten or a hundred literary kinds; there are as many kinds as there are individual poets." Nor is there any valid appeal *ad hominem.* The character and background of the poet are beside the mark; the poem itself is the thing. Oscar Wilde, weak and swine-like, yet wrote beautiful prose. To reject that prose on the ground that Wilde had filthy habits is as absurd as to reject "What Is Man?" on the ground that its theology is beyond the intelligence of the editor of the New York *Times.*

This Spingarn-Croce-Carlyle-Goethe theory, of course, throws a heavy burden upon the critic. It presupposes that he is a civilized and tolerant man, hospitable to all intelligible ideas and capable of reading them as he runs. This is a demand that at once rules out nine-tenths of the grown-up sophomores who carry on the business of criticism in America. Their trouble is simply that they lack the intellectual resilience necessary for taking in ideas, and particularly new ideas. The only way they can ingest one is by transforming it into the nearest related formula—usually a harsh and devastating operation. This fact accounts for their chronic inability to understand all that is most personal and original and hence most forceful and significant in the emerging literature of the country. They can get down what has been digested and re-digested, and so brought into forms that they know, and carefully labeled by predecessors of their own sort—but they exhibit alarm immediately they come into the presence of the extraordinary. Here we have an explanation of Brownell's loud appeal for a tightening of standards—i.e., a larger respect for precedents, patterns, rubber-stamps—and here we have an explanation of Phelps's inability to comprehend the colossal phenomenon of Dreiser, and of Boynton's childish nonsense about realism, and of Sherman's effort to apply the Espionage Act to the arts, and of More's querulous enmity to romanticism, and of all the fatuous pigeon-holing that passes for criticism in the more solemn literary periodicals.

As practiced by all such learned and diligent but essentially ignorant and unimaginative men, criticism is little more than a branch of homiletics. They judge a work of art, not by its clarity and sincerity, not by the force and charm of its ideas, not by the technical virtuosity of the artist, not by his originality and artistic courage, but simply and solely by his orthodoxy. If he is what is called a "right thinker," if he devotes himself to advocating the transient platitudes in a sonorous manner, then he is worthy of respect. But if he lets fall the slightest hint that he is in doubt about any of them, or, worse still, that he is indifferent, then he is a scoundrel, and hence, by their theory, a bad artist. Such pious piffle is horribly familiar among us. I do not exaggerate its terms. You will find it running through the critical writings of practically all the dull fellows who combine criticism with tutoring; in the words of many of them it is stated in the plainest way and defended with much heat, theological and pedagogical. In its baldest form it shows itself in the doctrine that it is scandalous for an artist—say a dramatist or a novelist—to depict vice as attractive. The fact that vice, more often than not, undoubtedly *is* attractive—else why should it ever gobble any of us?—is disposed of with a lofty gesture. What of it? say these birchmen. The artist is not a reporter, but a Great Teacher. It is not his business to depict the world as it is, but as it ought to be.

Against this notion American criticism makes but feeble headway. We are, in fact, a nation of evangelists; every third American devotes himself to improving and lifting up his fellow-citizens, usually by force; the messianic delusion is our national disease. Thus the moral *Privatdozenten* have the crowd on their side, and it is difficult to shake their authority; even the vicious are still in favor of crying vice down. "Here is a novel," says the artist. "Why didn't you write a tract?" roars the professor—and down the chute go novel and novelist. "This girl is pretty," says the painter. "But she has left off her undershirt," protests the head-master—and off goes the poor dauber's head. At its mildest, this balderdash takes the form of the late Hamilton Wright Mabie's "White List of Books"; at its worst, it is comstockery, an idiotic and abominable thing. Genuine criticism is as impossible to such inordinately narrow and cocksure men as music is to a man who is tone-deaf. The critic, to interpret his artist, even to understand his artist, must be able to get into the mind of his artist; he must feel and comprehend the vast pressure of the creative passion; as Major Spingarn says, "aesthetic judgment and artistic creation are instinct with the same vital life." This is why all the best criticism of the world has been written by men who have had within them, not only the reflective and analytical faculty of critics, but also the gusto of artists—Goethe, Carlyle, Lessing, Schlegel, Sainte-Beuve, and, to drop a story or two, Hazlitt, Hermann Bahr, Georg Brandes and James Huneker. Huneker, tackling "Also sprach Zarathustra," revealed its content in illuminating flashes. But tackled by Paul Elmer More, it became no more than a dull student's exercise, ill-naturedly corrected. . . .

So much for the theory of Major J. E. Spingarn, U.S.A., late professor of modern languages and literatures in Columbia University. Obviously, it is a far sounder and more stimulating theory than any of those cherished by the other professors. It demands that the critic be a man of intelligence, of toleration, of wide information, of genuine hospitality to ideas, whereas the others only demand that he have learning, and accept anything as learning that has been said before. But once he has stated his doctrine, the ingenious ex-professor, professor-like, immediately begins to corrupt it by claiming too much for it. Having laid and hatched, so to speak, his somewhat stale but still highly nourishing egg, he begins to argue fatuously that the resultant flamingo is the whole mustering of the critical *Aves*. But the fact is, of course, that criticism, as humanly practiced, must needs fall a good deal short of this intuitive recreation of beauty, and what is more, it must go a good deal further. For one thing, it must be interpretation in terms that are not only exact but are also comprehensible to the reader, else it will leave the original mystery as dark as before—and once interpretation comes in, paraphrase and transliteration come in. What is recondite must be made plainer; the transcendental, to some extent at least, must be done into common modes of thinking. Well, what are morality, trochaics, hexameters, movements, historical principles, psychological maxims, the dramatic unities—what are all these save common modes of thinking, short cuts, rubber stamps, words of one syllable? Moreover, beauty as we know it in this world is by no means the apparition *in vacuo* that Dr. Spingarn seems to see. It has its social, its political, even its moral implications. The finale of Beethoven's C minor symphony is not only colossal as music; it is also colossal as revolt; it says something against something. Yet more, the springs of beauty are not within itself alone, nor even in genius alone, but often in things without. Brahms wrote his Deutsches Requiem, not only because he was a great artist, but also because he was a good German. And in Nietzsche there are times when the divine afflatus takes a back seat, and the *spirochaetae* have the floor.

Major Spingarn himself seems to harbor some sense of this limitation on his doctrine. He gives warning that "the poet's intention must be judged at the moment of the creative act" —which opens the door enough for many an ancient to creep in. But limited or not, he at least clears off a lot of moldy rubbish, and gets further toward the truth than any of his former colleagues. They waste themselves upon theories that only conceal the poet's achievement the more, the more diligently they are applied; he, at all events, grounds himself upon the sound notion that there should be free speech in art, and no protective tariffs, and no *a priori* assumptions, and no testing of ideas by mere words. The safe ground probably lies between the contestants, but nearer Spingarn. The critic who really illuminates starts off much as he starts off, but with a due regard for the prejudices and imbecilities of the world. I think the best feasible practice is to be found in certain chapters of Huneker, a critic of vastly more solid influence and of infinitely more value to the arts than all the prating pedagogues since Rufus Griswold. Here, as in the case of Poe, a sensitive and intelligent artist recreates the work of other artists, but there also comes to the ceremony a man of the world, and the things he has to say are apposite and instructive too. To denounce moralizing out of hand is to pronounce a moral judgment. To dispute the categories is to set up a new anti-categorical category. And to admire the work of Shakespeare is to be interested in his handling of blank verse, his social aspirations, his shot-gun marriage and his frequent concessions to the bombastic frenzy of his actors, and to have some curiosity about Mr. W. H. The really competent critic must be an empiricist. He must conduct his exploration with whatever means lie within the bounds of his personal limitation. He must produce his effects with whatever tools will work. If pills fail, he gets out his saw. If the saw won't cut, he seizes a club. . . .

Perhaps, after all, the chief burden that lies upon Major Spingarn's theory is to be found in its label. The word "creative" is a bit too flamboyant; it says what he wants to say, but it probably says a good deal more. In this emergency, I propose getting rid of the misleading label by pasting another over it. That is, I propose the substitution of "catalytic" for "creative," despite the fact that "catalytic" is an unfamiliar word, and suggests the dog-Latin of the seminaries. I borrow it from chemistry, and its meaning is really quite simple. A catalyzer, in chemistry, is a substance that helps two other substances to react. For example, consider the case of ordinary cane sugar and water. Dissolve the sugar in the water and nothing happens. But add a few drops of acid and the sugar changes into glucose and fructose. Meanwhile, the acid itself is absolutely unchanged. All it does is to stir up the reaction between the water and the sugar. The process is called catalysis. The acid is a catalyzer.

Well, this is almost exactly the function of a genuine critic of the arts. It is his business to provoke the reaction between the work of art and the spectator. The spectator, untutored, stands unmoved; he sees the work of art, but it fails to make any intelligible impression on him; if he were spontaneously sensitive to it, there would be no need for criticism. But now comes the critic with his catalysis. He makes the work of art live for the spectator; he makes the spectator live for the work of art. Out of the process comes understanding, appreciation, intelligent enjoyment—and that is precisely what the artist tried to produce.

from Prejudices: First Series (*Alfred A. Knopf, 1919*).

◇◇◇

PORTRAIT OF AN AMERICAN CITIZEN

The theory lately held in Greenwich Village that the merit and success of *Main Street* constituted a sort of double-headed accident, probably to be ascribed to a case of mistaken identity on the part of God—this theory blows up with a frightful roar toward the middle of *Babbitt*. The plain truth is, indeed, that *Babbitt* is at least twice as good a novel as *Main Street* was—that it avoids all the more obvious faults of that celebrated work, and shows a number of virtues that are quite new. It is better designed than *Main Street;* the action is more logical and coherent; there is more imagination in it and less bald journalism; above all, there is a better grip upon the characters. If Carol Kennicott, at one leap, became as real a figure to most literate Americans as Jane Addams or Nan Patterson; then George F. Babbitt should become as real as Jack Dempsey or Charlie Schwab. The fellow simply drips with human juices. Every one of his joints is movable in all directions. Real freckles are upon his neck and real sweat stands out upon his forehead. I have personally known him since my earliest days as a newspaper reporter, back in the last century. I have heard him make such speeches as Cicero never dreamed of at banquets of the Chamber of Commerce. I have seen him marching in parades. I have observed him advancing upon his Presbyterian tabernacle of a Sunday morning, his somewhat stoutish lady upon his arm. I have watched and heard him crank his Buick. I have noted the effect of alcohol upon him, both before and after Prohibition. And I have seen him, when some convention of Good Fellows was in town, at his innocent sports in the parlors of brothels, grandly ordering wine at $10 a round and bidding the professor play "White Wings."

To me his saga, as Sinclair Lewis has set it down, is fiction only by a sort of courtesy. All the usual fittings of the prose fable seem to be absent. There is no plot whatever, and very little of the hocus-pocus commonly called development of character. Babbitt simply grows two years older as the tale unfolds; otherwise he doesn't change at all—any more than you or I have changed since 1920. Every customary device of the novelist is absent. When Babbitt, revolting against the irksome happiness of his home, takes to a series of low affairs with manicure girls, grass-widows and ladies even more complaisant, nothing overt and melodramatic happens to him. He never meets his young son Teddy in a dubious cabaret; his wife never discovers incriminating correspondence in his pockets; no one tries to blackmail him; he is never present when a joint is raided. The worst punishment that falls upon him is that his old friends at the Athletic Club—cheats exactly like himself—gossip about him a bit. Even so, that gossip goes no further; Mrs. Babbitt does not hear it. When she accuses him of adultery, it is simply the formal accusation of a loving wife: she herself has absolutely no belief in it. Moreover, it does not cause Babbitt to break down, confess and promise to sin no more. Instead, he lies like a major-general, denounces his wife for her evil imagination, and returns forthwith to his carnalities. If, in the end, he abandons them, it is not because they torture his conscience, but because they seem likely to hurt his business. This prospect gives him pause, and the pause saves him. He is, beside, growing old. He is 48, and more than a little bald. A night out leaves his tongue coated in the morning. As the curtain falls upon him he is back upon the track of rectitude—a sound business man, a faithful Booster, an assiduous Elk, a trustworthy Presbyterian, a good husband, a loving father, a successful and unchallenged fraud.

Let me confess at once that this story has given me vast delight. I know the Babbitt type, I believe, as well as most; for twenty years I have devoted myself to the exploration of its peculiarities. Lewis depicts it with complete and absolute fidelity. There is irony in the picture; irony that is unflagging and unfailing, but nowhere is there any important departure from the essential truth. Babbitt has a great clownishness in him, but he never becomes a mere clown. In the midst of his most extravagant imbecilities he keeps both feet upon the ground. One not only sees him brilliantly; one also understands him; he is made plausible and natural. As an old professor of Babbittry I welcome him as an almost perfect specimen—a genuine museum piece. Every American city swarms with his brothers. They run things in the Republic, East, West, North, South. They are the originators and propagators of the national delusions—all, that is, save those which spring from the farms. They are the palladiums of 100 percent Americanism; the apostles of the Harding politics; the guardians of the Only True Christianity. They constitute the Chambers of Commerce, the Rotary Clubs, the Kiwanis Clubs, the Watch and Ward Societies, the Men and Religion Forward Movements, the Y.M.C.A. directorates, the Good Citizen Leagues. They are the advertisers who determine what is to go into the American newspapers and what is to stay out. They are the Leading Citizens, the speakers at banquets, the profiteers, the corruptors of politics, the supporters of evangelical Christianity, the peers of the realm. Babbitt is their archetype. He is no worse than most, and no better; he is the average American of the ruling minority in this hundred and forty-sixth year of the Republic. He is America incarnate, exuberant and exquisite. Study him well and you will know better what is the matter with the land we live in than you would know after plowing through a thousand such volumes as Walter Lippmann's *Public Opinion*. What Lippmann tried to do as a professor, laboriously and without imagination, Lewis has here done as an artist with a few vivid strokes. It is a very fine piece of work indeed.

Nor is all its merit in the central figure. It is not Babbitt that shines forth most gaudily, but the whole complex of Babbittry, Babbittism, Babbittismus. In brief, Babbitt is seen as no more than a single member of the society he lives in—a matter far more difficult to handle, obviously, than any mere character sketch. His every act is related to the phenomena of that society. It is not what he feels and aspires to that moves him primarily; it is what the folks about him will think of him. His politics is communal politics, mob politics, herd politics; his religion is a public rite wholly without subjective significance; his relations to his wife and his children are formalized and standardized; even his debaucheries are the orthodox debaucheries of a sound business man. The salient thing about him, in truth, is his complete lack of originality—and that is precisely the salient mark of every American of his class. What he feels and thinks is what it is currently proper to feel and think. Only once, during the two years that we have him under view, does he venture upon an idea that is even remotely original—and that time the heresy almost ruins him. The lesson, you may be sure, is not lost upon him. If he lives, he will not offend again. No thought will ever get a lodgment in his mind, even in the wildest deliriums following bootleg gin, that will offer offense to the pruderies of Vergil Gunch, president of the Boosters' Club, or to those of old Mr. Eathorne, president of the First State Bank, or to those of the Rev. Dr. John Jennison Drew, pastor of the Chatham Road Presbyterian Church, or to those of Prof. Pumphrey, head of the Zenith Business College, or even to those of Miss McGoun, the virtuous stenographer. He has been rolled through the mill. He emerges the very model and pattern of a forward-looking, right-thinking Americano.

As I say, this *Babbitt* gives me great delight. It is shrewdly devised; it is adeptly managed; it is well written. The details, as in *Main Street*, are extraordinarily vivid—the speech of Babbitt before the Zenith Real Estate Board, the meeting to consider ways and means of bulging the Chatham Road Sunday-school, the annual convention of the real-estate men, Babbitt's amour with the manicure-girl, the episode of Sir Gerald Doak, the warning visit when Babbitt is suspected of Liberalism, the New Thought meeting, the elopement of young Theodore Roosevelt Babbitt and Eunice Littlefield at the end. In all these scenes there is more than mere humor; there is searching truth. They reveal something; they mean something. I know of no American novel that more accurately presents the real America. It is a social document of a high order.

from H. L. Mencken's *Smart Set* Criticism
(*Cornell University Press, 1968*), *edited by* William H. Nolte.

◇◇◇

STEPHEN CRANE

Next to Poe and Walt Whitman, Crane seems destined to go down into history as the most romantic American author of the Nineteenth Century. Even while he lived legend was busy with him. He was, by one story, a young man of mysterious and probably aristocratic origin, the scion of a Junker family in decay. He was, by another, a practitioner of strange, levantine vices—an opium smoker, a devotee of hashish. He was, by a third, the heaviest drinker known to vital statistics since Daniel Webster. He was, by a fourth, a consorter with harlots and the lover of Sarah Bernhardt. He was, by a fifth, sixth, seventh and eighth, the worst dead beat in New York.

All these yarns were fictions. Crane was actually the son of a respectable burgher in New Jersey and his mother was a member of the Methodist Church. If he drank somewhat freely when he was in funds, then so did all the other newspaper reporters of his era. If he borrowed money when he was out of a job, then ditto, ditto. If he took drugs, it was only to relieve his frequent and distressing infirmities, of which the last was the tuberculosis pulmonalis which took him off. As for his offenses against sex hygiene, they were chiefly imaginary. All through his youth he was romantically in love with a lady visibly his senior, and before he was much beyond 25 he married another lady still more his senior. In brief, a somewhat banal life. Even his war adventures were far less thrilling in fact than in his florid accounts of them. When he went to the Greek-Turkish War he came to grief because he could speak no language save English; when he went to the Spanish-American War he came down with severe cramps and had to be nursed by his fellow-correspondents.

But Crane could write, so some of his books have outlived their time. It was his distinction that he had an eye for the cold, glittering fact in an age of romantic illusion. The dignified authors of that time were such shallow, kittenish fellows as Howells, F. Hopkinson Smith and Frank R. Stockton, with Richard Watson Gilder as their high priest. The popular authors revolved around Richard Harding Davis. Crane's first writings alarmed Howells and shocked Gilder, but gradually a gang of younger men gathered around him, and before he died he was a national celebrity—in fact, a sort of American Kipling. He was, indeed, the head and forefront of the Young America movement in the middle nineties. No man of that movement was more vastly admired, and none has survived with less damage. How far would he have got if he had lived? It is useless to speculate. He died, like Schubert, at 30. He left behind him one superlatively excellent book, four or five magnificent short stories, some indifferent poems and a great mass of journalistic trash. The Gilders of his time left only trash.

from A Mencken Chrestomathy (*Alfred A. Knopf, 1949*).

◇◇◇

JOSEPH CONRAD

Some time ago I put in a blue afternoon re-reading Joseph Conrad's "Youth." A *blue* afternoon? What nonsense! The touch of the man is like the touch of Schubert. One approaches him in various and unhappy moods: depressed, dubious, despairing; one leaves him in the clear, yellow sunshine that Nietzsche found in Bizet's music. But here again the phrase is inept. Sunshine suggests the imbecile, barnyard joy of the human kohlrabi—the official optimism of a steadily delighted and increasingly insane Republic. What the enigmatical Pole has to offer is something quite different. If its parallel is to be found in music, it is not in Schubert, but in Beethoven—perhaps even more accurately in Johann Sebastian Bach. It is the joy, not of mere satisfaction, but of understanding—the profound but surely not merry delight which goes with the comprehension of a fundamental fact—above all, of a fact that has been coy and elusive. Certainly the order of the world that Conrad sets forth with diabolical eloquence and plausibility is no banal moral order, no childish sequence of virtuous causes and edifying effects. Rather it has an atheistic and even demoniacal smack: to the earnest Bible student it must be more than a little disconcerting. The God he visualizes is no loving papa in a house-coat and carpet-slippers, inculcating the great principles of Christian ethics by applying occasional strokes *a posteriori*. What he sees is something quite different: an extremely ingenious and humorous Improvisatore and Comedian, with a dab of red on His nose and maybe somewhat the worse for drink—a furious and far from amiable banjoist upon the human spine, and rattler of human bones. Kurtz, in "Youth," makes a capital banjo for that exalted and cynical talent. And the music that issues forth—what a superb *Hexentanz* it is.

One of the curiosities of critical stupidity is the doctrine that Conrad was without humor. No doubt it flows out of a more general error; to wit, the assumption that tragedy is always pathetic, that death itself is inevitably a gloomy business. That error, I suppose, will persist in the world until some extraordinary astute mime conceives the plan of playing "King Lear" as a farce—I mean deliberately. That it *is* a farce seems to me quite as obvious as the fact that "Romeo and Juliet" is another, this time lamentably coarse. To adopt the contrary theory—to view it as a great moral and spiritual spectacle, capable of purging and uplifting the psyche like marriage to a red-haired widow or a month in the trenches—to toy with such notions is to borrow the critical standards of a party of old ladies weeping over the damnation of the heathen.

This, at all events, is the notion that seems to me implicit in every line of Conrad. I give you "Heart of Darkness" as the archetype of his whole work and the keystone of his metaphysical system. Here we have all imaginable human hopes and aspirations reduced to one common denominator of folly and failure, and here we have a play of humor that is infinitely mordant and searching. Turn to pages 136 and 137 of the American edition—the story is in the volume called "Youth"—: the burial of the helmsman. Turn then to 178–184: Marlow's last interview with Kurtz's intended. The farce mounts by slow stages to dizzy and breath-taking heights. One hears harsh roars of cosmic laughter, vast splutterings of transcendental mirth, echoing and reëchoing down the black corridors of empty space. The curtain descends at last upon a wild dance in a dissecting-room. The mutilated dead rise up and jig. . . .

It is curious, re-reading a thrice-familiar story, how often one finds surprises in it. I have been amazed, toward the close of "The End of the Tether," to discover that the *Fair Maid* was wrecked, not by the deliberate act of Captain Whalley, but by the machinations of the unspeakable Massy. How is one to account for so preposterous an error? Certainly I thought I knew "The End of the Tether" as well as I knew anything in this world—and yet there was that incredible misunderstanding of it, lodged firmly in my mind. Perhaps there is criticism of a sort in my blunder: it may be a fact that the old skipper willed the thing himself—that his willing it is visible in all that goes before—that Conrad, in introducing Massy's puerile infamy at the end, made some sacrifice of inner veracity to the exigencies of what, at bottom, is somewhat too neat and well-made a tale. The story, in fact, belongs to the author's earlier manner; my guess is that it was written before "Youth" and surely before "Heart of Darkness." But for all that, its proportions remain truly colossal. It is one of the most magnificent narratives, long or short, old or new, in the English language, and with "Youth" and "Heart of Darkness" it makes up what is probably the best book of imaginative writing that the English literature of the Twentieth Century can yet show.

Conrad learned a great deal after he wrote it, true enough. In "Lord Jim," in "Victory," and, above all, in "A Personal Record," there are momentary illuminations, blinding flashes of brilliance that he was incapable of in those days of experiment; but no other book of his seems to me to hold so steadily to so high a general level—none other, as a whole, is more satisfying and more marvelous. There is in "Heart of Darkness" a perfection of design which one encounters only rarely and miraculously in prose fiction: it belongs rather to music. I can't imagine taking a single sentence out of that stupendous tale without leaving a visible gap; it is as thoroughly *durch componiert* as a fugue. And I can't imagine adding anything to it, even so little as a word, without doing it damage. As it stands it is austerely and beautifully perfect, just as the slow movement of the Unfinished Symphony is perfect.

I observe of late a tendency to examine the English of Conrad rather biliously. This folly is cultivated chiefly in England, where, I suppose, chauvinistic motives enter into the matter. It is the just boast of great empires that they draw in talents from near and far, exhausting the little nations to augment their own puissance; it is their misfortune that these talents often remain defectively assimilated. Conrad remained the Slav to the end. The people of his tales, whatever he calls them, are always as much Slavs as he is;* the language in which he describes them retains a sharp, exotic flavor. But to

* Conrad himself objected to this idea when it was first set forth in the *Smart Set*, Dec., 1919, p. 68, and remonstrated politely. But I stick to my guns.

say that this flavor constitutes a blemish is to say something so preposterous that only schoolmasters and their dupes may be thought of as giving it credit. The truly first-rate writer is not one who uses the language as such dolts demand that it be used; he is one who reworks it in spite of their prohibitions. It is his distinction that he thinks in a manner different from the thinking of ordinary men; that he is free from that slavery to embalmed ideas which makes them so respectable and so dull. Obviously, he cannot translate his notions into terms of every day without doing violence to their inner integrity. What Conrad brought into English literature was a new concept of the relations between fact and fact, idea and idea, and what he contributed to the complex and difficult art of writing English was a new way of putting words together. His style now amazes and irritates pedants because it does not roll along in the old ruts. Well, it is precisely that rolling along in the old ruts that he tried to avoid—and it was precisely that avoidance which made him what he is. No Oxford mincing is in him, despite his curious respect for Henry James. If he cannot find his phrase above the salt, he seeks it below. His English, in a word, is innocent. And if, at times, there gets into it a color that is strange and even bizarre, then the fact is something to rejoice over, for a living language is like a man suffering incessantly from small internal hemorrhages, and what it needs above all else is constant transfusions of new blood from other tongues. The day the gates go up, that day it begins to die.

A very great man, this Mr. Conrad. As yet, I believe, decidedly underestimated, even by many of his post-mortem advocates. Most of his first acclaimers mistook him for a mere romantic—a talented but somewhat uncouth follower of the Stevenson tradition, with the orthodox cutlass exchanged for a Malay *kris*. Later on he began to be heard of as a linguistic and vocational marvel: it was astonishing that any man bred to Polish should write English at all, and more astonishing that a country gentleman from the Ukraine should hold a master's certificate in the British merchant marine. Such banal attitudes are now archaic, but I suspect that they have been largely responsible for the slowness with which his fame has spread in the world. At all events, he is vastly less read and esteemed than he ought to be. When one reflects that the Nobel Prize was given to such third-raters as Benavente, Heidenstam, Gjellerup and Spitteler, with Conrad passed over, one begins to grasp the depth and density of the ignorance prevailing in the world, even among the relatively enlightened. One "Lord Jim," as human document and as work of art, is worth all the works produced by all the Benaventes and Gjellerups since the time of Rameses II. Nor is "Lord Jim" a chance masterpiece, an isolated peak. On the contrary, it is but one unit in a long series of extraordinary and almost incomparable works—a series sprung suddenly and overwhelmingly into full dignity with "Almayer's Folly." I challenge the nobility and gentry of Christendom to point to another Opus 1 as magnificently planned and turned out as "Almayer's Folly." The more one studies it, the more it seems miraculous. If it is not a work of genius then no work of genius exists on this earth.

from Prejudices: Fifth Series (*Alfred A. Knopf, 1926*).

◇◇◇

FIFTEEN YEARS

I

I began to write these book articles for *The Smart Set* in November 1908—that is, the first of them appeared in the magazine for that month. Since then, counting this one, I have composed and printed no less than one hundred and eighty-two—in all, more than nine hundred thousand words of criticism. An appalling dose, certainly! How many books have I reviewed, noticed, praised, mocked, dismissed with lofty sneers? I don't know precisely, but probably fully two thousand. But how many have I *read?* Again I must guess, but I should say at least twice as many. What? Even so. The notion that book reviewers often review books without having read them is chiefly a delusion; it may happen on newspapers, but certainly not on magazines of any pretensions. I remember printing notices of a number of books that were so dull, at least to me, that I couldn't get through them, but in every such case I printed the fact frankly, and so offered no complete judgment. Once, indeed, I read part of a book, wrote and printed a notice denouncing it as drivel, and then, moved by some obscure, inner necessity, returned to it and read it to the end. This experience gave me pause and taught me something. One cylinder of my vanity—the foul passion that is responsible for all book reviewers above the rank of slaves, as it is for all actor-managers, Presidents and archbishops—urged me to stick to my unfavorable notice, but the other cylinder urged me to make handsome amends. I did the latter, and trust that God will not forget it. I trust, too, that He will not overlook my present voluntary withdrawal from this pulpit. The insurance actuaries say that my expectation of life is exactly twenty-five years; in twenty-five years I might write and print three hundred more articles—another million and a half words. If I now resign the chance and retire to other scenes, then perhaps it may help me a few inches along the Eight-Fold Path. Men have been made saints for less.

II

Among the thousands of letters that have come to me from my customers and the public generally during the fifteen years of my episcopate have been a great many of a uraemic and acerbitous flavor, and not a few of these have set up the doctrine that whoever nominated me for my job was an idiot. To this day, curiously enough, I don't know who he was. At the time the poisoned pen was offered to me, I was not in practice as a literary critic, and had not, in fact, done much book reviewing. My actual trade was that of an editorial writer on a provincial newspaper, then in sad decay, and the subjects that I was told off to treat were chiefly (a) foreign politics, a topic then disdained by most American editorial writers, and (b) such manifestations of the naive and charming communal life of the Republic as are now grouped under the general head of Babbittry. I had a good time in that newspaper job, and invented a large vocabulary of terms of abuse of my countrymen; a number of these terms have since passed into the American language and are now used even by Babbitts. But I never reviewed books save when the literary critic of the paper was drunk, and that was not often. Some years before I had been the dramatic critic, but that office was already filled by another, to the great relief of the local Frohmans. Those were the palmy days of Augustus Thomas, Clyde Fitch and the dramatized novel. Mansfield was still the emperor of the American stage, Nazimova was a nine-days' wonder, Belasco was almost universally regarded as a Master Mind, and the late Joseph Jefferson still wobbled around the provinces with his tattered scenery and his company of amateurish sons, sons-in-law, cousins and second cousins. I am fond of recalling (to the disquiet of Comrade Nathan, who believed in the Belasco hocus-pocus so late as 1907, and once actually praised Nazimova's Nora in *A Doll's House*) that my observations upon these half-forgotten worthies brought many an indignant manager to the business office of my paper, and filled me with a fine sensation of bellicose sagacity. Some time ago I unearthed a bundle of clippings of my old dramatic notices, and their general sapience amazed and enchanted me. It was like meeting a precious one of 1902 and finding her still slim and sweet, with nightblack hair and eyes like gasoline pools on wet asphalt. Once, aroused to indignation by my derision of his mumming, Mansfield wrote me a letter denouncing me as an ass and inviting me to dinner. But I was not quite ass enough to accept his invitation. The fashionable way to fetch an anarchistic provincial critic in those days was to hire him as a press-agent; it is, in fact, still done. But I always had a few dollars in my pocket, and so resisted the lure. But by and by I tired of the theater, and took to writing facetious editorials, many of which were never printed. To this day I dislike the showhouse, and never enter it if I can help it.

But to return to my story. The assistant editor of *The Smart Set*, in 1908, was the late Norman Boyer, with whom, eight years before, I had worked as a police reporter in Baltimore. One day I received a polite note from him, asking me to wait upon him on my next visit to New York. I did so a few weeks later; Boyer introduced me to his chief, Fred Splint, and Splint forthwith offered me the situation of book reviewer to the magazine, with the rank and pay of a sergeant of artillery. Whose notion it was to hire me—whether Boyer's, or Splint's, or some anonymous outsider's—I was not told, and do not know to this day. I had never printed anything in the magazine; I had not, in fact, been doing any magazine work since 1905, when I abandoned the writing of short stories, as I had abandoned poetry in 1900. But Splint engaged me with a strange and suspicious absence of parley, Boyer gave me an armful of books, the two of us went to Murray's for lunch (I remember a detail: I there heard the waltz "*Ach Frühling wie bist du so schön!*" for the first time), and in November of the same year my first article appeared in this place. I have not missed an issue since. But now I shuffle off to other scenes.

III

Glancing back over the decade and a half, what strikes me most forcibly is the great change and improvement in the situation of the American imaginative author—the novelist, poet, dramatist, and writer of short stories. In 1908, strange as it may seem to the literary radicals who roar so safely in Greenwich Village today, the old tradition was still powerful, and the young man or woman who came to New York with a manuscript which violated in any way the pruderies and prejudices of the professors had a very hard time getting it printed. It was a day of complacency and conformity. Hamilton Wright Mabie was still alive and still taken seriously, and all the young pedagogues who aspired to the critical gown imitated him in his watchful stupidity. This camorra had delivered a violent wallop to Theodore Dreiser eight years before, and he was yet suffering from his bruises; it was not until 1911 that he printed *Jennie Gerhardt*. Miss Harriet Monroe and her gang of new poets were still dispersed and inarticulate; Miss Amy Lowell, as yet unaware of Imagism, was writing polite doggerel in the manner of a New England schoolmarm; the reigning dramatists of the nation were Augustus Thomas, David Belasco and Clyde Fitch; Miss Cather was imitating Mrs. Wharton; Hergesheimer had six years to go before he'd come to *The Lay Anthony;* Cabell was known only as one who provided the text for illustrated gift-books; the American novelists most admired by most publishers, by most readers and by all practicing critics were Richard Harding Davis, Robert W. Chambers and James Lane Allen. It is hard, indeed, in retrospect, to picture those remote days just as they were. They seem almost fabulous. The chief critical organ of the Republic was actually the Literary Supplement of *The New York Times.* The *Dial* was down with diabetes in Chicago; the *Nation* was made dreadful by the gloomy humor of Paul Elmer More; the *Bookman* was even more saccharine and sophomoric than it is today; the *Freeman,* the *New Republic* and the *Literary Review* were yet unheard of. When the mild and *pianissimo* revolt of the middle 90's—a feeble echo of the English revolt—had spent itself, the Presbyterians marched in and took possession of the works. Most of the erstwhile *révoltés* boldly took the veil—notably Hamlin Garland. The American Idealism now preached so pathetically by Prof. Dr. Sherman and his fellow fugitives from the Christian Endeavor belt was actually on tap. No novel that told the truth about life as Americans were living it, no poem that departed from the old patterns, no play that had the merest ghost of an idea in it had a chance. When, in 1908, Mrs. Mary Roberts Rinehart printed a conventional mystery story which yet managed to have a trace of sense in it, it caused a sensation. (I reviewed it, by the way, in my first article.) And when, two years later, Dr. William Lyon Phelps printed a book of criticism in which he actually ranked Mark Twain alongside Emerson and Hawthorne, there was as great a stirring beneath the college elms as if a naked fancy woman had run across the campus. If Hergesheimer had come into New York in 1908 with *Cytherea* under his arm, he would have worn out his pantaloons on publishers' benches without getting so much as a polite kick. If Eugene O'Neill had come to Broadway with *The Emperor Jones* or *The Hairy Ape,* he would have been sent to Edward E. Rose to learn the elements of his trade. The devilish and advanced thing, in those days, was for a fat lady star to give a couple of matinées of Ibsen's *A Doll's House.*

A great many men and a few women addressed themselves to the dispersal of this fog. Some of them were imaginative writers who found it simply impossible to bring themselves within the prevailing rules; some were critics; others were young publishers. As I look back, I can't find any sign of concerted effort; it was, in the main, a case of each on his own. The more contumacious of the younger critics, true enough, tended to rally 'round Huneker, who, as a matter of fact, was very little interested in American letters, and the young novelists had a leader in Dreiser, who, I suspect, was quite unaware of most of them. However, it was probably Dreiser who chiefly gave form to the movement, despite the fact that for eleven long years he was silent. Not only was there a useful rallying-point in the idiotic suppression of *Sister Carrie;* there was also the encouraging fact of the man's massive immovability. Physically and mentally he loomed up like a sort of headland —a great crag of basalt that no conceivable assault seemed able to touch. His predecessor, Frank Norris, was of much softer stuff. Norris, had he lived longer, would have been wooed and ruined, I fear, by the Mabies, Boyntons and other such Christian critics, as Garland had been wooed and ruined before him. Dreiser, fortunately for American letters, never had to face any such seduction. The critical schoolmarms, young and old, fell upon him with violence the moment he appeared above the horizon of his native steppe, and soon he was the storm center of a battle-royal that lasted nearly twenty years. The man himself was stolid, granitic, without nerves. Very little cunning was in him and not much bellicose enterprise, but he showed a truly appalling tenacity. The pedagogues tried to scare him to death, they tried to stampede his partisans, and they tried to put him into Coventry and get him forgotten, but they failed every time. The more he was reviled, sneered at, neglected, the more resolutely he stuck to his formula. That formula is now every serious American novelist's formula. They all try to write better than Dreiser, and not a few of them succeed, but they all follow him in his fundamental purpose—to make the novel true. Dreiser added something, and here following is harder; he tried to make the novel poignant—to add sympathy, feeling, imagination to understanding. It will be a long while before that aim is better achieved than he achieved it in *Jennie Gerhardt*.

IV

Today, it seems to me, the American imaginative writer, whether he be novelist, poet or dramatist, is quite as free as he deserves to be. He is free to depict the life about him precisely as he sees it, and to interpret it in any manner he pleases. The publishers of the land, once so fearful of novelty, are now so hospitable to it that they constantly fail to distinguish the novelty that has hard thought behind it from that which has only some Village mountebank's desire to stagger the booboisie. Our stage is perhaps the freest in the world—not only to sensations, but also to ideas. Our poets get into print regularly with stuff so bizarre and unearthly that only Christian Scientists can understand it. The extent of this new freedom, indeed, is so great that large numbers of persons appear to be unable to believe in it; they are constantly getting into sweats about the few taboos and inhibitions that remain, for example those nourished by Comstockery. But the importance and puissance of Comstockery, I believe, is quite as much overestimated as the importance and puissance of the objurgation still hurled at sense and honesty by the provincial prophets of American Idealism, the Genius of America, and other such phantasms. The Comstocks, true enough, still raid an occasional book, particularly when their funds are running low and there is need to inflame Christian men, but that their monkeyshines ever actually *suppress* a book of any consequence I very much doubt. The flood is too vast for them. Chasing a minnow with desperate passion, they let a whole school of whales go by. In any case, they confine their operations to the single field of sex, and it must be plain that it is not in the field of sex that the hottest battles against the old American tradition have been fought and won. *Three Soldiers* was far more subversive of that tradition than all the stories of sex ever written in America—and yet *Three Soldiers* came out with the imprint of one of the most respectable of American publishers, and was scarcely challenged. *Babbitt* scored a victory that was still easier, and yet more significant, for its target was the double one of American business and American Christianity; it set the whole world to laughing at two things that are far more venerated in the United States than the bodily chastity of women. Nevertheless, *Babbitt* went down so easily that even the alfalfa *Gelehrten* joined in whooping for it, apparently on the theory that praising Lewis would make the young of the national species forget Dreiser. Victimized by their own craft, the *Gelehrten* thus made a foul attack upon their own principles, for if their principles did not stand against just such anarchistic books, then they were without any sense whatever, as was and is, indeed, the case.

I shall not rehearse the steps in the advance from *Sister Carrie*, suppressed and proscribed, to *Babbitt*, swallowed and hailed. The important thing is that almost complete freedom now prevails for the serious artist—that publishers stand ready to print him, that critics exist who are competent to recognize him and willing to do battle for him, and that there is a large public eager to read him. What use is he making of his opportunity? Certainly not the worst use possible, but also certainly not the best. He is free, but he is not yet, perhaps, worthy of freedom. He lets the popular magazine, the movies and the cheap-John publisher pull him too hard in one direction; he lets the vagaries of his politics pull him too hard in another. In my first article in this place I predicted the destruction of Upton Sinclair the artist by Upton Sinclair the visionary and reformer. Sinclair's bones now bleach upon the beach. Beside them repose those of many another man and woman of great promise—for example, Winston Churchill. Floyd Dell is on his way—one novel and two doses of Greenwich Village psychology. Hergesheimer writes novelettes for the *Saturday Evening Post*. Willa Cather has won the Pulitzer Prize—a transaction comparable to the election of Charles W. Eliot to the Elks. Masters turns to prose fiction that somehow fails to come off. Dreiser, forgetting his trilogy, experiments rather futilely with the drama, the essay, free verse. Fuller renounces the novel for book reviewing. Tarkington is another Pulitzer prizeman, always on the verge of first-rate work but always falling short by an inch. Many of the White Hopes of ten or fifteen years ago perished in the war, as surely victims of its slaughter as Rupert Brooke or Otto Braun; it is, indeed, curious to note that practically every American author who moaned and sobbed for democracy between the years 1914 and 1919 is now extinct. The rest have gone down the chute of the movies.

But all this, after all, may signify little. The shock troops have been piled up in great masses, but the ground is cleared for those that follow. Well, then, what of the youngsters? Do they show any sign of seizing their chance? The answer is yes and no. On the one hand there is a group which, revolving 'round the *Bookman*, talks a great deal and accomplishes nothing. On the other hand there is a group which, revolving 'round the *Dial*, *Broom* and the *Little Review*, talks even more and does even less. But on the third hand, as it were, there is a group which says little and saws wood. I have, from time to time, pointed out some of its members in this place. There seems to be nothing in concert between them, no sign of a formal movement, with its *blague* and its bombast, but all of them have this in common: that they owe both their opportunity and their method to the revolution that followed *Sister Carrie*. Most of them are from the Middle West, but they are distinct from the Chicago crowd, now degenerated to posturing and worse. They are sophisticated, disillusioned, free from cant, and yet they have imagination. The raucous protests of the evangelists of American Idealism seem to have no more effect upon them than the advances of the Expressionists, Dadaists and other such café-table prophets. Out of this dispersed and ill-defined group, I believe, something will come. Its members are those who are free from the two great delusions which, from the beginning, have always cursed American letters: the delusion that a work of art is primarily a moral document, that its purpose is to make men better Christians and more docile cannon-fodder, and the delusion that it is an exercise in logic, that its purpose is to prove something. These delusions, lingering beyond their time, are responsible for most of the disasters visible in the national literature today—the disasters of the radicals as well as those of the 100 percent dunderheads. The writers of the future, I hope and believe, will carefully avoid both of them.

V

Inasmuch as I was immersed from the start in the struggle that I have briefly described, it is but natural that my critical treatises should have seemed, to many worthy souls, unduly tart, and even, in some cases, extravagantly abusive and unjust. But as I re-examine them in these closing days of my pastorate, I can't escape the feeling that that view of them is itself somewhat bilious. Tart, yes. But unjust—well, certainly not often. If I regret anything, it is that I have been, more than once, unduly tolerant. The spectacle of a man hard and earnestly at work is one that somehow moves me; I am often blinded to the falseness of his purpose by the agony of his striving. It is a sentimentality that quickly damages critical honesty, and I have succumbed to it more than once. I have overpraised books, and I have applauded authors incautiously and too soon. But, as the Lord God Jahveh is my judge and I hope in all humility to be summoned to sit upon His right hand upon the dreadful and inevitable Day of Judgment, when all hearts are bared and virtue gets its long-delayed reward, I most solemnly make my oath that, with the single exception noted on a previous page, I can't remember a time when I ever printed a slating that was excessive or unjust. The quacks and dolts who have been mauled in these pages all deserved it; more, they all deserved far worse than they got. If I lost them customers by my performances I am glad of it. If I annoyed and humiliated them I am glad of it again. If I shamed any of them into abandoning their quackery—but here I begin to pass beyond the borders of probability, and become a quack myself. Regarding false art, cheap cant, pious skullduggery, dishonest pretense—regarding all these things my position is this: that their practitioners have absolutely no rights that anyone is bound to respect. To be polite to them is not to be tolerant; it is simply to be silly. If a critic has any duty at all save the primary duty to be true to himself, it is the public duty of protecting the fine arts against the invasion of such frauds. They are insidious in their approach; they know how to cajole and deceive; unchallenged, they are apt to bag many victims. Once they are permitted to get a foothold, however insecure, it becomes doubly hard to combat them. My method, therefore, has been to tackle them at first sight and with an axe. It has led to some boisterous engagements, and, I sincerely hope, to a few useful unmaskings. So engaged, I do not hesitate to admit that I have been led by my private tastes quite as much as by any sense of professional duty. The man who tries to subjugate beautiful letters to the puerile uses of some bucolic moral scheme, or some nonsensical notion of the national destiny, or some petty variety of newfangled politics is a man who is congenitally and incurably offensive to me. He has his right, true enough, to be heard, but that right is not properly exercised in the field of *belles lettres*.

VI

A hundred times, during these fifteen years, I have been made aware painfully of a great gap in our domestic *apparatus criticus*, and I still wonder that no competent clerk of letters has ever thought to fill it. I allude to the lack of a comprehensive and intelligent history of American literature. Why does it remain unwritten? The existing books are all either conventional texts for the instruction of schoolboys, or histories of single periods, *e.g.*, Tyler's excellent work on the Colonial literature and Pattee's unimaginative but nevertheless often shrewd monograph on the period from 1870 to 1900. The *Cambridge History of American Literature* by no means meets the need. It is, in detail, accurate enough, and it shows some original exploration of the sources, but its defect is that it does not indicate the direction of the main currents, nor the non-literary forces behind them—that it is too much a series of essays on salient men, and views them only too often as phenomena *in vacuo*. Whole sections of the field are not entered at all—and often they are extremely interesting sections. Many of them are along the borders, with religion, politics or race enmity just over the fence. So far as I know, no literary historian, writing about Poe, has ever thrown up the fact that he came to manhood just as Andrew Jackson mounted the tin throne at Washington. Yet it seems to me to be a fact of capital importance; it explains many things about Poe that are otherwise inexplicable.

Poe, indeed, is a colossus who has never had a competent historian. His biographers have spent themselves upon vain efforts to find out the truth about his periodical drunkenness and his banal love affairs; meanwhile, the question of his artistic origins, like the question of his influence, is passed over with a few platitudes. The current doctrine in the high-schools seems to be that he was a superb poet and the inventor of the short story, or, at all events, of the tale of mystery and horror. He was actually neither. Nine-tenths of his poetry is so artificial that it is difficult to imagine even college tutors reading it voluntarily; as for his tales, they have long since passed over to the shelf of juveniles. But Poe was nevertheless a man with a first-rate head on him, and it seems to me that he proved it abundantly in his criticism, which the pedagogues now neglect. This criticism was not only revolutionary in its own time; it would have continued to seem revolutionary, had it been read, down to a few years ago. Who could imagine anything more subversive of the professorial categories—more direct, clear and hard-hitting, more fatal to literary cheese-mongers, more disconcerting to every hollow pretense and quackery. How did Poe come to write it? What set him on the track? And by what process was the whole body of it so neatly buried the moment he gasped out his last breath?

The equally strange case of Emerson I have discussed more than once in the past, but an adequate treatise upon him, alive and dead, yet remains to be written. It was obviously Emerson's central aim in life to liberate the American mind—to set it free from the crippling ethical obsessions of Puritanism, to break down herd thinking, to make liberty more real on the intellectual plane than it could ever be on the political plane. It is his tragic fate to be mouthed and admired today chiefly by persons who have entirely misunderstood his position—in brief, by the heirs and assigns of the very prigs and dullards he spent his whole life opposing. Certainly it would be difficult to imagine a greater irony than this. Emerson paved the way for every intellectual revolt that has occurred since his time, and yet he has always been brought into court, not as a witness for the rebels, but as a witness for the militia and the police. Three-fourths of the books and monographs written about him depict him as a sort of primeval Dr. Frank Crane; he was actually the first important American to give a hand to Whitman. . . . And Whitman himself! Who will work up the material so laboriously and competently unearthed by Prof. Holloway? . . . Who, indeed, will write the first history of American literature that fits such men as Poe, Emerson and Whitman into their true places, and reveals the forces that shaped them and describes accurately the heritage that they left to their countrymen? . . . I ask the question and pass on.

SOLI DEO GLORIA!

from H. L. Mencken's *Smart Set* Criticism.

Mencken *in* *His* LETTERS

Carl Bode

"Of all the varieties of biography perhaps the most unreliable is the kind based on letters." Having made this defiant pronouncement, Mencken then applies it specifically to his own life. An account of him would omit nine-tenths of the story if based on his letters.

Yes and no. It's true that where these were concerned he persistently tried to keep his private life private. The emotions, especially the deeper ones, which formed a part of that life seldom surfaced in his correspondence. When he did allow his feelings to flow over, he probably regretted it later on, even if the feelings weren't profound. For example. In the mid-1920s he and the effervescent Hollywood actress Aileen Pringle were fast friends. Their relationship had an air of lightness

---

Carl Bode teaches American literature and American Studies at the University of Maryland. He is the author of *Mencken* (1969) and the editor of *The Young Mencken* (1973) and *The New Mencken Letters* (1977). He is also the founder of the Mencken Society.

and gaiety which surely found its way into their correspondence. I doubt that any passion ever pulsed in its pages. Yet when Mencken became engaged to Sara Haardt at the end of the 1920s, he asked Aileen to return his letters as he returned hers. And when Sara died, after five happy years of marriage, he screened their correspondence before donating it to Goucher College, where she'd taught. Some of Sara's ardor remains, but little of what Mencken doubtless felt.

There's another reason for the dearth of highly charged passages in his letters. It's his marked distaste for the rhetoric of emotion. His very style hindered him from revealing himself fully. Sara's death ranked as the only real tragedy he ever encountered; it profoundly affected him. However, when he referred to it in a letter to an old acquaintance a week after it occurred, the most he could say was that he was "dashed and dismayed." So in searching for signs of his private life, we need to make allowance not only for reticence but for understatement.

Yet even after we acknowledge Mencken's practice of shutting out his private feelings, and private actions as well, from his letters they still tell us a vast amount about him. They can't help it: there are so many of them. According to his brother August's estimate, Mencken composed a hundred thousand during his career. He reported to his friend the publisher Alfred Knopf that at one point in 1926 he dictated 125 letters a day for ten days. Throughout the yeasty 1920s it seemed that every American thinker and author craved to communicate with him. When the hammer blows of the Great Depression hit America, Mencken's stance went out of fashion and his correspondence shrank. Still, it remained sizable enough to keep a secretary busy year after year until his catastrophic stroke in 1948.

The result is that, despite his disclaimer, we can comprehend his life through his letters; I think we can discover the essential Mencken. What sort of a man do we find? Some of us find a Nietzschean, the more so because Mencken conceded that many of his ideas were crystallized by the German philosopher's. I believe this is a sound view and I subscribe to it. But I also believe that there's a sounder one, sounder because it's more comprehensive. I believe that there's a better term for him than Nietzschean: Aristotelian.

For we can find in him a thorough-going Aristotelian. If we're all either Platonists or Aristotelians, Mencken was an Aristotelian inside and out. He admired rationality and order in others and evinced them in himself. Beneath the professional flamboyance of his writing lived a moderate. However, it should be added that once this moderate arrived at a mean, he wanted to stay there.

Mencken's daily life demonstrated that he detested change, whim, and chaos. He clothed the outer man, to take that first, in soberly cut suits which seldom shifted their style or color. At the height of his career, when he was often invited out in both Baltimore and New York, he had twenty such suits in his closet, all the work of a costly Manhattan tailor. Yet to Sara's longtime friend Anne Duffy, he always appeared to be attired in unalterable tin. Along with his suits he owned some twenty pairs of shoes. Though they varied somewhat in style, they also showed his love for the time-tested; for among them remained at least a few pairs of high-button blacks from years before. In a letter of December 2, 1927 to his artist friend Charlie Shaw, he volunteered that he didn't start buying brown shoes till after the world war. But now—surprise—he had even taken to brown oxfords. He noted in the same letter that he'd lowered his collar level two years earlier. But the fact was that he proved to be as reluctant to give up his high starched collars as Herbert Hoover would be.

In an equally unaltering and orderly way he took care of the inner man, nourishing him well but never to excess. His love affair with malt was permanent, but he drank only after work—and he spent nearly all of his days and many of his evenings working. He wrote to his first biographer, Isaac Goldberg, that he was at his desk at nine each morning. We know from other sources that, aside from taking time out for meals and a cat-nap, he didn't leave his upstairs study till 9:30 at night. Although he bragged to Charlie Shaw that he was "actually very lazy," I've always suspected that to be a bit of bravado. Regardless, he frequently met friends in the evening at the Rennert Hotel or Schellhase's Cafe to relax from ten on the dot to the stroke of midnight. During that time he customarily downed a couple of steins of Piel's or Michelob, though he assured Charlie Shaw that his favorite drink was beer "in any form." During the thirteen dire years of Prohibition he drank gin and rye whiskey also, partly as an act of defiance. A hearty eater all his life, he savored Maryland seafood and other tasty middle-class fare but never ate enough to make him fat. He kept his weight around 170 pounds despite the fact that he exercised infrequently. He claimed to enjoy laboring in his backyard but hardly overdid it, for he admitted that it took him seven years to build the brick wall which still bounds one side of the yard.

Most important, of course, his view of life was Aristotelian. He said just that, with complacence, in a letter of January 15, 1943 to Huntington Cairns. "I was simply born an Aristotelian, and nothing that you or I can do will ever change the fact. When I put my nose into 'Nicomachean Ethics' I began to feel at home at once, but the Platonic Dialogues irritate me constantly, and apparently incurably."

The principles of the Aristotle whom Mencken read posited a stable, concrete world in which our foremost function was to live a successful life. Our nature had a rational and an unrational side; both sides could help us to live such a life. The rational side in turn had two sides. The first was theoretical wisdom, which normally dealt with ideas and principles and had as its highest function our contemplating of unchanging truths. The second was practical wisdom, which normally dealt with actions and external objects. In ethical terms the rational gave us intellectual virtue, the unrational moral virtue. Moral virtue involved the control of our desires and was helped by good habits. When our desires confronted us with conflicting choices, we could usually make the proper choice by shunning extremes and adopting the mean.

Mencken's own world was a material one, containing nothing that couldn't be apprehended by the five senses. Physically and mentally it was remarkably stable. He lived and died in the family row-house at 1524 Hollins Street, the happy prisoner of his origins. He lived into his mid-seventies but had already firmed his two chief attitudes by his early twenties; he once summed these up for his biographer Goldberg: "I am strongly in favor of liberty and I hate fraud." In terms of his world, he managed his life very successfully, achieving eminence early as editor, journalist, and author. He even became that rarity, an affluent author. He regulated his affairs, public and private, with efficiency. Thoroughly competent himself, he valued competence in others. He assured his friend the naval officer Leland Lovette, "I like anyone who works at his business hard and knows something about it. This even extends to prostitutes." He wasn't exaggerating. Among his unpublished memos in the New York Public Library, there's a character sketch of Manhattan's leading call-girl during the late 1920s, Kay Laurel. He wrote that he admired her for her unemotional and businesslike methods.

His personal code of conduct was based on the avoidance of extremes; its guiding light was common sense. He grew much disturbed when persons he took an interest in acted outrageously. For instance, largely because he esteemed their novels, he wanted to be friends with Theodore Dreiser, Scott

Fitzgerald, and Sinclair Lewis. Yet he never could reconcile himself to their excesses: to Dreiser's political posturing or his greedy sexuality; to Fitzgerald's drunkenness or his spendthrift ways; to Lewis's raucousness or his rackety personal life. We can detect Mencken's internal conflict in the uneasiness of his correspondence with each of them.

Appropriately, his closest friends turned out to be Aristotelians, whether they knew it or not. Like him they were mostly Baltimore bourgeois who led sane, systematic lives. Solid citizens, they behaved as decent husbands and fathers should, with boisterous humor as their safety valve. Professionally, they managed their careers with competence at the least and with great distinction at the best. Two members of Mencken's circle stood at the top in their fields: Raymond Pearl in biological statistics and Max Broedel in anatomical art. Whether eminent or not, all were comfortable in a material world; and all were what used to be called clubbable men.

For the most part, the characteristics I've described show up in Mencken's correspondence with his friends. And there's a considerable amount of it. Although they inhabited the same city, he vastly preferred to write them rather than to telephone. When he commented about them to others or mentioned them in print, the nature of the kinship between him and them was obvious. Take the case of Raymond Pearl. In Pearl's obituary, which Mencken prepared for the *Sun* of November 24, 1940, he remarked that he himself was "especially stimulated by [Pearl's] relentless and effective war upon bogus facts and false assumptions within his own field." Furthermore, when Pearl encountered quackery and exposed it in print, "the result was often a piece of satirical writing of the first caliber."

An adjunct way of looking at Mencken is to view him as an eighteenth-century man, a man of the Age of Reason (itself an Aristotelian age). August Mencken, who loved him as a brother but knew him better than anyone else, said he thought of him as fitted for the eighteenth rather than the twentieth century. He saw him as skeptical, far beyond the average of his day in many matters; and ready to speak his mind even at a cost, like Voltaire. He saw him as satirical, again like Voltaire, sardonically surveying the pomposities and pretenses around him and then deflating them; he saw him as someone gleefully devoted to clearing away the rubbish of antiquity and ambiguity. He saw him as someone who prized clarity in thinking and writing; who made it a habit to define his ideas and then express them so that their shape was unmistakable.

August interpreted his brother as an eighteenth-century man in other diverse but significant directions. Despite Mencken's Punch-and-Judy polemics, which brought him international fame mixed with notoriety, he made consideration of the individual a watchword. In that sense he was an old-style gentleman, as August noted, never attacking anyone who couldn't fight back. As co-editor of the *Smart Set* magazine and as editor of the *American Mercury*, he wrote the letters of rejection to unsuccessful authors with unvarying kindness, often easing the blow with a touch of wit. But his kindness wasn't maudlin. Nor was it aimed at the masses. Beneath his bourgeois good-fellowship lay an elitist who all his life distrusted the democratic horde. He was an eighteenth-century man likewise in his amiable but not exalted view of the female sex, a view which August shared. To women Mencken showed a courtesy too elaborate for our own taste.

Lastly, Mencken was an eighteenth-century man to August, and surely to us, in his wit. With rare exceptions, it avoided the waspishness of Alexander Pope's and the contempt for mankind displayed in Jonathan Swift's. It considered mankind amusing rather than contemptible. It specially savored "Boobus Americanus." Mencken stayed in America, he said more than once, for the same reason that a small boy attends the circus. If we want to define Mencken's wit we can turn to a classic passage in his book *Minority Report*, where he identifies wit as a sense of humor. First he admits its drawback: "It is almost as dangerous to an author as to a politician to show a sense of humor." Then he defines it: wit is "a capacity to discover hidden and surprising relations between apparently disparate things, to penetrate the hollowness of common assumptions, and to invent novel and arresting turns of speech."

Throughout his career, his wit warmed and animated his writing, giving it a gusto which is perhaps its chief virtue. Much of what he printed was judged to be wrong-headed—he himself advertised that he was a prejudiced man—but it often made delightful reading, and still does, mainly if not entirely because of its buoyant cleverness. We find the wit in abundance in his private letters as well as in his publications. It is at its best in the correspondence with the Broadway impresario Phil Goodman. Between them the two men created a raunchy, comic German-Jewish community which can still bring grins to the reader.

On the whole, Mencken was much more frequently good-humored than not. However, it's illuminating that two different things irked him to an un-Aristotelian extent because they did violence to the Aristotelian mode. They were the telephone and the wind. The telephone's jangling was peremptory and usually unexpected; the response to it had to be hasty. It intruded on privacy; it opened the door to outsiders, to interruptions. "How often," Mencken exclaims in *A Mencken Chrestomathy*, "a single call has blown up my whole evening's work!" Mencken's dislike for the wind was pronounced; several of his associates, including the drama critic George Jean Nathan and the novelist James M. Cain, said so at one time or another. The reason surely was that the wind all too easily reduced order to chaos. It ruffled things, blew them about. It was whimsical and played tricks. It would snatch a man's hat off his head, and nothing looked sillier than a grown man in pursuit of a wheeling, rolling fedora.

For better or worse, Mencken stayed an Aristotelian till he died. In his final book he dryly commented: "Moderation in all things. Not too much life. It often lasts too long."

In the letters which follow, here published for the first time, we encounter Mencken in a variety of aspects, among them several we haven't mentioned. The letters range from the significant to the trivial, but they all show us something. We see his wry devotion to politics—he relished nothing more than covering a national political convention—and his detestation of political reformers, which peaked in his overflowing animosity toward Franklin Delano Roosevelt. We observe his affection for Germany, which even Hitler couldn't kill. We notice his struggle against injustice for blacks. We discover his approval of capital punishment. We see his love of travel. And we note his scorn for the sentimentality of the Christmas season.

Mencken was a man of stout convictions who gave them a sprightly expression in these letters. I believe they accurately represent the many more letters in which we can detect the essential Mencken, pungent and provocative.

I'd like to add my opinion that this Mencken has much to offer today's readers, particularly the younger ones, because the life style he embodies is so moderate that it's extreme, so conservative that it's revolutionary. His assumptions are rarely ours; his values have largely been discarded. His personal reticence provides a striking contrast to our current attitude, which young people sum up in the forthright slogan "Let it all hang out." His Aristotelianism has grown utterly unfashionable; the watchword today is far from "Moderation." The appeal to reason is seldom made. When it is, we assume that it won't work. We're usually correct, for reason can be easily submerged in tides of emotion or rhetoric. The orderly, scheduled life is regarded with disdain. Competence in one's job has become meaningless to many, whether we're blue-collar workers or memo-signing managers. It's also an era when we take for granted that the individual's sphere must shrink while the government's must grow. Mencken's skepticism about reform, whether engineered by the government or by private groups, is ignored by leaders who labor to enforce human rights by law throughout the planet. Yet I don't believe that Mencken would react to any of these developments with outrage. He'd be far more apt to turn to his typewriter with a grin, call on the armory of his wit, and exuberantly expose "the hollowness of common assumptions."

Thanks are due to the Mercantile-Safe Deposit & Trust Company, as trustee for the Mencken estate, for permission to publish the letters in this volume, and to the following for access to the letters themselves: American Philosophical Society; Cornell University Library; Marcella duPont; Enoch Pratt Library; Ruth Goodman Goetz; New York Public Library; University of Pennsylvania Library; Princeton University Library; and Stanford University Libraries.

For help with the letters, thanks are due to Andrea Nash, Betsy Swart, and Dorothy Zachmann, all of the University of Maryland.

◇◇◇

SELECTED LETTERS

◇◇◇

To Louis Untermeyer

H. L. MENCKEN
1524 HOLLINS ST.
BALTIMORE.

[*July 7, 1915*]

Dear Louis:–

As usual, we are both right. That swimmers pome, printed in the Yale Review, was excellent stuff, but it was not what (at the present instant) we conceive to be Smart Set stuff. The sweet, soft note — and short, short! Love lyrics. Appasionata. The sough of the towel. The present stock will last at least two numbers; I bought a lot back in May and June. You mention checks? Do we owe you anything? If so, I'll make a squawk. The rule is to pay on acceptance.

What a lousy lot the English are, to be sure! How beautifully they prove the German contention that they are overripe, and ready for the plucking.

von und zu Mackensen.

Mencken first met Untermeyer when he was on the road selling cheap jewelry so that he could survive as a poet. For years, even after Untermeyer became the country's leading editor of poetry anthologies and an established poet himself, the two men played the comedy roles illustrated in this letter: Untermeyer as the salesman and Mencken as the 6th Avenue buyer.

"What a lousy lot": *The British were protesting the ex-*

pansion of the Germans' submarine campaigns in World War I as well as their introduction of gas warfare.

"von und zu Mackensen": *Mencken is signing the name of a German field marshal.*

(*Letter courtesy University of Virginia Library*)

◇◇◇

To Theodore Dreiser

H. L. MENCKEN
1524 HOLLINS ST.
BALTIMORE.

Dec. 23, 1916.

Dear Dreiser:

Your eloquent arguments in favor of the high artistic purpose and noble intent of your play do not convince me at all and neither do the encomiums of the critics you mention. Any man who gives unqualified praise to such a loose and shambling piece of work simply confesses that he is incompetent to express an opinion. I haven't the slightest fear that any intelligent publisher will publish it, but what I am afraid of is that you will fall into the hands of some petty publisher who is eager to capitalize your present predicament, and who will at once rank you, and forever, with the pornographic authors whose books are so beautifully advertised in The Masses. In other words, you stand in serious danger, through this play, of being definitely labeled as a mere shocker of boobs. If the piece showed any sound thought, if it contributed a single intelligent idea to the subject, if it were in any sense a work of art, I'd be hot for it and you well know it. But for the life of me I can see nothing in it save a boyish desire to manhandle a subject that is fit only for black headlines in yellow journals. Why you waste your time on such futile quasi-pathology when there are so many tempting things to be done, is more than I can make out. I have thought of various theories and one that survives is that you are addicted to some secret and terrible drug — perhaps, castor oil or bicarbonate of soda. Theoretically, to be sure, such subjects may be handled on the stage, and it is possible, as you say, that certain Yiddish dramatists may have actually tackled them. But no theory is worth a hoot in the face of an immovable fact, and here we have the immovable fact that the thing you treat would never be discussed intelligently and decently by those who saw and reviewed the play, but would be immediately seized on as pornography. I could write a parody on this play and perhaps make it a much better play at bottom, in which a surgical operation for haemorrhoids constituted the principal scene. This, too, might be art, but surely you do not argue that it would be suitable for Broadway or even for Christendom.

Your allegation that I am a moralist is as intelligent as your treatment of your subject in your play. No one knows better than you that I am nothing of the sort. I have written ten times as much against the moralists as you have and perhaps twice as much as any other American. What is more, I shall continue to do so! But there is nothing that enrages me more than an attempt to put over banal improprieties on the ground that they are profound and artistic. That is why I urged you to cut out a lot of stuff in "The 'Genius.'" Don't forget that there is just as much freedom of speech in "The Titan" and that I never made the slightest complaint against it. The difference lies in the fact that "The Titan" is a sincere and creditable work of art while "The 'Genius'" in large part seems to be mere drivel. I offer these opinions, not for their novelty or authority, but merely because you seem to invite them. If I believed, for instance, that you seriously regarded your play as a piece of work worthy of your reputation, I'd apply for your commitment to an insane asylum. You know at bottom that it is silly stuff, and no matter how much you denounce my view of it, you will have to admit in the end that I am right. Masters has not seen it as it stands and neither has Wilkinson. As for Powys, I can't understand his criteria of judgment and therefore have no interest in his opinion.

Once more 10,000 damns upon all such enterprises. You are the one man in America who can write novels fit for a civilized man to read and here you waste yourself upon enterprises not worth ten minutes of your time. After all, what do you say about your pervert? Nothing that every child doesn't know. And what do you show regarding the influence of his crime upon his family? Nothing that even a newspaper reporter couldn't imagine. The whole thing is a mass of platitudes, and if the crime at the bottom of it were simply larceny or piracy, not a soul would show any interest in it. One of the things you have got to realize is that a childish interest in such things as perversion is one of the most salient proofs of an essentially moral mind. One step more and you will be writing sex hygiene books for use in nunneries.

The dinner on Wednesday had better be called off. You may be sure that I would, under no circumstances, show the play to Nathan or even describe it to him accurately. He views you with a great deal of respect. Meanwhile, I surely hope you celebrate the birthday of our Redeemer in a truly Christian manner and that you do not commit the infamy of going to bed sober. If I don't see you before my departure, my chaplain will attend to the daily prayers for you. God knows when I'll get back; it may be a few weeks and it may not be for months.

Yours,

M

Though Mencken ranked as Dreiser's premier advocate among the literary critics, he was more than once exasperated by Dreiser's moronic lack of judgment. Here Dreiser—already fighting the censors about his new novel The "Genius" *with Mencken's potent help—shows his wilfulness. He proposes to publish a play,* The Hand of the Potter, *which deals with a young man who rapes and murders a child. Because Mencken has expostulated, Dreiser now accuses him of being a mere moralist, to Mencken a direr insult than being called a cannibal.*

(*Letter courtesy University of Pennsylvania Library*)

◇◇◇

To Marion Bloom

1524 Hollins Street
Baltimore, Md.
[*September 21, 1918*]
Saturday evening

Dear Marion:–

I hope George delivered the tooth-paste promptly. He promised on the Bible I stole in Pittsburgh. The French are such idiots that they print their Bibles in French. If you need one in plain American, unexpurgated, let me know.

You were very sweet and nice yesterday evening. Somehow I came away full of a feeling that we'd meet again very soon. Maybe I am wrong, after all, about the length of the war. It may blow up suddenly. What I want you to do is to go ahead on the assumption that it will end soon and that we'll meet soon. New York, to me, is simply full of you. I'll be seeing your tracks everywhere, and wishing this and that — you know the fancies of a romantic young man. I shall dine in state now and then at the Wop's, and drink ceremonial seidels at Luchow's. Ah, that I were less windblown and wheezy, and could make love in true waltz time. As it is, you have it all.

I kiss both hands.

Yours,
H.

Beginning about three years before this, Mencken became close friends with a winsome Washington writer named Marion Bloom, so close that they spoke of marrying. When the United States entered World War I, she volunteered for nursing duty with the Army. Here she's about to embark in New York for service in France. No surviving letters of Mencken show more affection than this one.

(Letter courtesy Enoch Pratt Library)

◇◇◇

To Fielding H. Garrison

Baltimore
August 9, 1919.

Dear Col. Garrison:

A week or so ago you mentioned W. I. Thomas' "Source Book for Social Origins," and gave the University of Chicago Press as the publisher. I do not find the book in the latest catalogue of the Press. If you have a copy by you will you please take a look at the imprint? Probably some other university press prints it. I want to get a copy. I'll certainly be delighted to have Parkes-Weber's "Death in Art," if you can get me one without trouble. But don't bother.

As for my "Nietzsche," there is a good deal in it that Friedrich never heard of. Some time ago a philosophical man of

God in New England, Salter by name, published a very exhaustive tome on Nietzsche, and flayed me for my interpolations. But I do not repine. On the one hand, I was trying to write, not an exact text-book, but a volume that the average American would read and could understand, and so I tried to translate the thing into terms of his common concerns. And on the other hand, I was working out my own ideas for future use. Even so, those ideas were plainly *based* on Nietzsche; without him, I'd never have come to them. Last autumn, translating "Der Antichrist," I felt like a man going back to school. I hadn't read it for ten years. It is an amazing piece of work — wild, inchoate, deliberately offensive, and yet strangely sound.

It often seems to me that the chief merit of Nietzsche was in his manner rather than in his matter. He introduced a forthright style of criticism that blew up the old philosophical pussy-footing. When he came to the conclusion that a man was an ass, he said so plainly, however eminent the man. He constantly used the argument ad hominem, and with immense effect. (It is now at the bottom of Freudism.) He shook up all Europe, and it was a shaking up that was needed. Altogether, he was a first-rate man, though unfortunately somewhat Polish and hence partly dippy — and infested by spirochetae to boot. No doubt the spirochetae helped to make him. Genuine thinking is a sort of toxemia; the superstition monging of the mob is merely vegetative. I incline to think, with William James, that 98.6 is the wrong temperature for mental activity. It suits the liver, the stomach, and perhaps the gonads, but it is either too hot or too cool for the cerebrum.

Let me know about the Burlesques book and Europe After 8.15. If you ever feel like a novel, try "The Moon and Sixpence" by W. Somerset Maugham. It is the story of Gauguin, the French painter, capitally done. I put you down for another visit when the weather is cooler. From August 20 to September 15 I am usually soured by pollinosis. But after that I buck up.

Sincerely yours,
H. L. Mencken

A medical-corps colonel, Garrison had recently begun exchanging books with Mencken, and the two men were on their way to a closer acquaintance. Here we see Mencken's candid comment on his relation to Nietzsche.

(Letter transcription courtesy New York Public Library)

◇◇◇

To Herbert Parrish

H. L. MENCKEN
1524 HOLLINS ST.
BALTIMORE.

January 3rd. [1923?]

Dear Mr. Parrish:–

This story is the best managed of all that I have seen, but again I doubt that it is a Smart Set story. In detail it is splendid, but in essence it belongs to a standard type. I think, however, that you will sell it easily. Try it on Munsey's, Snappy Stories, Ainslee's and Short Stories.

Surely I'll be glad to see the novel. It sounds very promising. Maybe we can use it as a novelette. In any case I'll be delighted to go through it.

Believe me, I *do* believe that I have made a discovery in you. You write very well indeed, and know how to manage a story. I certainly hope you do not give up; no man should look for success until he has written at least 25 stories. I bought a story lately from a man who had been trying for three years. He is now a journeyman and will go ahead rapidly. Your fundamental error at the moment is this: you are trying to write stories of external intrigue, whereas your own interest lies chiefly in internal conflict. Once you apply the same humor, style and keen observation that you are now lavishing on plots (that is, mere anecdotes) to the elaboration of psychological situations and dilemmas, you will find yourself. I made a suggestion about your last story. Why not try to carry it out? Frankly, I am interested because the Smart Set wants the inward sort of story, and I think you could do it splendidly. So it is not mere politeness.

Sincerely yours,
H.L.M.

Mencken respected diligence and determination; Parrish showed both. As a result, this aspiring author and Episcopal clergyman finally made his way into Mencken's American Mercury. *When Mencken in 1930 was about to marry Sara Haardt, who insisted on a church wedding, he turned with a touch of desperation to Parrish. Parrish didn't fail him. He came from New Jersey to officiate in full style.*

(*Letter courtesy Enoch Pratt Library*)

◇◇◇

To Sara Powell Haardt

Baltimore, November 12, 1923

Dear Miss Haardt:–

The *Mercury* is down with 35 different diseases, all apparently fatal. But I'll surely be back by Saturday a week. What of lunch together then? I suggest avoiding the wop until he returns to normalcy. There is a marvellous beerhouse in Saratoga street, highly respectable outwardly but with superb Dunkles on tap. Or let us try the Southern Hotel, where a loud orchestra plays Massenet at meals and the drummers entertain the lady white-goods buyers. Or the Rennert, where the ceilings are 18 feet high but the food is excellent.

Yours,
H. L. Mencken

In May 1923, Mencken was lured into addressing a magazine-writing class at Goucher. Afterwards the professor in charge took him and two young ladies to supper. One was Sara Haardt, then an instructor in English. Mencken liked her and soon, in his humorous offhand way, was courting her. In evidence: their Saturday luncheons grew frequent.

"*The* Mercury": *Plans for publishing the magazine had been announced the previous month.*

"Drummers": *Traveling salesmen.*

(*Letter transcription courtesy Princeton University Library*)

◇◇◇

To Philip Goodman

H. L. MENCKEN
1524 HOLLINS ST.
BALTIMORE.

June 13th [1927]

Dear Phil:–

Eighty head of movie gals, bound for the Shriners' convention at Atlantic City, have been passing through Baltimore. They leave today. I'll be glad to get my pants on again.

If you used only one can of malt you will not get beer, but a weak variety of mule piss. The current malts are all feeble. I use three cans to eight gallons.

The large view of me is under way.

Yours,
H. L. Mencken

A lover of high living, Goodman for twenty years was one of Mencken's most frequent companions when he was in New York. Among the many things they had in common was the ambition to brew a drinkable beer all by themselves.

(*Letter courtesy Ruth Goodman Goetz*)

◇◇◇

To Bernard DeVoto

THE AMERICAN MERCURY
730 FIFTH AVENUE
NEW YORK

April 17, 1930.

Dear Mr. DeVoto:

My apologies, in the first place, for my delay in handing you this manuscript, and in the second place for its general badness. The simple truth is that when I read the book in detail I found myself less interested in it than I expected to be. In consequence, writing about it turned out to be a somewhat laborious business. I am afraid that that fact shows itself in the manuscript. If you think it is inadequate, please don't hesitate to send it back. I can imagine half a dozen other men who'd do the thing much better. I am perfectly serious here.

My pride of authorship is very slight, and I hate to see bad things get into print.

My best thanks again.

Sincerely yours,
H. L. Mencken

Trapped by his respect for the rising young author and editor Bernard DeVoto, Mencken agreed to write an introduction to James Fenimore Cooper's book The American Democrat *for a series DeVoto was editing. This letter shows Mencken's misgivings about the result and also his modesty about his own writing. They were unnecessary: Mencken even on Cooper was tonic.*

(*Letter courtesy Stanford University Library*)

◇◇◇

To Philip Goodman

H. L. MENCKEN
704 CATHEDRAL ST.
BALTIMORE

January 4th [1932]

Dear Phil:–

Aye, it is two years since we walked in the Tweeleries and the Pally Royal, and drank all that magnificent Kulmbacher, and got down that kolossale pink fish at the Rain Peeduck. And I wish to God we were at it now. And, if you ask me frankly, I believe we'll live to do it again. But the next time, as you say, we must move on to Munich. Joe Hergesheimer didn't like the town. Imagine THAT!

Now for a personal matter. My Uncle Otto, as you may have heard, had a natural child — a quite normal slip, for he was just emerging from puberty and the servant-girl, Freda, was a healthy, full-blooded, well-built wench. Their rooms adjoined, and nature took its course. My grandfather did the handsome thing by Freda. She was permitted to carry on her kitchen duties until within two hours of her confinement, and after her delivery she received a pension of $18 a month. Two years later, when she married Gustav Bergmann, she received a dot of $75. The child, a boy, grew up, went to school, was articled to the old Hanseatic firm of Gerhardt & Mumm, importers, and rose to be head bookkeeper. At 23 he married a virtuous girl named Blassmeyer, and they had, in due course, a daughter Geraldine.

It is of this daughter that I write. She is now 17, and somewhat wild. As her mother says, she thinks of nothing but dancing and fixing up. She has a distinct flair for the drama, and has appeared in half a dozen productions. Last Winter she played Yum Yum in the Westfalische Turnverein's notable production of "The Mikado." They say she can act anything. She appears under the name of Geraldine d'Arcy, and has become quite well known in lodge and club circles in Baltimore. But as you know, there is no future for a female histrion in a provincial town. She may get two or three parts a Winter, but there is much intrigue and backbiting, the papers vouchsafe only formal notices, and every young buck believes that because she is an actress she is easy meat.

Thus Geraldine's thoughts turn toward Hollywood, as you may well suspect. She is somewhat over the average height — five feet, eleven — but she is well proportioned, has a loud contralto voice, and can sing, dance and grimace. Her weight I should put at 165 lbs. Hair: real blonde. Complexion: ruddy. What I want to ask you is whether you think there is opportunity for her in the films, and if so, whether you are willing to speak to Schulberg or Louis B. Mayer in her behalf. Don't answer offhand, but give the matter thought. Are hill-horses coming back? If not, poor Geraldine must marry, and bear patiently the immemorial burdens of womenkind. But if her bulk is not against her, then she may have an honorable and even splendid career before her. Let me hear from you confidentially.

I'd approach the magnates myself, but it would be fatal. My mail would be filled with solicitations for encomiums of this and that film. Elder Hays would bombard me with questionnaires. I'd even, perhaps, have to appear before committees of Congress. But you are in the profession, and can get to the right ears without compromising yourself. I ask only one thing, and that is that you make no pass at Geraldine in case your good offices prevail and she comes to Hollywood.

Sara is in a hubbub about the W. Indian trip. She has never been to sea. I am giving her false directions for finding me in the smoke-room. We sail Saturday the 9th per Norddeutscher-lloydschnell-postluxusexpressdampfer Columbus. A swell boat.

Yours,
M

Goodman was struggling to establish himself in Hollywood after the Depression ended his career as a New York impresario. Mencken wrote him more often than usual, not only because he enjoyed doing so but because he hoped to hearten Goodman with his low-comedy routines.

(Letter courtesy Ruth Goodman Goetz)

◇◇◇

To the [George Schafer-H.C.] Pfaff Cigar Co.

October 26, 1932.

The Schaefer-Pfaff Cigar Co.,
Baltimore, Md.

Gentlemen:

Will you please send me 300 Uncle Willies, in 50s, without bands?

Sincerely yours,
(Signed) H. L. Mencken

These long, strong cigars remained Mencken's favorite over the decades.

(Letter transcription courtesy Enoch Pratt Library)

◇◇◇

To Philip Goodman

H. L. MENCKEN
704 CATHEDRAL ST.
BALTIMORE

June 22, 1933.

Dear Phil:

I spent the week-end in Pittsburgh with my brother. His daughter is graduating from high school next week, and heading for college in the Fall. I found that the Pittsburgh region shows a considerable degree of recovery. The steel mills are reopening one by one, and the coal mines and coke ovens are following. The railroad car-loadings show a steady increase, and already the depression seems to be passing off in the Black Country. As I wrote to you several weeks ago, there is something almost approaching a boom in the South.

The other day going to New York I met Ralph Hanes, of Winston-Salem, on the train. He and his brothers are textile men, and he himself runs a mill devoted to shrinking and dyeing cloth. He told me that he has been running it day and night for several weeks past. The truth is, of course, that the late depression was precisely like any other, despite all the insane whooping of bogus experts of all sorts. It lasted, like all the rest, precisely three and a half years. The low point was reached last Summer, and there has been a steady recovery ever since. It will probably be a couple of years before anything like normalcy is restored, but after that we may have a genuine boom, especially if there is a war in Europe.

Some time ago I dug up an article by Prince Kropotkin, the Russian radical, printed in 1885. He proved absolutely that the depression then prevailing was of a new and unprecedentedly bad kind, and that there could never be any recovery from it. His argument was so strikingly similar to the nonsense printed by Stuart Chase and other such quacks during the past few years that I sent it to Hamilton Owens, of the Baltimore *Evening Sun*, and he reprinted it verbatim. No doubt one could go even further back in the history of economic quackery and find precisely similar arguments.

It is good news that you are coming back early in August. You will find New York at its best, with the temperature running between 95 and 100, and the relative humidity playing around 90. I assume that when you stored your furniture you did not throw away your electric fans. So far, Manhattan Island has not developed any really pleasant drinking places. The best beer that I have so far encountered I drank at the Longchamps restaurant in 57th Street. Lüchow has a Würzburger on draft, but the high duty and the depreciation of the dollar forced him to charge fifty cents a Seidel for it, and that is too much. You will tell me, of course, that Piel's light is bad beer, but that will be only your joke. Find some place where it is decently served from the wood, and it will gradually win you.

So far, the show business does not seem to be recovering, but that will follow, no doubt, anon. Book publishing is showing a certain lift, and even the magazine business is not as bad as it was. We open with a page advertisement of Anheuser-Busch in August, and have a contract for the rest of the year. Some of the others, I suppose, will follow.

Yours,
M

Not suffering much himself, Mencken found it hard to believe that the Depression was really bad.

(*Letter courtesy Ruth Goodman Goetz*)

◇◇◇

To David Kemper

H. L. MENCKEN
704 CATHEDRAL ST.
BALTIMORE

July 7th [1933]

Dear Mr. Kemper:–

It goes without saying that I agree with you about Hitler, and I have said pretty much what you say in dozens of letters to German friends. It is depressing to see the good work of the years since the war blown up by so preposterous a mountebank. My hope is that he and his hoodlums will pass quickly, and that the monarchy will be restored. It offers the best chance, I believe, for the reliberalization of the country. Democracy is too unsafe for so exposed a spot.

If you have been following my articles in The Evening Sun you will have noticed that I have not discussed German affairs for ten years past. The Republic there interests me very little, and I can't think of it as permanent. It would be laboring the obvious to denounce Hitlerism. Moreover, it is surely done sufficiently by other hands.

My belief is that the boycott of all things German proposed by Rabbi Wise and other such fools is very ill advised. It is bound to fail, and there are better ways to achieve its ostensible end. My view of Wise is precisely that of President Roosevelt, expressed plainly eight or nine months ago. If he keeps on ranting he will only start an anti-Semitic movement in this country.

All this is for your private eye. My best thanks for your letter.

Sincerely yours,
H. L. Mencken

A Baltimore dry-goods merchant, Kemper had written Mencken the day before, noting that in Mencken's Sunpaper *pieces he'd seen nothing about the Nazis or Hitler. Because he believed Mencken to be a friend of justice and a defender of the weak and poor, he wondered if Mencken shouldn't attack the Hitler regime.*

(Letter courtesy Enoch Pratt Library)

◇◇◇

To A. C. Anderson

November 9, 1933.

A. C. Anderson, Esq.,
Lawton, N.D.

Dear Mr. Anderson:

Unfortunately, I must report that your arguments leave me unmoved. Certainly it is fair to hold the farmers responsible for the extravagant imbecility of their chosen leaders, and certainly it is preposterous to call teaching in the public schools "a noble art". Its true calibre, I think, is shown by the utterances of the great whales of the profession, as set forth in the Journal of the American Educational Association. I have been reading that publication for years, and I can't remember ever encountering anything in it that was much above the level of a harangue by a Methodist preacher. It supported Prohibition very violently until the last election and then dropped it with immense celerity.

I am willing to grant that public schools are necessary, but I see no reason why they should be converted into huge political machines ruinous to the taxpayer, or why the persons operating them should be permitted to poison the young with all sorts of puerile hocus pocus. It seems to me that the pedagogues of the country will be well advised if they get back to their proper business as promptly as possible and cease to cherish so many delusions of grandeur.

Sincerely yours,
(Signed) H. L. Mencken

Farmers and schoolteachers were among the targets Mencken found most alluring. He derided the farmers as rustic clowns and the teachers as overpaid idiots.

(*Letter transcription courtesy New York Public Library*)

◇◇◇

To Broadus Mitchell

December 7, 1933.

Dr. Broadus Mitchell
Johns Hopkins University,
Baltimore, Md.

Dear Dr. Mitchell:

I think the time has come when some effort should be made to smoke out the big-wigs who have been giving aid and comfort to the Eastern Shore lynchers. To that end I suggest a mild and discreet protest against both lynching itself and the abdication of the Eastern Shore courts, to be issued as soon as the Princess Anne case is officially shelved. I suggest presenting copies of this personally to every stuffed shirt in Baltimore, including especially to our venerable friend at the Johns Hopkins and the directors of the Associations of Commerce. I couldn't undertake this business myself, for my connection with it would offer the man approached a good excuse to refuse to sign. Your own name would probably affect them in much the same way, but I think they'd be forced to speak up if they were approached, say, by Dr. Lovejoy, the Rev. Peter Ainslie and one other completely Christian and reputable man. I propose that the names of those who refuse to sign be published. Certainly it is high time that we demanded a showdown from the prominenti who have been giving covert encouragement to the lynchers and above all to the Eastern Shore judges.

If the plan seems to you to be feasible and you can induce Dr. Lovejoy to undertake it, I'll be glad to suggest some names. Meanwhile, it lies between ourselves.

Yours,
(Signed) H. L. Mencken

In fall 1931 the lynching of a black man in Salisbury on Maryland's Eastern Shore had brought forth Mencken's most biting articles, including a Swiftian classic, "The Eastern Shore Kultur." Now, two years later, a second lynching had taken place, this time in Princess Anne. Again he criticized the Shore bitterly in public. But he did more; in private he tried to rally Baltimore's leaders against lynching. This letter shows how he went about it.

Broadus Mitchell, of the Hopkins Political Economy Department, was probably the University's leading activist; the "venerable friend" was the University's president, Joseph Ames; A. O. Lovejoy, of the Hopkins Philosophy Department, was another noted activist; and Ainslie was a Baltimore clergyman and advocate of good causes including racial toleration.

(*Letter transcription courtesy Enoch Pratt Library*)

◇◇◇

To Raymond Pearl

The Continental-Savoy
Cairo

March 15th [1934]

Dear Raymond:–

As for Egypt, it is yours with my compliments. The air is full of desert dust and the streets are full of thieves. All the bargemen and porters who used to practise at Naples have now moved to Port Saïd. And here in Cairo, in the block between this hotel and Shepheard's, there are at least 200 guides offering to show all comers "a boy fok a gerl en a gerl fok a boy". The ruins could be worse, but two days of them are enough. Even the Museum is tiresome after an hour or two. The cuisine of the hotels is militantly English. We have been eating at a Greek restaurant — very good seafood and capital vin ordinaire at 9 piastres a carafe.

The Holy Land, on the contrary, turned out to be swell. I have never seen more beautiful scenery, and everywhere there are good roads, and in Jerusalem a really first-class hotel. The Jews have spent millions developing some fine farm colonies. The Arabs retreat to the hills and wait. Armageddon is very handy.

The cruise has been pleasant, but we have made too many stops. We called at every port in Africa from Casablanca in Morocco to Port Said. Always the same Arabs and the same desert dust. Between Tripoli and Beiroot a dust storm came out from Libya, 200 miles to the south, and dam nigh suffocated us. It lasted 36 hours, and when it was over the whole ship was white. This was naturally bad for tender sinuses, and the ship's doctor has been doing a landoffice business ever since. Those who went up the Nile came back bitten by flies, fleas, scorpions, lizards, etc. The professing Christians seemed to suffer worst.

Now we head homeward, and along the European shore. We should be back in N.Y. by the Europa by April 5th. On the 7th I hope to be in my old stall at Schellhase's. The ship's beer is not bad, but it left Bremen two months ago, and begins to be shaken. Ashore I have had nothing but bad stuff in quart bottles.

As in duty bound I humbly pray, etc.,

Yours,
M

Early in 1934 Mencken took Sara on a Mediterranean cruise. Here he reports on it to his friend Raymond Pearl, the celebrated biometrician at Johns Hopkins.

(*Letter courtesy American Philosophical Society*)

◇◇◇

To Leland P. Lovette

March 4, 1935.

My dear Commander:

It was grand to hear from you again, and your picture of morning in the tropics almost made me bust into sobs. Well do I recall the first time I ever saw a palm tree. I had arrived off the little port of Port Antonio on the northern coast of Jamaica about 4 A.M. I was aboard a nine hundred ton banana boat just at dawn. The captain invited me to go ashore. If I live to be three thousand years old I'll never forget the sounds and colors of that tropical morning. In those days I was stuck in Lafcadio Hearn's Two Years in the French West Indies, and so I was well primed to receive a powerful impression. Certainly it left a deep mark behind it.

The American Mercury has now been sold to two young fellows who promise to restore it, and what is more to make money with it. One of them is Paul Palmer, who has married money and has a considerable amount of editorial experience behind him. The other is Spivak, who has been business manager during the past year. The damage done during Angoff's editorship will pass off rapidly. People seldom remember such things. I have been a sort of innocent by-stander in the matter myself. I sold all my stock to Knopf six years ago and have absolutely no voice in the magazine since my retirement as editor, but I am naturally somewhat interested.

My guess about the Philippines is that the Japs will gobble them within a year after the last American soldier leaves. I see no way to hold the Japanese Vormarsch in Asia. It appears to be ordained by God personally and so it must go on. The chances of a war between Japan and the United States have always seemed to me to be rather remote. The Japanese would not be fools enough to tackle us if our hands were untied. They'll wait until we are engaged elsewhere and then grab what they want. This is what they tried to do during the World War. To be sure, they were forced later to disgorge, but certainly they didn't disgorge all. Probably everything they really wanted is still in their hands.

But here I am discussing with my grandmother the art of sucking eggs. When you get back I shall incarcerate you in a room long enough to hear what has really been going on in the East. If you protest that your oath binds you to reticence, I shall ply you with alcohol until you forget it.

What a pleasure it will be to see you at 704 again! My wife has been making good progress, but at the moment she is suffering a little set-back. I don't think it is serious, but the chiropractors swarm into the house. If they don't restore her promptly I shall have at them with artillery.

My brother begs to be remembered.

Yours,
(Signed) H. L. Mencken

(Letter transcription courtesy New York Public Library)

◇◇◇

To Roscoe Peacock

H. L. MENCKEN
704 CATHEDRAL ST.
BALTIMORE

August 3, 1935

Dear Peacock:

It seems to me that Roosevelt is an even worse quack than the Communists. He is talking just as loudly as they are about soaking the rich, and he knows better than they do that it will yield him nothing. His public utterances for the past month or two have been pure demagoguery. I can recall no American president who was a more transparent fraud. Now I hear from Washington that he is preparing for a violent onslaught upon the opposition newspapers. Part of that onslaught is embodied in the McCormack bill. It seems to me to be a thoroughly dishonest and vicious piece of legislation. Aimed ostensibly at Communists, it will actually invade the rights of all of us, and especially of those of us who are not deceived by the Roosevelt blather.

Obviously enough, the American Civil Liberties Union is largely in the hands of Communists and other such fools. Nevertheless, it seems to me to be doing a useful work. I don't belong to it and never have, but I have often supported it in its fights for free speech. It is a tragedy that such fights have to be carried on mainly by radicals. The lawyers who ought to rise to the defense of the Constitution are usually magnificently silent when some political mountebank tries to invade the Bill of Rights.

Yours,
H. L. Mencken

Peacock, who ran a magazine subscription agency, was perhaps the most strident of Mencken's many conservative friends.

(Letter courtesy Princeton University Library)

◇◇◇

To Theodore Dreiser

The HOLLENDEN
CLEVELAND, OHIO
August 15th [1936]

Dear Dreiser:–

Your letter reaches me here. I am doing the Coughlin convention — an inspiring sight to us old sons of Holy Church. Imagine 9000 morons crowded into one hall, and all of them bawling.

I'll probably be engaged on such jobs until October 1st, at the least, and maybe until election day. New ones are popping up all the time, and you know how I enjoy them. Thus, if I wait on you at Mt. Kisco, it will most likely be well after October 1st. More of this anon. My very best thanks.

I have half made up my mind to vote for Landon. He is far less dumb than he looks. I had a long talk with him in Topeka and came away convinced that he is a shrewd fellow and would make a very fair President. He realizes that people will be voting in November either for or against Roosevelt, and he plans to take every advantage of the fact that he is Roosevelt's complete antithesis. Thus he will not attempt any tenor oratory, nor will he pretend to be a wizard. He believes the people are tired of wizards, and I agree with him. He is a Pennsylvania Dutchman, and shows all the stigmata of the race. That is, he works hard, says little, and pays his debts.

Yours,
M

The year 1936 offered Mencken a bonus: four national political conventions to attend instead of the ordinary two. Besides covering the Republican and Democratic conventions for the

Sunpapers, *he reported on the cavortings of the followers of Dr. Francis Townsend, the apostle of old-age benefits, and of the Rev. Charles Coughlin, the activist Catholic priest and radio personality.*

(Letter courtesy University of Pennsylvania Library)

◇◇◇

To Edith Sheridan

May 17, 1937.

Miss Edith Sheridan,
152 E. 28th St.
New York

Dear Miss Sheridan:

On the whole I am inclined to favor capital punishment—at least for crimes against strangers. The late Judge Bausman, of Portland, Oregon, a very competent judge, once proposed that our categories of murder be revised. He argued that the punishment for murders which any rational persons could imagine committing under the circumstances should be made relatively mild. But that criminals who kill strangers for gain should be put to death as quickly as possible. I am inclined to believe that this notion is a good one. Certainly there is no rational reason for sparing the lives of professional and incorrigible criminals. Many of them are young, and when they are sent to prison for life the taxpayer is saddled with their keep for long years. It is much cheaper and more sanitary to put them to death at once. Moreover, executing them gives the public a feeling that something has really been done to them. When it hears of them being imprisoned it always assumes that they will get out soon or late.

Sincerely yours,
(Signed) H. L. Mencken

Criminal justice was one of Mencken's interests. Several Baltimore judges were among his friends and correspondents, and half a dozen convicts received his help because he liked their writing, some of which he published. But no one could accuse him of wanting to coddle criminals.

(*Letter transcription courtesy New York Public Library*)

◇◇◇

To Alf M. Landon

November 22, 1940

Alf M. Landon, Esq.,
Topeka, Kansas.

My dear Governor:

I needn't tell you that it was pleasant to hear from you. If I were a wholly free agent I'd hop a freight at once and come out to Topeka to eat both the fried rabbit and the hog meat. As it is, I can only hope and pray that there will be something left by the time I am able to make the trip. I can imagine nothing pleasanter than sitting down with you for a palaver.

My own feeling about the Republican party apparently differs somewhat from yours. I believe that it has been injured mainly not by standing too far aloof from the New Deal but by embracing it too fervently. In brief, I think it can succeed only as a genuine opposition and there can be no genuine opposition that does not directly attack the New Deal's various schemes to buy proletarian votes with public money. Obviously, the rights of labor must be maintained and even augmented, but I don't believe that labor deserves some of the privileges that the New Deal has given it. If you have ever attended a trial before the National Labor Relations Board you will know what I mean. The proceedings are inconceivably unfair. The employer apparently has no rights whatsoever. I believe that this is a bad idea and that it is bound to produce bitter reprisals. Every time the Republican party encourages it, even indirectly, it prepares the way for its own destruction. Soon or late we are bound to have a vigorous conservative party, for the great majority of Americans are still probably conservative at heart. I think that the Republican party's chance lies in organizing that movement. In order to do so it must tackle the New Deal much more vigorously than it has in the past.

These, of course, are the ideas of an old man, now fast approaching Hell. I have been a Democrat all my life and still incline toward democratic ideas. In the days of the Coolidge-Hoover prosperity I bawled and hollered against it with the best of them and I am still convinced that I was right. But I am still convinced that giving the proletariat large and unfair advantages is quite as injurious as giving the same advantages to the plutocracy. If democracy means anything whatsoever, it means equality between man and man. That massive fact has been forgotten by both parties.

Are you likely to be in these wilds at any time in the near future? If so, I surely hope you give me a chance to see you.

Sincerely yours,
(Signed) H. L. Mencken

This letter is one of the most balanced statements of Mencken's political position.

(*Letter transcription courtesy New York Public Library*)

◇◇◇

WESTERN UNION

1940 Dec 23

MRS ALFRED V DUPONT=

ALL THE USUAL CHRISTMAS BLAH=

H L M.

BLAH.

Mencken had met Marcella and Alfred duPont when he took Sara on a Caribbean cruise in early 1932. They found Marcella charming, and after Sara's death the friendship between him and Marcella grew close. She came to share some of his prejudices, among them the one against Christmas.

(Telegram courtesy Marcella duPont)

◇◇◇

To George Jean Nathan

H. L. MENCKEN
1524 HOLLINS ST.
BALTIMORE.

March 17, 1941

Dear George:

Prior's beer is completely unknown to me. I'll certainly get down a couple of vats of it the next time I come within its orbit. There is a swell beer here in Baltimore called National Premium, but unhappily it has begun to degenerate since the supply of Bohemian hops was cut off. American hops I simply can't abide. They seem to me to show distinct traces of Coca Cola.

You missed a charming party at Schellhase's last night. It was Schellhase's birthday, and many members of the intelligentsia gathered to celebrate it. Schellhase made an excellent speech, though I should add that it was somewhat long. The first two hours were devoted to a really remarkable review of the life and times of Bismarck. After that his discourse became less instructive.

Yours,
M

Mencken had forced his friend and former co-editor of the Smart Set *out of the co-editorship of the* American Mercury *after its initial year, 1924. Although the friendship withered, Nathan refused to admit it; so occasional correspondence with Mencken continued. By the time of this note they were meeting again at intervals as well as exchanging letters.*

(*Letter courtesy Cornell University Library*)

To Joseph Katz

H. L. MENCKEN
1524 HOLLINS ST
BALTIMORE-23

May 20, 1946

Dear Joe:

The only thing that consoles me about the present pestilence of jobholders is that I am occasionally in receipt of the forms used in England. The bureaucracy there has had a long start, and in consequence has developed a superb technique. If any Englishman wants anything so trivial as a pane of glass, he must make out a form comparable to an income tax return.

I hope, but don't predict, that the American people will one day raise up in moral indignation and shoot at least two million jobholders.

God help us all.

Yours,
M

A Baltimore advertising executive, Katz admired Mencken and was an avid collector of his writings.

(*Letter courtesy Enoch Pratt Library*)

In November 1948 a massive stroke ended Mencken's reading and writing, although he lived on for another seven years.

H. L. Mencken
A MEMOIR

Alfred A. Knopf

I knew Mencken for more than forty years, intimately for well over thirty. During all of this time I published his books and I could describe our relationship as author and publisher in just a single word: perfect. He was the ideal author, for he believed that while his job was to write his books it was mine to publish them. We both had a high regard for competence. He was probably the most competent writer I have ever dealt with, and he respected my competence as a publisher of books—especially his.

I went to Baltimore in late 1913 and first saw Henry in the offices of the *Sun*, for which he was writing a rather celebrated column, "The Free Lance." As was his habit, he was sitting in his shirt sleeves at his typewriter with a corncob pipe in his mouth and his glasses probably raised to his forehead. Henry recalled that meeting twenty-seven years later when he wrote, "What we talked of chiefly when we met was

---

Alfred A. Knopf has published books under his own imprint since 1915.

his grandiose scheme to bring out a complete edition of Joseph Conrad at the cost and risk of 'The Captain Barabbas' for whom I worked as 'only a humble deckhand.' "

I think we took to each other at once, and as I was beginning to consider establishing my own firm I thought of Henry as a likely author to join me. He had already published *George Bernard Shaw: His Plays* in 1905 (possibly the first book on Shaw by an American), *The Philosophy of Friedrich Nietzsche* in 1908, *The Gist of Nietzsche, Arranged by Henry L. Mencken,* in 1910, and an amusing trifle, *The Artist: A Drama Without Words,* in 1912. All of these bore the imprint of John W. Luce and Company in Boston, a small firm owned by Harrison Hale Schaff, an old friend of Henry's. As far as I know, these books went out of print in due course and were not reprinted.

John Lane, then a very distinguished English publisher, had an American branch whose list included Mencken, George Jean Nathan, Willard Huntington Wright, and Theodore Dreiser's *The "Genius."* Henry published the following books with Lane: *A Book of Burlesques* (1916), *A Little Book in C Major* (*Opus 11*) (1916), and *Europe After 8^{15}* (1914), of which Nathan and Wright were co-authors. Lane also brought out at least two books by Wright, who had preceded Mencken as editor of the *Smart Set* and was at the time very much a kindred spirit. (Later, in a new incarnation, he became S. S. Van Dine, the enormously successful writer of the popular Philo Vance detective stories.) Before this, in 1910, Henry Holt & Company had published *Men Versus The Man,* a correspondence between Rives La Monte, Socialist, and H. L. Mencken, Individualist.

When Henry and Nathan became editors of the *Smart Set* in 1908, they established a close and friendly association that lasted for a great many years. By 1916 they decided to come over to us, and next year we issued *A Book of Prefaces* and

Mr. George Jean Nathan Presents. We did not publish Mencken again until two years later. He had a great friend in a maverick advertising man, Philip Goodman, whom I never met except with Mencken and then very casually. Goodman had a hankering for the publishing business and an idea of selling vast quantities of books in drug stores, and it was over his imprint that *In Defense of Women* and *Damn!* appeared in 1918, as did Nathan's *A Book Without a Title.* However, Goodman had no organization, his publishing venture failed, and he turned to theatrical production, where he became very successful. We took over his stock and in 1919 reissued *In Defense of Women* and *Damn!* (under the title *A Book of Calumny*), as well as *A Book Without a Title.**

The Mencken-Nathan partnership was in full swing at this time and in 1920, 1921, and 1927 we published different editions of *The American Credo* signed by both men as well as, in the earlier year, a play, *Heliogabalus: A Buffoonery in Three Acts,* in a limited edition which was quickly sold out. We were able to have printed and to sell a limited number of copies on fine Japan vellum signed by both authors.

The year 1919 marked a watershed in Henry's writing career, for in that year we published the first version of *The American Language*—a subject which would engage him busily for the rest of his active life. The first edition was an octavo of fewer than four hundred pages, limited to fifteen hundred copies. To our surprise, the edition sold out immediately;

* Henry and Philip Goodman remained warm friends for many years. But when Goodman died of a heart attack in 1940, years after the breakup of his friendship with Mencken, he had not for some years been well off. Henry, though he tried, never succeeded in getting anything from Goodman to publish in the *American Mercury.* Just before he died, however, Goodman had completed a book of reminiscences of Philadelphia. The following year his daughter, Ruth Goetz, sent Henry the manuscript. He was so delighted by the memoir that he forwarded it to us and we published it under the title *Franklin Street.*

and the second edition, greatly revised, which ran to five hundred pages, did not appear until 1921, and it too sold out quickly. This edition was a monstrous piece of bookmaking, printed on outrageously heavy paper. But Henry had written me, "All I ask is that you make 'The American Language' good and thick. It is my secret ambition to be the author of a book weighing at least five pounds."

By now I began to believe we had a classic on our hands, but Henry was not quite so optimistic, for he wrote me, " 'Subsequent printings' *sagt der Kerl*. I refuse to engage in any such astronomical speculations. But if God is kind and you ever have to reprint, I see no objection to reducing the thickness of the book. Me, I like it as it is, but I can still see the force of the objection to its present weight."

The third edition, again revised, appeared in 1923, at which point Henry let the book rest for a long time. But in 1936 we published the fourth edition. The book had been completely rewritten and now ran to nearly eight hundred pages.

Henry continued to amass much new material both from his own researches and with the help of innumerable correspondents. But we had reached the limit of what could be put in a single volume. So in 1945 we published *Supplement One*—again, nearly eight hundred pages—and in 1948 *Supplement Two*, more than a hundred pages longer.

A letter written December 28, 1944, tells in more detail the kind of labor *The American Language* involved: "The new material includes an immense mass of matter. For many years past I have had clipping bureaus send me everything printed about the American language in the United States, Great Britain and the British colonies. Before the war I also received all the discussions of the subject from the other countries of Europe and from Japan. I have received, first and last, probably 3,000 letters from readers, some of them embodying corrections and suggestions. I have also kept in close touch with the discussions of the subject by professional philologians since 1936. The *Dictionary of American English* has been completed, the *Linguistic Atlas of the United States and Canada* has been begun, and there has been a great deal of discussion in the philological periodicals. All of this material is to be worked into the two Supplements. In format they will follow the fourth edition of 1936 precisely, and Supplement 1 will be of about the same bulk.

"Here are the facts. I trust your bright young ladies to put them into useful form. Please tell them that they are not expected to avoid encomiastic adjectives. I have passed the page proofs on Supplement 1 and am now at work on the two indexes. One of them runs to more than 11,000 entries, so the labor is onerous."

By this time our relationship with Henry had become far more than that of publisher and author. I was devoted to him, and so was my wife, Blanche. He had more influence over me and my beliefs than anyone except possibly my father, who in the early 1920s became treasurer of the firm and a full partner, as Blanche had been almost from the very beginning. I know Henry soon conceived an affection for all three of us, and his later joining the Board of Directors was a mere formality. He was an unpaid member of our editorial staff, and his advice and enterprise on our behalf were very, very considerable indeed.

Early in my association with Mencken, probably by 1921, it had become clear that he was not happy editing the *Smart Set* with George Jean Nathan as co-editor. The title was vulgar, the production cheap, and the owner-publisher, Eltinge F. Warner, had really no interest in the kind of magazine it had become. Henry had developed interests of the most varied kind, while Warner cared chiefly about sports, and Nathan's only real love—apart from pretty women—was the theater. Around this time, we were beginning to think about starting a new magazine. Since it had long been my conviction that a magazine could be no better than its editor and that in Henry we had a great editor, we approached him with the idea. He immediately showed interest.

I had hoped that he would part company with Nathan, leaving him with the *Smart Set*, where he seemed to me to be quite happy. But the collaboration of the two could not be ended at this time, and so we incorporated the *American Mercury*, dividing the stock one-third to my father as business manager, one-third to me as publisher, and one-sixth each to Nathan and Mencken. We hoped for a circulation of perhaps twenty thousand copies,* and no salaries were to be paid to any stockholder, including the editors, who were given what they would insist upon, an absolutely free hand in deciding what to print. If any important difference arose between them, I was to cast the deciding vote. Such a difference arose very soon over Eugene O'Neill's short play, "All God's Chillun Got Wings." Nathan wanted to print it, Henry did not. Ironically, I agreed with Nathan, and it appeared in the second issue.

The interests of the two men drifted apart, and in a couple of years Henry insisted that George be eliminated from any connection whatever with the magazine. It took repeated meetings of the two with Father, Blanche, and me before we were able to persuade George to agree to sell back his stock in the *Mercury*. He was in a position to make any demands, however unreasonable, and then simply refuse to budge from them. George abandoned all pride and self-respect when Henry deprived him of an office of his own, had his name removed from the directory in the lobby, and gave him a desk among those of the stenographers. Besides the bitterness that

* The readership of the *Mercury* exploded, however, and its circulation reached 80,500 in 1926, a remarkable figure for a 50¢ magazine in those times.

Henry felt toward George, their quarrel had its trivial side as well. For example, Nathan objected to our advertising the *Mercury* on the wrappers of his books. Mencken retaliated by objecting to our advertising George's books in the *Mercury*.

As late as 1930 Henry wrote me, "If he [George] will withdraw his prohibition not only with respect to his new book but also with respect to all his other books, my objections will fall down." But then came the essential Mencken: "In any case it is only an objection. The advertising is in your hands and I will agree to any decision you make."

In 1920 we had published *The American Credo*. In December, 1934, Mencken sent me this memorandum: "At the time the last edition of 'The American Credo' was brought out—in 1927—I resigned all my rights in it to Nathan. This was on condition that my preface be omitted, that my name be removed from the title page, and that no mention of me be made elsewhere in the book or on the dust-cover or in any announcement relating to it. I have no objection to its reissue on the same terms, but they must be observed strictly." Eugene Reynal's firm, Reynal & Hitchcock, planned to bring out a *Smart Set* anthology, but Mencken refused to permit the inclusion of anything by him. Mencken, distrusting Reynal, wrote me: "I suggest that Reynal be required to enter into some sort of contract to avoid the use of it [Mencken's name]. His conduct in the Rascoe business* convinces me that he is a bounder without any comprehension of the common decencies. He would make an ideal publisher for Nathan." But in the end, George was the only one of us to get any cash out of the magazine. For many years he maintained publicly that there had never been any break in the friendship, but this was not the case, even though years later they would resume superficial social relations.

* Burton Rascoe was editor of the *Smart Set* anthology.

We got our old friend Elmer Adler to design the *Mercury*'s typography and the circular which we sent out soliciting charter subscribers. President Nicholas Murray Butler of Columbia was number one and sent in his check with a personal note.

We regarded the Rumford Press at Concord, New Hampshire, as the best magazine printers in the country and intended to use them even though their estimate was twenty percent higher than that of other printers. For the first issue, January 1924, Mencken planned to run an article which was very critical of labor unions and their leaders. Rumford refused to print the *Mercury* if we ran that article. Mencken's reaction was violent, and we felt exactly as he did. We immediately placed the magazine in the hands of the Haddon Craftsmen in Camden, New Jersey, who turned out to be very satisfactory indeed. And they had in stock the typeface we wished to use—Monotype Garamond. We printed on a special Esparto paper imported from England which was expensive but very light in weight. It was indeed a handsome magazine; Henry called Adler's design of it "whorish"—high praise.

During all the time that Henry edited the *Mercury*, he came to New York for no more than one week during each month and really carried on from his study on the second floor front of the old Baltimore home on Hollins Street. The Algonquin Hotel on Forty-fourth Street, west of Fifth Avenue, was owned in those days by a remarkable couple, Frank and Bertha Case, who made it a particularly comfortable home for out-of-town writers and others in the arts, and Henry always stayed there. In New York, he usually spent some time, especially evenings, with Blanche and me, but he had a host of friends among journalists, of whom Harold Ross, of *The New Yorker*, was one. We had a box for the Boston Symphony concerts, then conducted by Serge Koussevitzky, where he often joined us; and he frequently stayed a night or a weekend at our country house in Purchase, N.Y. After ten years, which was as long as he thought a man should hold down any one job, he was not only becoming bored with the magazine, but he had done most of what he had set out to accomplish in 1923. When he left, the *Mercury* fell on first difficult and soon evil days, and I soon realized that he was so closely identified with the magazine that once he left it we should have closed it down for keeps.

Mencken so delighted in the attacks made on him by his many enemies that he made selections from them into a small book, *Menckeniana: A Schimpflexikon*, which we published in 1928. And in 1932 *Making a President* was a collection of his dispatches from the Republican and Democratic conventions of that year. This little book was my idea and I expected a similar one would be published every fourth year. Henry was always against the whole plan, and he was dead right. There was never a second volume.

To go backward, the famous *Prejudices* began to appear in 1919. I think it was Richard Laukhuff, a most admirable smallish bookseller in Cleveland, who suggested to me—I traveled the Middle West in those days to sell my own books—that we ought to publish a collection of Mencken's magazine and newspaper articles. Henry liked the idea, and we soon brought out *Prejudices, First Series*. These were not mere reprints, for, as he said, "There was always a great deal of expansion and rewriting." Five more volumes were issued, the last in 1927.

Henry was seriously interested in his learned ancestors and in 1937 we published a translation of *De Charlataneria Eruditorum*, a learned discourse by a scholarly forebear of his. We were to issue this book for him on terms which he set forth:

"1. I am to take 150 copies at a price to be fixed by the contract, and am to pay cash for them on delivery.

"2. I am to indemnify you for any loss incurred up to the end of the first year, or up to any other time you may prefer.

"3. You are to catalogue the book and announce it, but not to advertise it.

"4. Any copies remaining unsold at the time of the indemnification are to come to me on terms fixed by the contract, and I am to acquire the copyright. The book is never to be remaindered."

Later, when we billed Henry in accordance with our agreement for the unsold copies of this book, he wrote: "I see nothing outrageous about that bill. On the contrary, it seems to me to be rather low. Have you noticed that it amounted to less than the actual cost of the books? I think it should be at least that much and probably more. Certainly I don't want the office to show a net loss on the transaction."

Notes on Democracy was published in 1926, *Treatise on the Gods* in 1920 (a revised edition appeared sixteen years later), and *Treatise on Right and Wrong* in 1934.

Meanwhile Blanche had been urging him—perhaps nagging would be not too strong a way to put it—to get on with his autobiographical papers, which had begun to appear from time to time in *The New Yorker*. *Happy Days*, which covered roughly the years 1880 to 1892, came out in 1940; *Newspaper Days*, which went down to 1906, in 1941; and *Heathen Days* (1890 to 1936) in 1943. None of these delightful volumes has ever had a wide sale, a sad fact which I find extremely difficult to understand.*

But the first of them drew this from Otis Ferguson in the *New Republic*: " 'Happy Days' gives me a springboard I don't often find for boasting; I can read the general run of stuff in the prints of these later days and say, 'Well, I'm no big

* A one-volume selection from these three books, edited by Edward Galligan, was published in 1980 on the centenary of Mencken's birth.

burst of shrapnel myself, but where I come from, you had to learn how to write. Ever hear of Aitchel Mencken? He was around then and set the pace, and he was a very tough man to follow; he wrote like a bat out of hell, and he picked his words like weapons.' "

Ferguson wrote me, "I will lay you he would rather have had a panning from the *NR* as it must mortify him to death to have a disciple actually on that staff." But Henry said, "Tell Otis Ferguson that I forgive him for reviewing my book so generously. It was a shock, but in these days of horror such things can be borne. Tell him that there is now a brewery in Baltimore that surpasses all others in America and that I crave the honor of taking him to it the next time he is in these latitudes."

For years Henry had been working on a *Dictionary of Quotations*, which we published in 1942. W. A. Dwiggins designed the book handsomely, and the production was placed with the Plimpton Press at Norwood, Massachusetts. Henry, always appreciative of competence, wrote the Press when the book was completed: "My very best thanks for the excellent work that the gentlemen of the Plimpton Press did on the book. It presented many serious difficulties, but they were all surmounted with great skill. Will you please convey my thanks to the linotype operators, to the proofroom, and above all, to the make-up man? I was struck constantly by the good judgment shown by the linotype operators, by the cogency and good sense of the proof-room's queries, and by the ingenuity with which the make-up man solved his problems. In forty years of dealing with composing rooms I have encountered few such excellent jobs."

We always admired Dwiggins' work. He stamped the Mencken coat of arms on the front cover of many of his books. Once Henry didn't approve of Dwiggins' sketch and wrote me, "The animal is a Rehbock (roe-deer). The tree is a linden. The stamp now used on Supplement One to 'The American Language' probably comes closer to the heraldic accuracy than Mr. Dwiggins' sketch. In particular, the forelegs in the stamp are properly bent. They should not be spread out. The rules of German heraldry often differ from those of English heraldry." I sent this to Dwiggins, who wrote across the bottom, "Far be it from me to separate a man from his house-badge! Use the 'American Language' one."

He almost always admired the work of our printers and cooperated very effectively with them. But one time he protested violently, and this was against charges made by the Plimpton Press for his alterations in the proofs of *Supplement One* of *The American Language*. "I am sending a check for my author's corrections. I suspect and allege that you have whittled them down unduly* and so laid an unfair burden on the house. I believe we should go into these matters at length when we meet."

Unlike most writers, Henry was concerned that his publisher should find publishing his books profitable. He once wrote me: "I gather from your letter that you are proposing to pay me the new royalty retroactively. Is that a fact? If so, I must protest against it as over-generous. But in all such matters I am disposed to follow your lead without question, so I do not protest too much." Another time: "In drawing up the contract for Supplement One (of 'The American Language') please don't forget that its sale will be very much less than those of the 'American Language' fourth edition." And later, concerning the same book: "I also note your very generous proposal regarding the royalties on the supplement. I have a real fear that the book will not do very well and so I think it would be better to fix the royalties at some modest

* They were whittled down, largely, I suspect, by Plimpton, with whom our relations were astonishingly frank and friendly and who always cooperated with us far beyond the call of duty.

level. However, if you prefer your own plan I'll certainly go along with you."

For some years after his stroke in 1948, his books, except for the *American Language* volumes, suffered an eclipse, but in 1954 his friend Alistair Cooke edited a selection from his writings which would "give the new Mencken reader a running account of his life as he wrote and lived it." This was *The Vintage Mencken*, a paperback which we published in 1955, and which within a year sold more than one hundred thousand copies.

Shortly thereafter, Henry's secretary discovered a book-length manuscript described by him in his preface to it as "not a book, but a notebook . . . made up of selections chosen more or less at random from the memoranda of long years devoted to the pursuit, anatomizing, and embalming of Ideas." Published in 1956 as *Minority Report: H. L. Mencken's Notebooks*, this too did surprisingly well and sold over twenty thousand copies.

Two other books did not do so well. One, published in 1958, *A Bathtub Hoax and Other Blasts and Bravos from the Chicago Tribune*, reprinted fifty-four of the columns he had published in that paper from 1924 to 1927. The other, *H. L. Mencken on Music*, a selection by his old friend and member of the Saturday Night Club, Louis Cheslock, appeared in 1961.

I cannot recall precisely when Henry and I started going to the great Bach Festival in Bethlehem, Pennsylvania, each spring, but we attended for several years. Sometimes we met there but more often Henry came to Purchase to spend the night and we then drove to Bethlehem. He always bragged that he could locate good beer in 15 minutes or so in any town, but one year during Prohibition his touch ran out in

Allentown. The next day the taxi driver heard us talking and turned to ask, "Do you gentlemen want beer?" He then drove us to a conventional-looking home in a middle-class part of town. We knocked at the door—we were both carrying scores of the B Minor Mass—and Henry asked if they could help two poor musicians to some liquid refreshment. We were told to come right in, turn to the left, walk down a long hallway at the end of which we would find a bar that served good sandwiches and quite good beer, very reasonably priced. The local politicos were sitting in cane-bottomed chairs tilted against the wall. One year we stayed at the Elks Club, no other quarters being available, but in the end we settled down to using the Hotel Bethlehem which required, I think, that you pay for two nights minimum. Sometimes at the conclusion of the second day's performance—the B Minor Mass—Henry would return to Purchase with me, but most of the time he found a train that took him back to Baltimore through lovely country of which he was very fond. I remember that several days before the death of John Frederick Wolle, who conducted the Festival, which he had inaugurated in 1900, Henry had a letter from the widow-to-be asking him to be pallbearer at the funeral. I think Henry and I went together every year until 1948, when he suffered his first stroke.

He was for a long time a faithful member of the Saturday Night Club in Baltimore, whose sessions I often attended. Each member played host in turn, and during Prohibition he was expected to have on hand not only food but a generous supply of home brew.

Henry and Max Broedel took care of the piano (Henry played *secondo*); Raymond Pearl the French horn. There was a flute, a cello or two, and several violins.

Whenever he came to New York, Henry used to visit Schirmer's to find more music for the club to perform, not always easy when you consider one report of his: "We actually played 'Don Juan' (Strauss) for four-hand piano, double string quartet and basset-horn. I had to play the French horn part on the piano." By and large, it is only fair, I think, to report that the music was enjoyed more by the players than by their audience. However, the rule was to stop playing promptly at ten o'clock and go on to the beer and vittles. After Repeal, the club foregathered in a small private room in Henry's favorite saloon, Schellhase's. At one of these meetings Heinie Buchholz, a non-playing but very old member, sat at the head of the table and acted as a sort of sergeant-at-arms. A group of young roughs turned up and demanded that they be admitted to the room. Buchholz told them it was a private party and that they could not come in, whereupon one of them struck him on the ear and drew a little blood. But before any further blows, the police arrived, dragged the intruders off to the station-house, and locked them up for the night.

According to Henry: "The Buchholz case succumbed to the Christmas spirit. Pearl, Strube, Hazlehurst, Schellhase, Mlle. Schellhase and I turned out at 9 o'clock this morning, and the assassins were brought from their dungeon. They looked very sick and were full of remorse. They had a lawyer hired by friends—an ex-traffic court judge I happened to know. He entered pleas of guilty and they were at the mercy of the court. Then Buchholz melted, asked that they be released, and there was handshaking all around. Their excuse was that they were tight. The lawyer drew up and handed to Buchholz a document admitting that they were guilty, asking for absolution, and agreeing not to sue Buchholz or anyone else for false arrest. It was unnecessary legally, but seemed advisable, to stave off possible blackmail by some Communist lawyer. At the end the cops, news photographers, criminals, complainant and witnesses wished one another many happy returns of the day."

After one of our visits to Bethlehem, Henry wrote in a piece for the *Evening Sun:* "Bach, as everyone knows, cannot be sung on well-water. Nor for that matter, heard. His grand and heavenly music is not for teetotallers brought up on the obscene rubbish of Moody and Sankey. It presumes a civilized and robustious spirit in both singers and hearers. In this department the Bethlehem boosters plainly neglect a civic duty. The town is full of comfortable and respectable saloons, and all of them have good beer on tap. Save in a few dives, no hard liquor is sold, for the Moravian theology frowns upon it, but a sound Helles is everywhere obtainable, and at very neat prices. Moreover, the town booticians are humane and hospitable men, and during the Bach Festival they trust any stranger carrying the score of the B Minor Mass. Unfortunately, no arrangements are made to lead strangers to the right places. They are left to find their own way, and many of them never find it."

In the mid-1920s Leopold Stokowski organized a brass band of a hundred and forty players. Forty clarinets, as I recall it, took the place of violins. The men were given gorgeous yellow and gold uniforms, and the stage of the Academy of Music at Philadelphia was curtained off so that the audience first saw the band with every man in his place. Stokowski led a few concerts for an invited audience before the musicians' union forced him to give up the band. Sousa marches, Strauss waltzes, Wagner, and Bach made up the greater part of the programs and everything was scored for the band by Stokowski himself. Henry wrote a characteristic piece for the *Evening Sun* after one of these concerts: "Stokowski's conducting was quite as remarkable as the skill he showed at writing for his band. He had the advantage, of course, of starting off with highly competent performers. His first trumpet, name unknown to me, was a genuine virtuoso; he had the best trombones I have ever heard. Superb music, too, came from the French horns, from his flutes, and from his lower woodwinds, and his drummers and cymbal beaters showed immense skill. But there must have been plenty of second-rate players in the band, especially among the clarinets. If they were there, then good conducting concealed them. The band played almost perfectly. There was not a grunt or a bray from end to end."

Henry was a great admirer of the Johns Hopkins Hospital and accompanied many a friend who came there for treatment. I once went down to Baltimore for a tonsillectomy and what is called, I think, a mucous subsection. On the night before the operation, I attended the Saturday Night Club, of which the surgeon, Frank Hazlehurst, was a member. As usual the homemade beer was bottled and nestled in ice water in the bathtub. Member after member warned me not to worry, that the more of the brew Hazlehurst drank the safer he would be at the operating table next morning. The hospital was a Catholic one—not Hopkins—and when I arrived I was promptly greeted by a Sister who demanded to know why this surgery had to be performed on a Sunday. I can't remember exactly what Henry told her, but it sounded as if my very life depended on having the job done that very day. He said that after the operation a priest would visit me and attempt to convert me: my only chance was to draw my hand across my throat and shake my head. This worked perfectly. I remember that the bill was so low that I felt I had to leave at least a modest donation to the hospital when I paid it. Before I went home, Henry gave me a bottle of unlabeled old whiskey. I kept it around for some time before sampling it. It turned out to be admirable bourbon—the first bourbon I had ever tasted, and the whiskey I have preferred to all others ever since.

I had never been to a national convention and in 1928 I decided to watch the Republican performance in Kansas City, where I had a close and distinguished friend, Logan Clendening; I had also published a book or two by Henry Haskell, who was editor of the Kansas City *Star* for many years. I was looking forward to seeing what Mencken always described as the greatest show on earth and, in addition, Mencken himself in his capacity of professional reporter. Somehow I got myself a ticket and a room in a hotel on the edge of the city.

On the train the next morning I saw Nicholas Murray Butler in the dining car. Although I had been an undergraduate at Columbia, I had never before laid eyes on this controversial figure who was president of that university. I knew that at the convention Butler, always a power in Republican politics, was going to make a strong attack on Prohibition. When I arrived at the hall, I found my seat in the uppermost gallery and I remember hearing the raucous voice of Mabel Walker Willebrandt, then a lady of some power in the Department of Justice and an ardent Prohibitionist. The microphones of those days were fairly crude, and her voice was scratchy and hard on one's ear. The chairman was Senator George H. Moses of New Hampshire, best known for his reference to the Western progressives as sons of the wild jackass. When Butler finished his speech, Moses brought down his gavel and it was as if the president of Columbia had never been present.

When Mencken discovered where I was seated, he got me a pass as a photographer, as I had a small Bell & Howell movie camera with me, and from that time on I sat on the floor with the Baltimore *Sun* contingent led by Paul Patterson (under whose guidance the *Sunpapers* had risen to great eminence) and with Frank Kent, Hamilton Owens and several others. Later at his desk in the *Sun* hotel suite I saw Mencken at work in his rolled-up shirt sleeves and perhaps his BVD's if it was hot, as it probably was, pounding away at his typewriter, corncob pipe in his mouth.

The convention lasted, I believe, only four days and everything seemed to move smoothly under the management of the Hoover machine. My recollection is that the only serious opposition for the nomination—and it wasn't very serious—came from Frank Lowden, governor of Illinois, who had an important connection with the Pullman Company so that he was able to have porters parade the streets on his behalf. There were great social activities, details of which I cannot remember, except that Arthur Krock of *The New York Times* seemed to be flitting here, there and everywhere and Logan Clendening cheerfully christened his handsome new home Roaring Toilet. I had the strong impression that Hoover's nomination was very distasteful to the press, not to the owners but rather to the working newspapermen.

Henry was a man of great humor. When I sent him a copy of Wilfred E. Binkley's "American Political Parties" he wrote, "The Binkley book sounds very interesting. So far as I know, there is no other good history of political parties in the U.S.A. The story should be done of course by a criminologist."

When I told him early in the war that Berry Brothers in London were shipping me five cases of old German wines which they had been holding for me since long before Hitler, he wrote: "Let us avoid all public festivities the next time I am in New York. That will give us a chance to stick our noses into that 1921 Moselle." And again when I wrote him that I had discovered I had a hitherto unsuspected case of a good

German wine, he replied next day, "If you are really a lover of humanity you will reserve at least a bottle of that Hitzler Caselay against my next visit to Purchase."

After the Republican convention in Philadelphia in 1940, he wrote me: "I suppose you heard that an angel appeared in the gallery at the precise moment Willkie stepped before the Republican convention. Among those who saw it were Dorothy Thompson and Oswald Garrison Villard—not a hot Willkie man! A fact! As for me, my back was turned and I missed it. It must have been a Portent."

Once when I was summoned for jury duty, he wrote, "I have just discovered that it is possible to escape jury duty in Maryland by confessing to atheism. It is a valuable thing to know. Maybe the same rule prevails in New York. Try it next time."

Another time: "Will you please send a letter to ——— saying that I have suggested that you add him to your staff; that you welcome the idea with great enthusiasm, if only because of your high admiration for his late father, but that by one of those unhappy strokes of fate that baffle human desire, you only lately made such additions to your staff that there is no opportunity at the moment to make him an offer? Tell him, finally, that you will certainly not forget him and that if any opportunity to bring him in offers itself you will leap upon it."

Only once did he violate the agreement he forced me to live up to of no birthday presents. This letter accompanied his gift: "Your moustache has no greater admirer than I am; nevertheless, I am not unaware of the penalties that you must pay for cultivating it. It practically cuts you off from noodle soup, and makes you justifiably uneasy every time a salad dressed with mayonnaise is brought on the table. Above all, it deprives you of the great boon of having Schlagsahne on your coffee. In a day when vibrissae were more common on men such difficulties were thought of, and human ingenuity surmounted them. The moustache-cup was invented, and came into wide use. My father had one, and my grandfather had a whole set, some of them specially designed to take care of his chin whiskers. Now they have gone out, but in the antique shoppes of Baltimore specimens are still discoverable. At immense labor and expense Sara and I have assembled a battery of four, with saucers for the drip. They go to you to gladden your birthday. For the first time you are now free to wallow in Schlagsahne. Find out which cup fits you best, and keep it for your private use. The rest are for moustachioed guests."

His correspondence was extensive with people all over the United States and much of Western Europe. He was constantly suggesting books to us that other people might write and authors we should solicit. Thus December 13, 1919: "Put down the name of J. V. A. Weaver, Display Advertising Dept., *Daily News*, Chicago, as likely for your next year's poetry list. Weaver is gradually accumulating some excellent stuff, and it is very original. It represents an attempt to turn the common language of America into beauty. I think his book, when it is ready, will cause a lot of gabble. I'll be glad to do a preface for it. In the end, of course, it may turn out impossible, but meanwhile it might do no harm to get a sort of option on it." This book was *In American*.

He read innumerable manuscripts for us. The notion that he could or should have charged for this work would, I am sure, have shocked and insulted him. He also read with an eye to censorship, which was still active in these early days. Thus in April 1921, when we asked him to read the translation of a novel by a Norwegian author, he wrote: "This is now absolutely safe. It is also one of the worst novels I have ever read, or heard of. Such banality is really quite magnificent. . . . I have made small changes in verbiage here and there. I have also cut out the absurd honorific Jomfru. It is quite unnecessary. The translation, even as it stands, seems idiotic, but I am sure that the original Norwegian is far worse."

Frequently people wrote in invoking his name. When a preacher sent us a manuscript for which he said Mencken had promised to write an introduction, I asked Henry if this were so and he replied: "The book is psychical crap, but it might sell. ——— is a high church Episcopal rector in a fashionable suburb. Most of his congregation are rich ex-Methodists, Presbyterians, Dunkards, Jews, Lutherans, etc. I shall certainly write no introduction for it. More, ——— is well aware that I shall not. Never believe a clergyman."

He was, of course, very early interested in the American language and he wrote me this report on a manuscript submitted by Professor Philip Krapp: "The Krapp book is extremely interesting, but, despite its size, not exhaustive. I have a feeling that it should be, not one work in two volumes, but a series of volumes. The second volume, on American pronunciation, is complete enough as it stands, and I advise you to do it as a separate book, but the chapters on American literary style, American spelling, American proper names, etc., in the first volume are by no means as comprehensive as they might be. I think it would be a good idea to take the second volume, and to suggest to Krapp that he expand each of these chapters into a separate volume. This second volume, coming after my book, should arouse a good deal of interest in American English, and so pave the way for others. Thus you would have a monopoly on the subject. Krapp's stuff necessitates very few changes in my book. In many cases my treatment of the subject is more thorough than his."

In April 1923 he recommended that we try to get from Cape, the English publisher, "a book by an Australian physician called 'Post Mortem' "; that Xavier Scharwenka had written a book of reminiscences ("If you care to risk a musical book it might be a very good bet"); and that Doubleday was after a book on American politics by his colleague, Frank R. Kent of the Baltimore *Sun*. This turned out to be *The Great Game of Politics*, which Doubleday did publish with great success. I regretted very much indeed that we were unable to make a contract with Kent, a first-rate man, whose writings I found very interesting.

At about this time, Mencken and I agreed that a popular physiology was not only needed but might have a very wide sale. He was an avid reader of the *Journal of the American Medical Association*, and one day he ran across a review there of a medical textbook called "Modern Methods of Treatment" by Logan Clendening. He saw in Clendening the man we had been looking for, and the letter which he wrote the doctor—this was in December 1925—is, I think, a model of what an editor's proposal ought to be but seldom is:

"What I suggested to Mr. Knopf was not a book on physiology in the technical sense, but a general work on the human body and its operations for the intelligent layman. Strangely enough, there is no such book in print. Old time school texts are all stupid, and the later books for general reading are full of pious propaganda.

"What I suggest is a volume describing the anatomy of the human body with constant reference to function and ending with a brief statement of pathological principles, say along the run of McCallum's well-known textbook. The layman reads about such things as blood counts, blood pressures, kidney functions, Wassermann reactions and fallen arches, and yet he finds it almost impossible to discover precisely what they mean. The book I have in mind ought to avoid useless physiological and anatomical minutiae; nevertheless, it should contain a few pages devoted to histology. I believe that such a book would have a large and permanent sale and that it would do a great deal of good. Its value as a counterblast to the grotesque quackeries now prevailing must be obvious."

Logan Clendening agreed to write the book, and in due course he delivered his manuscript, which struck everyone who read it as superb. We published *The Human Body* with great enthusiasm in October 1927, and of that first edition sold something over thirty-seven thousand copies. In 1945 Clendening revised the book, and of this new edition we sold something over thirty thousand copies. It did not go out of print until 1978. Meanwhile a Doubleday subsidiary, Garden City Books, had started a dollar reprint series of clothbound non-fiction books. In this form *The Human Body* sold over two hundred and thirty thousand copies. Finally, some two hundred thousand copies were sold by Pocket Books as a paperback.

For a long time both Blanche and I tried to find someone to write on surgery a companion to *The Human Body*. We never succeeded, though I went with Logan to St. Louis, where we spent an evening trying to persuade a surgeon friend of his, Dr. Major Seelig, to undertake the book. Henry prepared a characteristic outline of the volume he wanted:

"I think this book should cover the whole history of surgery from prehistoric days (there are plenty of archeological evidences) down to the present. There should be chapters on Egyptian and Greek surgery, and on the great advances made in the Middle Ages and thereafter, for example, by Ambroise Paré. Then he should come down to modern times, with chapters on anaesthetics and asepsis, and plenty of stuff about the men who brought them in. The history of the principal operations of today should be told—appendectomy, the Billroth breast operations, tonsillectomy, etc. The history of cutting for the stone will naturally fall into its place. At the end there should be some discussion of the different schools of surgery. Of late there have been three main movements—toward reducing hemorrhage, toward the use of block anaesthesia to cut off shock, and toward the careful handling of exposed tissues. I think the book should be illustrated, and that it should mention as many concrete surgeons as possible. Every advance had a beginning in a definite man."

We showed him any manuscript which we thought had possibilities for the *American Mercury*. One of these was Mabel Dodge Luhan's "Lorenzo in Taos." His comment casts an interesting light on what had made him such a good editor: "The Mabel Dodge book is very interesting stuff, but I have found it impossible to dig an article out of it. The separate episodes are too long; moreover, one hangs upon another, so that an attempt to isolate one of them would involve writing long explanations. Any single article, standing by itself, would seem thin, and probably idiotic. La Dodge is a New Thoughter, and a vain and preposterous old baggage, but she was precisely the person to do a book about Lawrence. What a fellow she makes him out!"

In 1934: "Do you ever see such magazines as *Real Detective* and *True Detective?* They are made up of accounts of real crimes, and they seem to have enormous circulations. I have been wondering if some of their contents wouldn't make a couple of salable books. In *Real Detective* a man named Stuart Palmer has been running a series of articles on the famous crimes of the last thirty or forty years. They are extraordinarily well written and very amusing."

Five years later he suggested we do a volume of Justice Hugo L. Black's dissenting opinions. But this time I had beaten him to the gun and had already called in Washington on the man who became one of the people I most admire and a good friend. Henry's comment was characteristic: "I should have suspected that your visit to Hugo had no good purpose. I only hope he comes across. Who writes his decisions I don't know, but now and then they are very well done. His fundamental theory, of course, seems to me to be loony. If he had his way no one would have any rights in this great republic save Alabama sharecroppers."*

From another letter: "God willing, I should be in your great city by Monday, July 23rd, to stay a few days. The *Sun* is in the midst of a gory bout with the local Catholic archbishop, and I have been employed in it as theologician and assassin. It may end in a compromise, but I hope not. The *Sun* was in the wrong in the first place, but His Excellency has run amuck, and so I think we have him."

And again: "Why doesn't someone print a really decent looking King James Bible? All those issued by the regular publishers have a funereal air, and most of them are bound idiotically. There are some better Bibles in modern translation, but no sensible man wants to read a modern translation. What is needed is a simple Bible without notes, giving the King James text precisely, and bound so that it looks like a good book, not like a scarecrow to alarm sinners. If you ever think of doing such an edition, I'll be glad to write an introduction for it. The King James is a really magnificent work, and deserves to be read as literature. It is stupendously superior to all the other texts, and it should be read in the orthodox form."

Sometimes, to our loss, we did not follow Henry's suggestions, as when in October 1933 he wrote: "In the *Symposium* for October just out there is an article on Dr. William Carlos Williams which says that he is putting together a volume of his poems, and that his publishing arrangements are still 'pending.' I incline to think that such a volume might have a chance.

* Knowing Hugo Black as well as I did, I think I am safe in assuring my readers that if ever a man did his own work it was Hugo, and I doubt very much indeed if he ever let anyone else take any substantial part in the writing of his opinions.

Williams has been printed off and on by Jitney Publishers, but there is no big collection of his writings." Unfortunately, we had just turned down Williams' poems. I did this after a good deal of consideration and consulting Louis Untermeyer, whose judgment in such matters, from both a purely editorial and a commercial point of view, was usually sound. To which Henry replied, "Untermeyer's opinion about Williams is worth far more than mine." We were both mistaken.

Once we discussed the desirability of a history of Christianity. He commented: "My belief is that the only kind of history of Christianity that would have a chance must be rather agnostic in tone—that is to say, it must describe Christianity completely objectively, and without any pious qualms. There are thousands of good histories done by Christians, and even better ones by mild skeptics. What is needed is a book that gets rid of the religious prejudice altogether. I don't mean a slating, of course, for a large part of the history of Christianity is not discreditable, and all of it is immensely interesting. But the general tone of the book ought to be that of Huxley, not that of Bishop Manning."

However, the most important of all the suggestions he made to us was back in 1921: "If you can get 'Buddenbrooks' at a reasonable price, grab it. It is probably the solidest novel done in Germany in years. It is well worth having."

The last book in the preparation of which Henry participated actively was *A Mencken Chrestomathy*. He was in love with the word *chrestomathy* and could not be persuaded against using it in the title. But I guess he was right, for the book, which was a fascinating selection from his out-of-print writings, mostly from books but also from magazines and newspapers, with a few notes never previously published at all, sold very well indeed.

For the most part, Henry never worked at anything that didn't interest him, but the jobs he kept running simultaneously were fantastic in their number and variety. His first loyalty was always to the *Sunpapers,* but for nearly a decade he edited the *American Mercury,* produced the different and increasingly elaborate editions of *The American Language,* edited the six volumes in *The Free Lance Books,* one of which was his own translation of Nietzsche's *The Antichrist,* co-authored with Nathan their "buffoonery" *Heliogabalus,* and turned out more than a dozen books of his own. All this time he was compiling what became *A New Dictionary of Quotations on Historical Principles.*

Henry was a chronic hay fever sufferer. I joined the ranks in the summer of 1921. After a couple of years of fussing with non-specialists, I went to Robert A. Cooke. Relief was almost immediate, and after a few years I was one of Cooke's best exhibits. Finally I persuaded Henry to go to him, although he expressed a complete disbelief in the efficacy of Cooke's vaccines. In New York you visited Cooke for your injections, but if you lived in another city or traveled, Cooke supplied vaccine to take with you. Henry wrote me in 1932: "The injections will be inserted here by George Walker, an old friend of mine. He gets a lot of practice shooting arsenic, bismuth and mercury into the arms of the wicked."

He was something of a hypochondriac and many of his letters dealt with his physical ills. I quote from one: "December is always my unluckiest month. As far back as I can remember, I have always been in some sort of trouble at Christmas—in fact, I'd be delighted if the holiday could be wiped from the calendar and at the same time the carcasses of the twelve Apostles could be dug up and burned."

On November 23, 1948, Henry went to the apartment of his secretary of many years, Mrs. Rosalind Lohrfinck, to pick up a manuscript and take her to dinner. There, at seven-thirty, he suffered a severe stroke. As soon as I heard the news the next day, I telephoned his physician, Dr. Benjamin Baker, Jr., and I have never forgotten Dr. Baker's wise comment: "Mr. Mencken has suffered a stroke and I am sorry to say he is recovering from it." He did recover in a physical sense, but he was never afterward able to read and his speech suffered severe impediments, chiefly an inability to summon up the right word at the right time. For a time he was very cheerful, but soon he became fully aware of what had happened to him and that his progress, if indeed it could be called that, was painfully slow.

On February 20, 1950, I wrote August, "I wonder how Henry feels about the announcement that he is to receive the gold medal for essays and criticism of the National Institute at the American Academy of Arts and Letters on May 25th." August replied: "My brother feels the same way about that gold medal as he would have felt in the old days." August wrote later that the previous fall Louis Untermeyer had informed Henry that he had proposed him for the medal. Untermeyer had not asked permission, but Lohrfinck would seem to have written an ambiguous acknowledgment to Untermeyer, which "must have made it appear to him that my brother was not only willing to take the medal but was flattered by the idea."

In January, Douglas Moore of the Institute apparently wrote Henry that the medal had been awarded to him. Then, in March, the Institute asked Lohrfinck whether Henry could write a short acceptance and designate someone to read it at the presentation. Lohrfinck replied that Henry was too ill to do this or take any part in the ceremony. August adds, "Had he been in good health, you know as well as I do that there would never have been any question about the medal. He would have refused it as he has all others."

On April 24, Lohrfinck wrote Moore: "After carefully considering the matter, Mr. Mencken has concluded that the gold medal to be awarded him by the National Institute of Arts and Letters had better not be given at this time. Due to his health, it is quite impossible for him to be present at the celebration in May, and it is equally impossible for him to write a statement to be read by somebody else. He therefore thinks that it is very unwise for the Institute to award the medal while he is unable to accept it personally. He offers his best thanks to the members of the Institute for their kind thought of him, and regrets that his condition prevents his acceptance of the award."

I then wrote August, "The trouble is that Untermeyer as an old friend of Henry's must have known damn well that what he was proposing was something that Henry if he were well would certainly not have considered for a moment. It is inconceivable to me that after all these many years of his friendship for Henry he hadn't been fully aware of what Henry's attitude has always been toward the Institute and the Academy of Arts and Letters."

Shortly afterward Moore telephoned me and we had a long talk. He felt that Lohrfinck's last letter was provoked solely by his request to Henry for a statement, and that they were therefore quite willing to award him the medal without any such statement. He said that the medal had already been engraved and their publicity release sent to the press and that it would be enormously embarrassing to announce Henry's withdrawal. He said furthermore that when they offered Henry the medal they realized that he had once upon a time refused membership in the Institute and were quite prepared to have him refuse the medal. Instead they got a gracious (and ambiguous) letter from Lohrfinck.

On June 17, August wrote me that the medal had arrived "a week or so ago, but no message came with it and none has followed." Henry refused to acknowledge its receipt.

. . .

August told me that on September 12, 1955, Henry's 75th birthday, more than a thousand letters, as well as hundreds of telegrams, came to their Hollins Street house in Baltimore. The night of January 29, 1956, Henry died quietly in his sleep. The funeral was a very simple one, with neither services nor eulogy. A handful of friends simply gathered together for a few minutes of silent contemplation—Hamilton Owens, James M. Cain, August, myself, and three or four others. Robert McHugh, then with the Associated Press in Baltimore, was present to prevent any reports of a religious service from getting around.

After Mencken's death, Henry Hazlitt—who served briefly after Mencken's resignation as editor of the *American Mercury* —wrote in *Newsweek* (February 20, 1956): "In his political and economic opinions Mencken was from the beginning, to repeat, neither 'radical' nor 'conservative,' but libertarian. He championed the freedom and dignity of the individual. Therefore he always considered Socialism preposterous."

The tribute to Henry which I found most moving came from my old friend, Harry M. Lyndenberg, Director of the New York Public Library. He had secured a great batch of Henry's letters for the noble institution he headed. He wrote me: "Well, he's gone. No, not so. His heart stopped pumping, but Henry Mencken will be alive and pulsing for the literate long after the multitude has been dead and buried. You must count your work with him as fruitful beyond much of your other connections in the field, like some outwardly but with flavor all its own. Congratulations for your early recognition of his stature. . . . I know the end was certain, but that makes the sense of loss not one bit less keen."

I never knew his like and expect never to see it again.

A NOTE ON THE TYPE

The text of this book was set in Electra, a typeface designed by W(illiam) A(ddison) Dwiggins for the Mergenthaler Linotype company and first made available in 1935. Electra cannot be classified as either "modern" or "old-style." It is not based on any historical model, and hence does not echo any particular period or style of type design. It avoids the extreme contrast between thick and thin elements that marks most modern faces, and is without eccentricities that interfere with reading. In general, Electra is a simple, readable typeface that attempts to give a feeling of fluidity, power, and speed.

During the nineteen-thirties and forties, Dwiggins designed many of the books by H. L. Mencken published by Knopf. The use of a Dwiggins typeface in the design of this book and the elegant Dwiggins ornament on the title page, with selective segments repeated in the chapter openings, help to make the book a tribute to this distinguished typographer as well as to Mencken.

Composed by American–Stratford Graphic Services, Inc.,
Brattleboro, Vermont.

Printed and bound by The Haddon Craftsmen, Inc.
Scranton, Pennsylvania.

Designed by Judith Henry.

21 DAY BOOK
PUBLIC LIBRARY